NEXT GENERATION
GRAMMAR
1

Christina M. Cavage

Steve Jones

Series Editor
David Bohlke

Next Generation Grammar 1

Pearson Education, 10 Bank Street, White Plains, NY 10606

Staff credits: The people who made up the *Next Generation Grammar 1,* team—representing editorial, production, design, and manufacturing—are Andrea Bryant, Aerin Csigay, Dave Dickey, Nancy Flaggman, Gosia Jaros-White, Mike Kemper, Maria Pia Marrella, Amy McCormick, Liza Pleva, Massimo Rubini, Ruth Voetmann, and Adina Zoltan.

Development: Goathaus Studio
Cover art: Diane Fenster
Text composition: ElectraGraphics, Inc.
Text font: Minion Pro

Library of Congress Cataloging-in-Publication Data
Cavage, Christina.
 Next generation grammar 1 / Christina Cavage, Stephen T. Jones.
  p. cm.
 ISBN 978-0-13-256063-4 — ISBN 978-0-13-276054-6 — ISBN 978-0-13-276055-3 — ISBN 978-0-13-276057-7
1. English language—Grammar—Study and teaching. 2. English language—Study and teaching—Foreign speakers.
I. Jones, Stephen T. II. Title. III. Title: Next generation grammar one.
 PE1065.C528 2013
 428.2'4—dc23

2012024734

For text, photo, and illustration credits please turn to the page following the index in the back of the book.

PEARSON ELT ON THE WEB

PearsonELT.com offers a wide range of classroom resources and professional development materials. Access our course-specific websites, product information, and Pearson offices around the world.

Visit us at **pearsonELT.com**

Printed in the United States of America

ISBN 10: 0-13-256063-1 (with MyEnglishLab)
ISBN 13: 978-0-13256063-4 (with MyEnglishLab)

1 2 3 4 5 6 7 8 9 10—V082—18 17 16 15 14 13

Welcome to *Next Generation Grammar*

When do we use one of the present forms for future, as opposed to using *will* or *be going to*? Which modal verbs do we tend to use to make requests, from least formal to most formal? In what types of writing might we find more instances of passive forms than active forms? And how and why do we reduce certain adverbial clauses? These and many other questions are all answered in *Next Generation Grammar,* a groundbreaking new series designed to truly meet the needs of today's students. In addition to learning through the textbook, learners engage with innovative digital content, including interactive learning software, video, and continuous online assessment.

At its heart, *Next Generation Grammar* is a comprehensive grammar course that prepares students to communicate accurately in both writing and speaking. The grammar points are presented naturally, through a variety of high-interest reading texts followed by extensive practice and application. Each new grammar point is practiced using all four skills, with extra emphasis on grammar for writing. This task-centered approach allows immediate feedback on learning outcomes so students can track their own progress.

The series is truly for a new generation—one that is busy, mobile, and demanding. It respects that learners are comfortable with technology and use it as part of their daily lives. The series provides a traditional textbook (in either print or eText format) along with dynamic online material that is an integral, not a supplementary, part of the series. This seamless integration of text and digital offers a streamlined, 21st century learning experience that will engage and captivate learners.

Next Generation Grammar boasts a highly impressive author team. I would like to thank Sigrun Biesenbach-Lucas, Donette Brantner-Artenie, Christina Cavage, Arlen Gargagliano, Steve Jones, Jennifer Recio Lebedev, and Pamela Vittorio for their tireless dedication to this project. I would also like to thank Pietro Alongi, Andrea Bryant, Gosia Jaros-White, Amy McCormick, Massimo Rubini, and the entire Pearson editorial, production, and marketing team for their vision and guidance through the development of this series.

David Bohlke
Series Editior

About the Series Editor. David Bohlke has 25 years of experience as a teacher, trainer, program director, editor, and materials developer. He has taught in Japan, Korea, Saudi Arabia, and Morocco, and has conducted multiple teacher-training workshops around the world. David is the former publishing manager for adult courses for Cambridge University Press and the former editorial manager for Global ELT for Cengage Learning. He is the coauthor of *Listening Power 2* (Pearson Education), *Four Corners* (Cambridge University Press), and *Speak Now* (Oxford University Press), and is the series editor for *Interchange,* Fourth Edition (Cambridge University Press).

What's next in grammar?

Imagine a grammar course that gives you the freedom to devote class time to what you think is most important; a grammar course that keeps students engaged and on-track; a grammar course that extends learning beyond the classroom through compelling digital content.

Introducing *Next Generation Grammar*

Print or eText?
You make the choice. The course book content is presented in two formats, print or eText, offering maximum flexibility for different learning styles and needs.

Blended instruction
Optimize instruction through a blend of course book (in either print or eText format) and online content. This seamless integration will allow for spending more class time on meaningful, communicative work. Learners will practice and apply new language online and can also access our engaging video reviews if they have missed a lesson, or simply need additional help with a grammar point.

Rich online content
Explore the online component. It offers a wealth of interactive activities, grammar reference material, audio files, test material, and video reviews with our Grammar Coach, Jennifer Lebedev, YouTube's *JenniferESL*. The dynamic multimedia content will keep learners focused and engaged. You can also track class progress through an intuitive and comprehensive learner management system.

Ongoing assessment
Use the extensive assessment suite for targeted instruction. The interactive nature of the assessments (including timely feedback, goal tracking, and progress reports) allows you to track progress, and also allows learners to see for themselves which areas have been mastered and which require more effort. In the course book, assessment occurs at the end of each unit. The online component offers pre- and post-unit tests, as well as end-of-chapter tests.

The **next generation of grammar** courses is here. Anytime, anywhere, anyplace.

Teacher-directed

Student-centered

Print or eText

Practical tasks

Seamless integration of course book and digital

Grammar coach

Ongoing assessment

Anytime, anywhere, anyplace

CONTENTS

UNIT 1 BACK TO SCHOOL	Student Book Outcomes	MyEnglishLab
Chapter 1 page **2** **Welcome, Students!** Nouns and pronouns Simple present: Statements with *be*	Getting Started Reading: *Welcome to English 1 class! / We're from Around the World!* Grammar Focus 1 and 2 Listening, Speaking, Writing	Vocabulary Check + Reading Comprehension Grammar Plus 1 and 2 Listen for it, Sounding Natural Linking Grammar to Writing Diagnostic Test
Chapter 2 page **10** **The Class of 2016** Simple present: *Yes / No* questions and short answers with *be* *This, that, these, those* Simple present: *Wh-* questions with *be*	Getting Started Reading: *Profiles* Grammar Focus 1, 2, and 3 Listening, Speaking, Writing	Vocabulary Check + Reading Comprehension Grammar Plus 1, 2, and 3 Listen for it, Sounding Natural Linking Grammar to Writing Diagnostic Test
Unit Assessments page **20**	Grammar Summary Self-Assessment Unit Project	Grammar Summary Unit Test Search it!

UNIT 2 A DAY IN THE LIFE	Student Book Outcomes	MyEnglishLab
Chapter 3 page **24** **Journal Writing** Simple present: Statements Third person singular: Irregular and other forms Expressing frequency	Getting Started Reading: *Email to Gita* Grammar Focus 1, 2, and 3 Listening, Speaking, Writing	Vocabulary Check + Reading Comprehension Grammar Plus 1, 2, and 3 Listen for it, Sounding Natural Linking Grammar to Writing Diagnostic Test
Chapter 4 page **34** **Blogging** Simple present: *Yes / No* questions Simple present: *Wh-* questions	Getting Started Reading: *Blog FAQs* Grammar Focus 1 and 2 Listening, Speaking, Writing	Vocabulary Check + Reading Comprehension Grammar Plus 1 and 2 Listen for it, Sounding Natural Linking Grammar to Writing Diagnostic Test
Unit Assessments page **42**	Grammar Summary Self-Assessment Unit Project	Grammar Summary Unit Test Search it!

UNIT 3 WHERE IN THE WORLD?	Student Book Outcomes	MyEnglishLab
Chapter 5 page **46** **Mapping It Out** Simple present: *There is* and *There are* Prepositions of place	Getting Started Reading: *Where's Amy? A Blog about Travel and Adventure* Grammar Focus 1 and 2 Listening, Speaking, Writing	Vocabulary Check + Reading Comprehension Grammar Plus 1 and 2 Listen for it, Sounding Natural Linking Grammar to Writing Diagnostic Test
Chapter 6 page **54** **Traveling Through Time** Simple past: *There + be* statements Simple present and past: *Be + there* questions	Getting Started Reading: *A Conversation about Dr. John Snow* Grammar Focus 1 and 2 Listening, Speaking, Writing	Vocabulary Check + Reading Comprehension Grammar Plus 1 and 2 Listen for it, Sounding Natural Linking Grammar to Writing Diagnostic Test
Unit Assessments page **62**	Grammar Summary Self-Assessment Unit Project	Grammar Summary Unit Test Search it!

UNIT 4 ENGLISH FUN	Student Book Outcomes	MyEnglishLab What do you know?
Chapter 7 page 66 **Proverbs** Parts of speech: Nouns, pronouns, verbs, prepositions, and adjectives Sentences: Subjects, verbs, and objects Question forms	Getting Started Reading: *English 1 Notes* Grammar Focus 1, 2, and 3 Listening, Speaking, Writing	Vocabulary Check + Reading Comprehension Grammar Plus 1, 2, and 3 Listen for it, Sounding Natural Linking Grammar to Writing Diagnostic Test
Chapter 8 page 76 **Changing Language** Sentence patterns with *be* Prepositional phrases / Object pronouns	Getting Started Reading: *A Class Discussion* Grammar Focus 1 and 2 Listening, Speaking, Writing	Vocabulary Check + Reading Comprehension Grammar Plus 1 and 2 Listen for it, Sounding Natural Linking Grammar to Writing Diagnostic Test
Unit Assessments page 84	Grammar Summary Self-Assessment Unit Project	Grammar Summary Unit Test Search it!
UNIT 5 GENERATIONS	Student Book Outcomes	MyEnglishLab What do you know?
Chapter 9 page 88 **Different Points of View** Expressing advice: *Should* Infinitives	Getting Started Reading: *Jin-woo's Letter* Grammar Focus 1 and 2 Listening, Speaking, Writing	Vocabulary Check + Reading Comprehension Grammar Plus 1 and 2 Listen for it, Sounding Natural Linking Grammar to Writing Diagnostic Test
Chapter 10 page 96 **Generational Differences** Possessive nouns and adjectives Gerunds	Getting Started Reading: *Understanding Immigrant Families and Their Challenges* Grammar Focus 1 and 2 Listening, Speaking, Writing	Vocabulary Check + Reading Comprehension Grammar Plus 1 and 2 Listen for it, Sounding Natural Linking Grammar to Writing Diagnostic Test
Unit Assessments page 104	Grammar Summary Self-Assessment Unit Project	Grammar Summary Unit Test Search it!
UNIT 6 WE'RE COOKING NOW	Student Book Outcomes	MyEnglishLab What do you know?
Chapter 11 page 108 **Culinary Science** Present progressive: Statements Present progressive: Questions Simple present vs. present progressive	Getting Started Reading: *Garden in the Sky* Grammar Focus 1, 2, and 3 Listening, Speaking, Writing	Vocabulary Check + Reading Comprehension Grammar Plus 1, 2, and 3 Listen for it, Sounding Natural Linking Grammar to Writing Diagnostic Test
Chapter 12 page 118 **Around the Global Dinner Table** Count and noncount nouns *How many . . . ? How much . . . ? /* Quantifiers	Getting Started Reading: *The Global Table Project* Grammar Focus 1 and 2 Listening, Speaking, Writing	Vocabulary Check + Reading Comprehension Grammar Plus 1 and 2 Listen for it, Sounding Natural Linking Grammar to Writing Diagnostic Test
Unit Assessments page 126	Grammar Summary Self-Assessment Unit Project	Grammar Summary Unit Test Search it!

UNIT 7 THE FUTURE IS COMING SOON		Student Book Outcomes	MyEnglishLab What do you know?
Chapter 13 **My Future** Future: *Be going to* Future: Present progressive	page **130**	Getting Started Reading: *My Future: School, Work, Family* Grammar Focus 1 and 2 Listening, Speaking, Writing	Vocabulary Check + Reading Comprehension Grammar Plus 1 and 2 Listen for it, Sounding Natural Linking Grammar to Writing Diagnostic Test
Chapter 14 **Our Future** Future: *Will* Quantifiers: Comparisons	page **138**	Getting Started Reading: *Futurists at Work: How Will the Future Be Different?* Grammar Focus 1 and 2 Listening, Speaking, Writing	Vocabulary Check + Reading Comprehension Grammar Plus 1 and 2 Listen for it, Sounding Natural Linking Grammar to Writing Diagnostic Test
Unit Assessments	page **146**	Grammar Summary Self-Assessment Unit Project	Grammar Summary Unit Test Search it!
UNIT 8 ARCHITECTURE		Student Book Outcomes	MyEnglishLab What do you know?
Chapter 15 **House and Climate** Descriptive adjectives *Very, too, enough*	page **150**	Getting Started Reading: *Housing Styles Around the World* Grammar Focus 1 and 2 Listening, Speaking, Writing	Vocabulary Check + Reading Comprehension Grammar Plus 1 and 2 Listen for it, Sounding Natural Linking Grammar to Writing Diagnostic Test
Chapter 16 **International Designs** Comparative adjectives *As . . . as* and other expressions	page **158**	Getting Started Reading: *A Conversation about Design* Grammar Focus 1 and 2 Listening, Speaking, Writing	Vocabulary Check + Reading Comprehension Grammar Plus 1 and 2 Listen for it, Sounding Natural Linking Grammar to Writing Diagnostic Test
Unit Assessments	page **166**	Grammar Summary Self-Assessment Unit Project	Grammar Summary Unit Test Search it!
UNIT 9 HIDDEN HISTORY		Student Book Outcomes	MyEnglishLab What do you know?
Chapter 17 **Uncovering the Past** Simple past: Regular verbs Simple past: Irregular verbs	page **170**	Getting Started Reading: *From Dock Creek to Dock Street* Grammar Focus 1 and 2 Listening, Speaking, Writing	Vocabulary Check + Reading Comprehension Grammar Plus 1 and 2 Listen for it, Sounding Natural Linking Grammar to Writing Diagnostic Test
Chapter 18 **City of Angels** Simple past: Questions Time signals	page **178**	Getting Started Reading: *A Tour of the City of Angels* Grammar Focus 1 and 2 Listening, Speaking, Writing	Vocabulary Check + Reading Comprehension Grammar Plus 1 and 2 Listen for it, Sounding Natural Linking Grammar to Writing Diagnostic Test
Unit Assessments	page **186**	Grammar Summary Self-Assessment Unit Project	Grammar Summary Unit Test Search it!

UNIT 10 PATHWAYS		Student Book Outcomes	MyEnglishLab What do you know?
Chapter 19 **Their Stories** Past progressive: Statements Past progressive: Questions	page **190**	Getting Started Reading: *The Journey Begins* Grammar Focus 1 and 2 Listening, Speaking, Writing	Vocabulary Check + Reading Comprehension Grammar Plus 1 and 2 Listen for it, Sounding Natural Linking Grammar to Writing Diagnostic Test
Chapter 20 **Intersecting Lives** Time clauses: *While* and *when* Simple past vs. past progressive	page **198**	Getting Started Reading: *An Interview with Former Slave Martha Miller* Grammar Focus 1 and 2 Listening, Speaking, Writing	Vocabulary Check + Reading Comprehension Grammar Plus 1 and 2 Listen for it, Sounding Natural Linking Grammar to Writing Diagnostic Test
Unit Assessments	page **206**	Grammar Summary Self-Assessment Unit Project	Grammar Summary Unit Test Search it!

Appendices

A Spelling rules for -s endings on regular plural nouns .... page A-1
B Spelling of irregular plural nouns .... page A-1
C Pronunciation and spelling rules for final -s on verbs with *he, she, it* subjects .... page A-2
D Subject pronouns, object pronouns, and possessive adjectives .... page A-3
E Spelling rules for -ing endings .... page A-3
F Non-action verbs: Verbs not commonly used in progressive tenses .... page A-4
G Noncount nouns .... page A-4
H Spelling rules for comparative adjectives .... page A-4
I Spelling rules for -ed endings .... page A-5
J Verbs with irregular simple past forms .... page A-6
K World map .... page A-8
Index .... page I-1

Tour of a Unit

Each unit in *Next Generation Grammar* begins with an engaging opener that provides a quick overview of the unit. A list of learning outcomes establishes each chapter's focus and helps students preview the grammar content. The outcomes can also be used as a way to review and assess progress as students master chapter content.

MyEnglishLab

Before they begin the unit, students go online and complete the *What do you know?* section to assess what they already know about the grammar featured in the unit. This directs students' focus to the grammar and also helps teachers target instruction to their learners' specific needs.

UNIT 7

Relationships

Outcomes
After completing this unit, I will be able to use these grammar points.

Chapter 13
Grammar Focus 1
Enough and *too*
Grammar Focus 2
Permission: Modals and expressions
Grammar Focus 3
Requests: Modals and expressions

Chapter 14
Grammar Focus 1
Reflexive and reciprocal pronouns
Grammar Focus 2
Unreal conditional

MyEnglishLab
▶ What do you know?

The ***Getting Started*** section begins with the introduction of the chapter's themes. Students engage in lighthearted, motivating, and personal tasks that introduce and preview the chapter's grammar points.

In the ***Reading*** section students are further exposed to the chapter's grammar through high-interest, real-world texts that reflect the unit's theme. Beginning with a pre-reading warm-up, tasks progress from schema building to a detailed comprehension check.

MyEnglishLab

The ***Vocabulary Check*** activities on *MyEnglishLab* allow students to review and practice the vocabulary necessary for reading comprehension. Students are encouraged to complete these activities before they begin the ***Reading*** section.

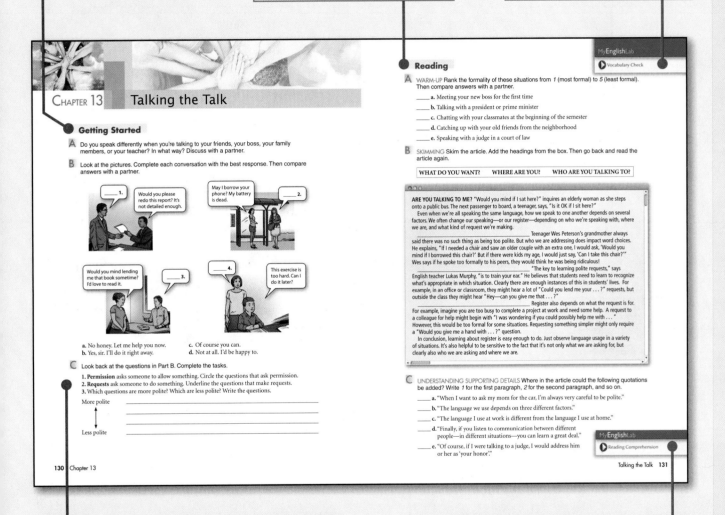

This section culminates with an important inductive step that asks students to look back at the previous tasks and focus on form or function. By circling, underlining, charting, or answering questions, students focus on differences in meaning.

MyEnglishLab

Upon completion of the ***Reading*** section, students can further engage with the chapter's reading selection on *MyEnglishLab*. The ***Reading Comprehension*** activities provide students with an additional check of understanding.

The **Grammar Focus** sections present the chapter's target structures in clear, easy-to-read charts. Each chart presents example sentences taken from the chapter reading that illustrate the structure in context.
The language notes give short and clear explanations of the form, meaning, and use of the target structure.

Grammar Focus 1 *Enough and too*

Examples	Language notes
(1) She was **smart enough**, but she didn't try. Did he finish **quickly enough**? I didn't **study enough**. I failed the test.	As we saw in Chapter 11, the word *enough* means "sufficient" or "the right amount." It has a positive meaning. In addition to modifying nouns, *enough* can also modify **adjectives, adverbs,** and **verbs.** Use: **adjective / adverb / verb + enough**
(2) This report is **not detailed enough**. He didn't work **fast enough**. You aren't eating **enough**.	*Not enough* means that something is insufficient or less than the right amount. Use: *not* + **adjective** + *enough* *not* + verb + **adverb** + *enough* helping verb + *not* + verb + *enough*
(3) He didn't move fast **enough to get** a seat. Do you think she has **enough to do**?	We often add an **infinitive:** *enough* + infinitive
(4) Don't be **too friendly** with strangers. Does he speak **too formally** to his peers?	As we saw in Chapter 11, the word *too* means "more than is needed." The meaning is usually negative. In addition to modifying quantifiers, *too* can also modify **adjectives** and **adverbs.**
(5) My kids aren't **too interested** in history. Don't work **too hard**!	We use *not too* to say that something is lacking. Use: *not* + *too* + adjective / adverb
(6) You are **too busy to complete** a project. Did he arrive **too late to get** into the movie?	We often add an **infinitive:** *too* + adjective / adverb + infinitive
(7) There are **too many people** on the bus. There are **too few seats** on the bus. Q: Did the teacher present **too much information**? A: No, she presented **too little**. / She didn't present **enough**.	As we saw in Chapter 11, we can also use *(not) enough* and *too* with count and noncount nouns. • The opposite of *too many* is *too few* (for count nouns). • The opposite of *too much* is *too little* (for noncount nouns). We more commonly say "not enough."

Grammar Practice

MyEnglishLab
▶ Grammar Plus 1 Activities 1 and 2

A Complete the sentences. Use *enough* or *too*.

1. I don't have _____ money to pay my taxi fare. Could you lend me some?
2. You are speaking _____ quickly. Would you mind slowing down?
3. Kevin hates to wait. He has _____ little patience.
4. I had no trouble finding your house. Your directions were easy _____
5. Your instructions aren't clear _____. Can you say it in a different way?
6. Hal is _____ short to get the book off the shelf. He needs a ladder.
7. Nancy doesn't have a driver's license. She's not old _____.

132 Chapter 13

8. The movie is sold out. We arrived _____ late.
9. My grandma says I'm too thin. She always says, "You don't eat _____."

B Rewrite these sentences to say the opposite. Use *enough* or *too*. More than one correct answer may be possible.

1. She is walking too quickly. *She is not walking fast enough.*
2. He is old enough to enter the contest. _____
3. We were too slow to get seats on the subway. _____
4. There are too many people in our discussion group. _____
5. She was strong enough to lift the box. _____
6. There are too few grammar exercises in this book. _____

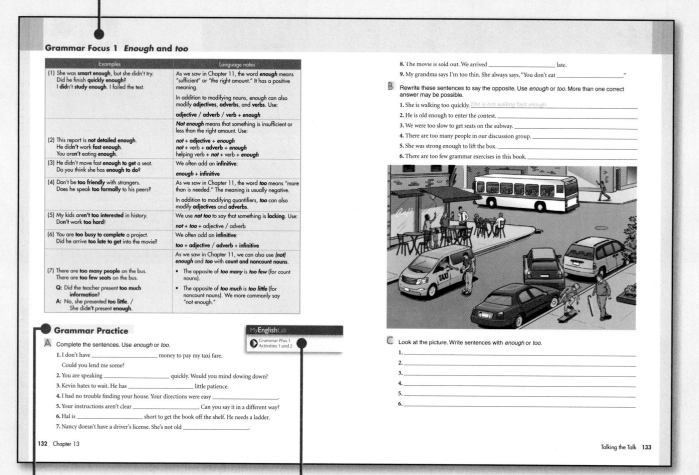

C Look at the picture. Write sentences with *enough* or *too*.

1. _____
2. _____
3. _____
4. _____
5. _____
6. _____

Talking the Talk 133

In the **Grammar Practice** sections, students are given the opportunity to apply the grammar structures in a variety of contextualized, controlled exercises that allow them to practice both the forms and the uses of the new structures.

MyEnglishLab

Grammar practice continues online in the **Grammar Plus** activities. Each **Grammar Plus** includes two additional practice activities to further reinforce new structures. Instant scoring and meaningful feedback show students their progress and highlight areas that may require more effort. Students also have the opportunity to see a video review featuring our expert grammar coach. The videos provide a quick, engaging review—perfect for allowing students to check their understanding before proceeding to further assessment.

In the **Listening** sections students have the opportunity to hear the target grammar in context and to practice their listening skills. Activities are developed to practice both top-down and bottom-up listening skills.

Listening activities continue online with **Listen for it**. These activities assess both grammar in context and listening comprehension, and include instant scoring and feedback.

Before students do the **Writing**, they go online to complete **Linking Grammar to Writing**. Several guided writing tasks link the grammar to the skill of writing, enabling students to then move back to the textbook and complete the **Writing** section with full confidence.

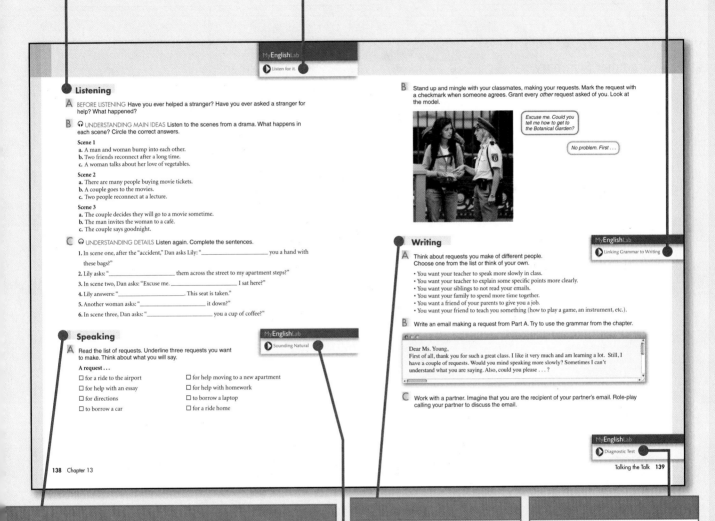

Listening

A BEFORE LISTENING Have you ever helped a stranger? Have you ever asked a stranger for help? What happened?

B 🎧 UNDERSTANDING MAIN IDEAS Listen to the scenes from a drama. What happens in each scene? Circle the correct answers.

Scene 1
a. A man and woman bump into each other.
b. Two friends reconnect after a long time.
c. A woman talks about her love of vegetables.

Scene 2
a. There are many people buying movie tickets.
b. A couple goes to the movies.
c. Two people reconnect at a lecture.

Scene 3
a. The couple decides they will go to a movie sometime.
b. The man invites the woman to a café.
c. The couple says goodnight.

C 🎧 UNDERSTANDING DETAILS Listen again. Complete the sentences.

1. In scene one, after the "accident," Dan asks Lily: "_____ you a hand with these bags?"
2. Lily asks: "_____ them across the street to my apartment steps?"
3. In scene two, Dan asks: "Excuse me. _____ I sat here?"
4. Lily answers: "_____. This seat is taken."
5. Another woman asks: "_____ it down?"
6. In scene three, Dan asks: "_____ you a cup of coffee?"

Speaking

A Read the list of requests. Underline three requests you want to make. Think about what you will say.

A request . . .
☐ for a ride to the airport
☐ for help with an essay
☐ for directions
☐ to borrow a car
☐ for help moving to a new apartment
☐ for help with homework
☐ to borrow a laptop
☐ for a ride home

B Stand up and mingle with your classmates, making your requests. Mark the request with a checkmark when someone agrees. Grant every *other* request asked of you. Look at the model.

Excuse me. Could you tell me how to get to the Botanical Garden?

No problem. First . . .

Writing

A Think about requests you make of different people. Choose one from the list or think of your own.
• You want your teacher to speak more slowly in class.
• You want your teacher to explain some specific points more clearly.
• You want your siblings to not read your emails.
• You want your family to spend more time together.
• You want a friend of your parents to give you a job.
• You want your friend to teach you something (how to play a game, an instrument, etc.).

B Write an email making a request from Part A. Try to use the grammar from the chapter.

Dear Ms. Young,
First of all, thank you for such a great class. I like it very much and am learning a lot. Still, I have a couple of requests. Would you mind speaking more slowly? Sometimes I can't understand what you are saying. Also, could you please . . . ?

C Work with a partner. Imagine that you are the recipient of your partner's email. Role-play calling your partner to discuss the email.

The **Speaking** section provides students with the opportunity to use the chapter's grammar naturally and appropriately in a variety of engaging interactive speaking activities.

The **Sounding Natural** activities are pronunciation activities relating to the chapter's grammar and alternating between productive and receptive tasks. In the receptive tasks, students listen to prompts and select correct answers. In the productive tasks, students listen to prompts, record themselves, and compare their submissions with a model.

The **Writing** section provides students with the opportunity to use the chapter's grammar naturally and appropriately in a variety of activities. Students are provided with a whole or partial model and a more open-ended writing task.

Each chapter culminates with an online **Diagnostic Test** that assesses students' comprehension and mastery of the chapter's grammar structures. The test tracks students' progress and allows teachers to focus on the specific student needs.

The **Grammar Summary** chart provides a concise, easy-to-read overview of all the grammar structures presented in the unit. It also serves as an excellent reference for review and study.

A quick 20- or 25-point **Self-Assessment** gives students an additional opportunity to check their understanding of the unit's target structures. This gives students one more chance to assess what they may still need to master before taking the online **Unit Test**.

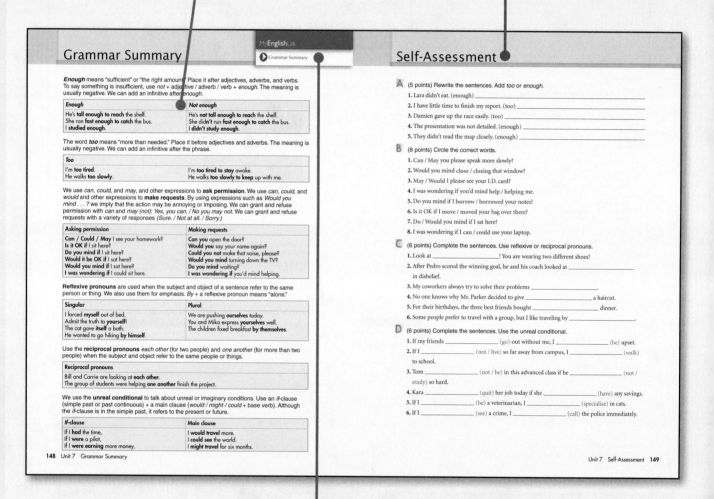

Grammar Summary

MyEnglishLab
▶ Grammar Summary

Enough means "sufficient" or "the right amount." Place it after adjectives, adverbs, and verbs. To say something is insufficient, use *not* + adjective / adverb / verb + *enough*. The meaning is usually negative. We can add an infinitive after *enough*.

Enough	Not enough
He's **tall enough to reach** the shelf. She ran **fast enough to catch** the bus. I **studied enough**.	He's **not tall enough to reach** the shelf. She **didn't run fast enough to catch** the bus. I **didn't study enough**.

The word *too* means "more than needed." Place it before adjectives and adverbs. The meaning is usually negative. We can add an infinitive after the phrase.

Too	
I'm **too tired**. He walks **too slowly**.	I'm **too tired to stay** awake. He walks **too slowly to keep** up with me.

We use *can*, *could*, and *may*, and other expressions to **ask permission**. We use *can*, *could*, and *would* and other expressions to **make requests**. By using expressions such as *Would you mind . . . ?* we imply that the action may be annoying or imposing. We can grant and refuse permission with *can* and *may* (*not*): *Yes, you can. / No you may not.* We can grant and refuse requests with a variety of responses (*Sure. / Not at all. / Sorry.*)

Asking permission	Making requests
Can / Could / May I see your homework? **Is it OK if** I sit here? **Do you mind if** I sit here? **Would it be OK if** I sat here? **Would you mind if** I sat here? **I was wondering if** I could sit here.	**Can you** open the door? **Would you** say your name again? **Could you not** make that noise, please? **Would you mind** turning down the TV? **Do you mind** waiting? **I was wondering if** you'd mind helping.

Reflexive pronouns are used when the subject and object of a sentence refer to the same person or thing. We also use them for emphasis. *By* + a reflexive pronoun means "alone."

Singular	Plural
I forced **myself** out of bed. Admit the truth to **yourself**! The cat gave **itself** a bath. He wanted to go hiking **by himself**.	We are pushing **ourselves** today. You and Mika express **yourselves** well. The children fixed breakfast **by themselves**.

Use the **reciprocal pronouns** *each other* (for two people) and *one another* (for more than two people) when the subject and object refer to the same people or things.

Reciprocal pronouns
Bill and Carrie are looking at **each other**. The group of students were helping **one another** finish the project.

We use the **unreal conditional** to talk about unreal or imaginary conditions. Use an *if*-clause (simple past or past continuous) + a main clause (*would / might / could* + base verb). Although the *if*-clause is in the simple past, it refers to the present or future.

If-clause	Main clause
If I **had** the time, If I **were** a pilot, If I **were earning** more money,	I **would travel** more. I **could see** the world. I **might travel** for six months.

Self-Assessment

A (5 points) Rewrite the sentences. Add *too* or *enough*.
1. Lara didn't eat. (enough) _____
2. I have little time to finish my report. (too) _____
3. Damien gave up the race easily. (too) _____
4. The presentation was not detailed. (enough) _____
5. They didn't read the map closely. (enough) _____

B (8 points) Circle the correct words.
1. Can / May you please speak more slowly?
2. Would you mind close / closing that window?
3. May / Would I please see your I.D. card?
4. I was wondering if you'd mind help / helping me.
5. Do you mind if I borrow / borrowed your notes?
6. Is it OK if I move / moved your bag over there?
7. Do / Would you mind if I sat here?
8. I was wondering if I can / could use your laptop.

C (6 points) Complete the sentences. Use reflexive or reciprocal pronouns.
1. Look at _____! You are wearing two different shoes!
2. After Pedro scored the winning goal, he and his coach looked at _____ in disbelief.
3. My coworkers always try to solve their problems _____.
4. No one knows why Mr. Parker decided to give _____ a haircut.
5. For their birthdays, the three best friends bought _____ dinner.
6. Some people prefer to travel with a group, but I like traveling by _____.

D (6 points) Complete the sentences. Use the unreal conditional.
1. If my friends _____ (go) out without me, I _____ (be) upset.
2. If I _____ (not / live) so far away from campus, I _____ (walk) to school.
3. Tom _____ (not / be) in this advanced class if he _____ (not / study) so hard.
4. Kara _____ (quit) her job today if she _____ (have) any savings.
5. If I _____ (be) a veterinarian, I _____ (specialize) in cats.
6. If I _____ (see) a crime, I _____ (call) the police immediately.

MyEnglishLab

Students can go to *MyEnglishLab* for a **Grammar Summary** review, which includes activities and a video to help students prepare for the **Self-Assessment** and **Unit Test**.

Each unit ends with an interesting and engaging group **Unit Project** that encourages students to synthesize the new grammar structures and to integrate the unit's theme and skills. The project promotes collaboration, creativity, and fluency and exposes students to a variety of real-world situations.

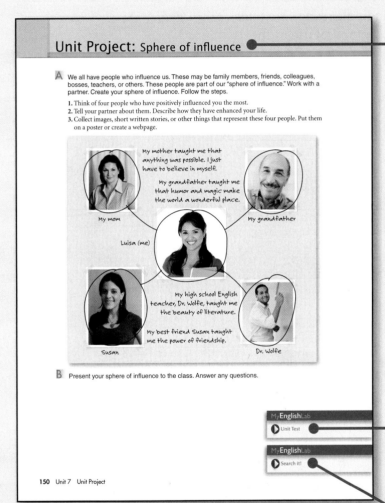

Unit Project: Sphere of influence

A We all have people who influence us. These may be family members, friends, colleagues, bosses, teachers, or others. These people are part of our "sphere of influence." Work with a partner. Create your sphere of influence. Follow the steps.

1. Think of four people who have positively influenced you the most.
2. Tell your partner about them. Describe how they have enhanced your life.
3. Collect images, short written stories, or other things that represent these four people. Put them on a poster or create a webpage.

My mother taught me that anything was possible. I just have to believe in myself.

My grandfather taught me that humor and magic make the world a wonderful place.

My mom

Luisa (me)

My grandfather

My high school English teacher, Dr. Wolfe, taught me the beauty of literature.

My best friend Susan taught me the power of friendship.

Susan

Dr. Wolfe

B Present your sphere of influence to the class. Answer any questions.

MyEnglishLab
► Unit Test

MyEnglishLab
► Search it!

MyEnglishLab

The unit's final, cumulative assessment is a comprehensive online **Unit Test**. This test allows students to check their mastery of the unit's grammar structures, see their progress, and identify areas that may need improvement. The test allows teachers to track students' progress and to focus on areas that might benefit from more attention.

MyEnglishLab

The **Search it!** activity allows students to do a fun online search for content that relates to the chapter's theme. Teachers may choose to have students complete these real-world tasks individually, in pairs, or in small groups.

Next Generation Grammar Digital

MyEnglishLab

A dynamic, easy-to-use online learning and assessment program, integral to the *Next Generation Grammar* program

▶ **Original activities** focusing on grammar, vocabulary, and skills that extend the *Next Generation Grammar* program

▶ **Multiple** reading, writing, listening, and speaking activities that practice grammar in context, including *Linking Grammar to Writing*, which guides students in the practical use of the chapter's grammar

▶ **Video** instruction from a dynamic grammar coach that provides an engaging and comprehensive grammar review

▶ **Extensive** and ongoing assessment that provides evidence of student learning and progress on both the chapter and unit level

▶ **Individualized** instruction, instant feedback, and study plans that provide personalized learning

▶ A **flexible gradebook** that helps instructors monitor student progress

And remember, *Next Generation Grammar* is available both in print and as an eText.

ActiveTeach

A powerful digital resource that provides the perfect solution for seamless lesson planning and exciting whole-class teaching

◐ A **Digital Student Book** with interactive whiteboard (IWB) software

◐ **Useful notes** that present teaching suggestions, corpus-informed grammar tips, troublesome grammar points, and culture notes

◐ Instant one-stop **audio** and **video grammar coach**

◐ **Printable** audio scripts, video scripts, and answer keys

◐ **Capability** for teachers to:
  • Write, highlight, erase, and create notes
  • Add and save newly-created classroom work
  • Enlarge any section of a page

> **P Teacher's Note** ⎯ □ ✕
>
> Teacher's Note p3
> **Unit 1, Chapter 1**
> **B Reading Skills**
> When you **skim** a text, you look it over quickly to get a general idea of what it is about. Do not read every word and do not use a dictionary. Instead, look at the title, pictures, bold, or italicized words, and the first line of each paragraph to get a sense of the general idea.

About the Authors

Christina M. Cavage is a professor of ESL at Savannah College of Art and Design. Prior to joining SCAD in 2011, she was an associate professor of ESL and the department chairperson at Atlantic Cape Community College. She has authored several articles on blended learning and technology in ESL. Additionally, she is the author of two textbooks: *Working At It!* and *Talking About It!* Christina is a regular presenter at TESOL.

Steve Jones has taught ESL in academic, community, and vocational settings for over 25 years, in addition to teaching college composition and linguistics. He is currently an assistant professor of English/ESL at Community College of Philadelphia. He is the series editor and an author of *Catalyst: Writing from Reading* (Cengage) and the author of *College Oral Communication 4* in Cengage's *English for Academic Success* series.

Acknowledgments

The creation of these materials was a group effort. We appreciate the expertise and support of the wonderful people at Pearson in making this project a success, especially Massimo Rubini, Leigh Stolle, Amy McCormick, David Bohlke, Andrea Bryant, and Malgorzata (Gosia) Jaros-White.—*SJ & CC*

I am thankful for having had the opportunity to work with such a great team. A big thanks to my partner Steve Jones for challenging me to be a bit less organized, and a lot more aware. My never-ending gratitude goes to the numerous students at Atlantic Cape and SCAD who have helped me refine the way I think about grammar and grammar teaching. A special thanks to friends and colleagues Gwen McIntyre and Kristi Bergman for our fruitful conversations about language teaching and the ESL world. Lastly, my deepest gratitude to Bill and Emma for always having the right words, and giving me my space when I needed it.—*CC*

I am grateful for the energy and integrity of my writing partner Christina Cavage, and of the work of the team at Pearson in making these materials as useful to teachers and students as they are. Thank you to my colleagues Todd Jones and Michael Remshard for helpful discussions about college counseling, and to my colleagues Si Ah Yoo and Yun Yoo for advice about Korean culture. Jeremy H. Picker was instrumental in the creation of fictional college towns. I gratefully acknowledge the work of Venita Wilson, Charles H. Walker, and Leita E. Jones in preserving the writings of Susan Tallmon. Love and thanks to Grace, David, and Daniel, who were my constant advisers. Finally, gratitude goes to my students at Community College of Philadelphia, who were always ready to give advice and encouragement in the creation of this work.—*SJ*

Reviewers

We are grateful to the following reviewers for their many helpful comments:

Yukiko Arita, Ibaraki University, Mito, Japan; **Asmaa Awad,** University of Sharjah, Sharjah, United Arab Emirates; **Kim Bayer,** Hunter College CUNY, New York, NY; **Michelle Bell,** University of South Florida, Tampa, FL; **Jeff Bette,** Westchester Community College SUNY, Valhalla, NY; **Leslie Biaggi,** Miami Dade College, Miami, FL; **Celina Costa,** George Brown College, Toronto, Ontario, Canada; **Eric Dury,** University of Sharjah, Sharjah, United Arab Emirates; **Katie Entigar,** Kaplan's English Scool, Boston, MA; **Margaret Eomurian,** Houston Community College, Central College, Houston, TX; **Liz Flynn,** San Diego Community College, San Diego, CA: **Ruth French,** Hunter College CUNY, New York, NY; **Jas Gill,** University of British Columbia, Vancouver, British Columbia, Canada; **Joanne Glaski,** Suffolk County Community College, Selden, NY; **Sandra Hartmann,** University of Houston, Houston, TX; **Cora Higgins,** Boston Academy of English, Boston, MA; **Carolyn Ho,** Lone Star College-Cyfair, Cypress, TX; **Gretchen Irwin-Arada,** Hunter College CUNY, New York, NY; **Bob Jester,** Hunter College CUNY, New York, NY; **Patricia Juza,** Baruch College CUNY, New York, NY; **Liz Kara,** Alberta College, Alberta, Canada; **Jessica March,** American University of Sharjah, Sharjah, United Arab Emirates; **Alison McAdams,** Approach International Student Center, Boston, MA; **Kathy Mehdi,** University of Sharjah, Sharjah, United Arab Emirates; **April Muchmore-Vokoun,** Hillsborough Community College, Dale Mabry Campus, Tampa, FL; **Forest Nelson,** Tokai University, Toyko, Japan; **Dina Paglia,** Hunter College CUNY, New York, NY; **DyAnne Philips,** Houston Community College, Southwest College, Gulfton Center, Houston, TX; **Russell Pickett,** Sam Houston State University, Huntsville, TX; **Peggy Porter,** Houston Community College, Northwest College, Houston, TX; **Tahani Qadri,** American University of Sharjah, Sharjah, United Arab Emirates; **Alison Rice,** Hunter College CUNY, New York, NY; **Kevin Ryan,** Showa Women's University, Tokyo, Japan; **Yasser Salem,** University of Sharjah, Sharjah, United Arab Emirates; **Janet Selitto,** Seminole State College of Florida, Sanford, FL; **Laura Sheehan,** Houston Community College, Southwest College, Stafford Campus, Houston, TX; **Barbara Smith-Palinkas,** Hillsborough Cummunity College, Dale Mabry Campus, Tampa, FL; **Maria Spelleri,** State College of Florida Manatee-Sarasota, Venice, FL; **Marjorie Stamberg,** Hunter College CUNY, New York, NY; **Gregory Strong,** Aoyama Gakuin University, Tokyo, Japan; **Fausto G. Vergara,** Houston Community College, Southeast College, Houston, TX; **Khristie Wills,** American University of Sharjah, Sharjah, United Arab Emirates; **Nancy Ramirez Wright,** Santa Ana College, Santa Ana, CA.

UNIT 1

Back to School

OUTCOMES

After completing this unit, I will be able to use these grammar points.

CHAPTER 1

Grammar Focus 1
Nouns and pronouns

Grammar Focus 2
Simple present: Statements with *be*

CHAPTER 2

Grammar Focus 1
Simple present: *Yes / No* questions and short answers with *be*

Grammar Focus 2
This, that, these, those

Grammar Focus 3
Simple present: *Wh-* questions with *be*

MyEnglishLab

 What do you know?

CHAPTER 1 Welcome, Students!

 **Getting Started**

A Read the sentences. Circle your answers.

1. I am a new student.	Yes	No
2. The classroom is small.	Yes	No
3. My classmates are from different countries.	Yes	No
4. We are in the computer lab.	Yes	No

B Look at the picture. Read about the students and teacher. Then write *T* for the true statements and *F* for the false statements.

We're in English 1!

José is 21 years old. He is a returning student. He's from Colombia.

Yan is 19 years old. She is a new student. She's from China.

They aren't in English 2. They're in English 1. They are classmates.

Emma is the English 1 teacher. Class isn't boring—it's fun.

José, Emma, and Yan

_____ **1.** One student is from China.

_____ **2.** One student is from Venezuela.

_____ **3.** José and Yan are classmates.

_____ **4.** They're in English 2.

_____ **5.** José isn't in English 2.

_____ **6.** Yan isn't a returning student.

_____ **7.** Emma is a teacher.

_____ **8.** Class isn't boring.

C Look back at Parts A and B. Complete the tasks.

1. We use **nouns** and **pronouns** to talk about people, places, and things. Nouns and pronouns are singular (one: *book, girl, it, she*) or plural (two or more: *books, girls, they*). Plural nouns usually end in -*s*. Write *1* for singular. Write *2+* for plural.

_____ classmates _____ countries _____ I _____ student _____ we

2. The verb *be* has three forms in the simple present: *am*, *is*, *are*. Underline the forms of *be* in Part A.

3. A **contraction** is two words put together with an apostrophe ('). It's a shorter way of saying something. Circle the contractions in Part B.

Reading

A WARM-UP What kind of student are you? Check (✓) the sentences that describe you and your habits.

☐ I'm hardworking.　☐ I work with a tutor.　☐ I go to the computer lab.

☐ I'm curious.　☐ I ask questions in class.　☐ I study with friends.

☐ I'm friendly.　☐ I help my classmates.　☐ I talk to the teacher before and after class.

B SCANNING Scan the newsletter for school-related words. Underline them. Then go back and read the whole newsletter.

Welcome to English 1 class!

My name is Emma. I am an English teacher. Here is some helpful information:
* English classes are in classrooms 224, 226, and 228. English 1 is in room 224.
* My office is in room 264. I am in my office before and after class.
* The tutors are in room 216. Tutoring sessions are free.
* The computer labs are open every day.
* You need two books for this class. The books are in the bookstore. The bookstore also has dictionaries. The bookstore is in Building A. It isn't open on weekends.

We're from around the world!

The students in my English 1 class are from many different countries.
* Yuliy is a new student. He's from Bulgaria. He's 19 years old. He's a computer science major. His classes are about computers and computer programming.
* Mai, 22, isn't a new student. She's a returning student. She's from Japan. She's a business major.
* Pavil and Dharva are returning students, too.
* Pavil is a second-year student. She's 21 years old. She is a nursing major.
* Dharva is also a second-year student. She's 19 years old. She is an education major.
* Su is a new student. She's Vietnamese. She is 18 years old.

C UNDERSTANDING DETAILS Write *T* for the true statements and *F* for the false statements.

_____ 1. Emma is a teacher.

_____ 2. English classes are in rooms 220, 226, and 228.

_____ 3. The tutors aren't in room 216.

_____ 4. The two English books are in the bookstore.

_____ 5. Yuliy isn't a new student.

_____ 6. Pavil and Dharva aren't returning students.

_____ 7. Mai and Su are from Vietnam.

Grammar Focus 1 Nouns and pronouns

Examples	Language notes
(1) The **students** are from different **countries**. The **bookstore** is in **Building A**. The **books** are in the **bookstore**.	We use **nouns** for **people**, **places**, and **things**.
(2) **Dharva** is from **India**.	The specific name of a person or place is called a **proper noun**.
(3) The computer **lab** is open all week. The two computer **labs** are open all week.	Some nouns are **singular** = 1. Some nouns are **plural** = 2 or more.
(4) **The man** is a new student. → **He** is a new student. **Dharva and Pavil** are new students. → **They** are new students.	**Pronouns** replace nouns. *I, you, he, she, it, we,* and *they* are **subject pronouns**. They come before the verb.
(5) **I** am your teacher. **He** is from Bolivia. *(Pedro)* **She** is a teacher. *(Emma)* **It** is closed. *(the bookstore)*	*I, he, she,* and *it* are **singular** pronouns.
(6) **We** are from Brazil. *(Pedro and I)* **They** are here. *(Pavil and Dharva)*	*We* and *they* are **plural** pronouns.
(7) **You** and Mika are in English class. *(one person)* **You** are both returning students. *(two people)*	*You* can be **singular**, meaning one person. Or it can be **plural**, meaning two or more people. The situation determines the meaning.

Spelling: Plural nouns		
situation	how to make plural	examples
Most nouns, including nouns that end in **vowel + y** and **vowel + o**	Add -*s*	book → books key → keys lab → labs radio → radios
Nouns that end in -*s*, -*ss*, -*sh*, -*ch*, and -*x* Nouns that end in **consonant + o**	Add -*es*	bus → buses class → classes dish → dishes lunch → lunches box → boxes tomato → tomatoes
Nouns that end in **consonant + y**:	Change *y* to *i* and + -*es*	country → countries
Nouns that end in -*f* or -*fe*	Change *f* to *v* and + -*es*	leaf → leaves wife → wives
Nouns with **irregular** plural forms		child → **children** people → **person** man → **men** woman → **women**

See Appendices A and B on page A-1 for more examples of plural nouns and for spelling rules for -s endings.

Pronouns	
singular	plural
I	we
you	you
he	
she	they
it	

Grammar Practice

A Complete the chart. Use the words from the box.

book	desks	Sam	tutor
computers	dictionaries	schools	university
country	men	they	woman

Singular	Plural

B Write the plural form.

1. pencil *pencils* _____ **6.** watch _____

2. office _____ **7.** city _____

3. glass _____ **8.** zoo _____

4. bus _____ **9.** dish _____

5. box _____ **10.** man _____

C Write the singular form.

1. dictionaries *dictionary* _____ **5.** people _____

2. offices _____ **6.** sandwiches _____

3. potatoes _____ **7.** keys _____

4. radios _____ **8.** leaves _____

D Rewrite the sentences. Replace the underlined words with the correct pronouns.

1. <u>Dharva</u> is a second-year student. *She is a second-year student.* _____

2. <u>Yuliy and Yan</u> are students. _____

3. <u>Fatima and I</u> are in the bookstore. _____

4. <u>The dictionary</u> is on the desk. _____

5. <u>Patrick</u> is a teacher. _____

6. <u>Maria</u> is from Colombia. _____

Grammar Focus 2 Simple present: Statements with *be*

Example	Language notes
(1) I **am** your teacher. Julie **is** happy. The tutors **are** in room 216.	The verb *be* connects a person, place, or thing to information about the person, place, or thing.
(2) **Present** Past ——————— X ————→ Future I **am** your teacher. He **is** from Taiwan. She **is** from Mongolia. It **is** on the table. We **are** students. You **are** a new student. *(one person)* You **are** new students. *(2+ people)* They **are** in the classroom.	The verb *be* has three forms in the simple present: **am**, **is**, and **are**. To form **affirmative statements**, use: *I* + *am* *he, she, it,* singular subjects + *is* *we, you, they,* plural subjects + *are*
(3) I am → **I'm** a student. He is → **He's** American. She is → **She's** 21 years old. It is → **It's** old. We are → **We're** in the classroom. You are → **You're** from Fiji. They are → **They're** Canadian.	A **contraction** is a shorter way of saying two words. The two words are connected by an apostrophe ('). We use contractions with **subject pronouns** + *be*, especially in speech and informal writing. Use: *am* → *'m* *is* → *'s* *are* → *'re*
(4) I **am not** a student. It **is not** my book. They **are not** from Japan.	To form **negative statements**, use: subject + *be* + *not* + more information
(5) **I'm not** from here. **He's not / isn't** American. **She's not / isn't** 21 years old. **It's not / isn't** old. **We're not / aren't** in the classroom. **You're not / aren't** from Kenya. **They're not / aren't** Canadian.	To form **contractions** with *be* + *not*, use: *am not* → *'m not* *is not* → *'s not* OR *isn't* *are not* → *'re not* OR *aren't*

Affirmative statements with *be*			Negative statements with *be*				
I	**am**		I	**am**			
He She It	**is**	at school.	He She It	**is**	**not**	at home.	
We You They	**are**		We You They	**are**			

Grammar Practice

A Complete the sentences. Use the correct form of *be*. Use the simple present.

1. Juan _is_____ a teacher.

2. Marta and Yuan _____ tutors.

3. I _____ a new student.

4. We _____ in the classroom.

5. The book _____ on the table.

B Rewrite the sentences. Make negative statements with *not*. Use the simple present.

1. She is a new student. _She is not a new student._____

2. I am 20 years old. _____

3. You are from Japan. _____

4. It is in the bookstore. _____

5. They are in the computer lab. _____

C Complete the student ID. Use your information.

Name: _____

Home country: _____

Age: _____ Class: _____

☐ New student ☐ Returning student

D Stand up and talk with your classmates. Look at their IDs. Complete the sentences with your classmates' names.

1. _____ is a new student.

2. _____ is a returning student.

3. _____ is _____ years old.

4. _____ and _____ are from _____.

E Rewrite the sentences. Use contractions.

1. I am a student. _____

2. We are in the classroom. _____

3. They are tutors. _____

4. It is on the table. _____

5. She is not 20 years old. _____

6. You are not from Japan. _____

Speaking

A Complete the sentences with information about you.

My name is **1.** _____. I'm from **2.** _____. I'm

3. _____ years old. I'm a **4.** _____ student. I'm not a

5. _____ student. I'm a(n) **6.** _____ major.

B Work with a partner. Read your sentences from Part A. Listen and take notes as your partner reads. Then tell the class about your partner. Look at the model.

Name: _____ Status (new or returning): _____
Country: _____ Major: _____
Age: _____

This is Kushi. She's from Mongolia. She's not from the United States. She's 18 years old. She's a new student. She's not a returning student. She's a math major.

Listening

A BEFORE LISTENING It is the first day of class. What do teachers talk about on the first day? Check (✓) your guesses.

Introductions
☐ students' countries
☐ students' jobs
☐ students' status (new / returning)
☐ students' majors

Supplies
☐ pens and pencils
☐ clothes
☐ bilingual dictionary
☐ snacks

B 🎧 UNDERSTANDING MAIN IDEAS Listen to the teacher welcome the students. Check (✓) the kinds of information you hear.

Name	Status (new / returning)	Home country	Age	Major
Lin	✓	✓	✓	
Alex				
Maria				
Marta				
Ahmed				

C 🎧 UNDERSTANDING DETAILS Listen again. Circle the correct answers.

1. Lin is _____ years old. **a.** 22 **b.** 23

2. Alex is from _____. **a.** Iceland **b.** Poland

3. Maria is _____. **a.** 24 **b.** 44

4. Marta is a(n) _____ major. **a.** art **b.** math

5. Ahmed is from _____. **a.** Mongolia **b.** Morocco

Writing

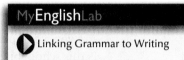

A Read about the English 3 students. Check (✓) the kinds of information in the article.

We're new students!
by Lin

Marta, Ahmed, Alex, Maria, and I are new students. We aren't returning students. We're from all around the world! Maria and Marta are from Ecuador. Ahmed is from Morocco. Alex is from Poland. I am from Korea. In class, we use two books and one dictionary. Our class isn't boring. It's interesting!

Marta, Ahmed, Alex, Maria, Lin

☐ students' names   ☐ students' favorite foods   ☐ students' majors

☐ students' ages   ☐ students' addresses   ☐ students' status

☐ students' home countries ☐ students' birthdays   ☐ students' opinions about class

B Talk to your classmates. Then write a short paragraph about your new classmates. Include the kinds of information you checked (✓) in Part A. Try to use the grammar from the chapter.

C Exchange paragraphs with a partner. Tell your partner what you like about his or her paragraph. Use the questions to review your partner's paper. Help your partner fix mistakes.

• Does your partner's paragraph include classmates' names? Home countries? Ages? Majors?

• Does your partner use the forms of *be* (*am, is, are*) correctly?

• Does your partner use *not* and contractions correctly?

CHAPTER 2   The Class of 2016

Getting Started

A Read the questions. Circle your answers.

1. Are you a new student?   **Yes**   **No**
2. Is your class in the morning?   **Yes**   **No**
3. Are you a computer major?   **Yes**   **No**
4. Is this school big?   **Yes**   **No**

B Look at the pictures. Then match the answers to the questions.

Darya   **Jung**   **Sam**

Questions	Answers
_____ 1. Who is from Cameroon?	**a.** *Engineering Today.*
_____ 2. Where is Darya?	**b.** 10 A.M.
_____ 3. What is the name of Darya's book?	**c.** To learn English.
_____ 4. How is Sam?	**d.** In the library.
_____ 5. Why is Jung in class?	**e.** Happy.
_____ 6. When is Jung's class?	**f.** Sam.

C Look back at Parts A and B. Complete the tasks.

1. **Yes / No questions** can be answered *yes* or *no*. What words do the *yes / no* questions in Part A start with?

   _____ and _____

2. **Wh- questions** ask for details and information. What words do the *wh-* questions in Part B start with?

   Who _____   _____   _____

   _____   _____   _____

Reading

A WARM-UP Think back in time to your first day of school or work. Are you relaxed? Nervous? Why? Is it a good experience?

B SKIMMING Skim the profiles and the conversation. Answer the questions. Then go back and read the profiles and conversation again.

1. Who are the students? _____

2. Who is the teacher? _____

PROFILES

Mark is a student at City College. He is 19 years old. He's an engineering major.

Luda is a student at City College, too. She is 24 years old. She's a nursing major.

Jason is an English professor at City College.

MARK: Excuse me. I'm in English 2. Where's room 224?

LUDA: That's room 224.

MARK: Thank you. I'm Mark.

LUDA: Hi, I'm Luda. It's nice to meet you. Are you a new student here?

MARK: Yes. Are you?

LUDA: No. This is my second year. Where are you from?

MARK: I'm from Russia. Where are you from?

LUDA: I'm from Ukraine.

MARK: Who's he?

LUDA: He's the English 2 teacher. His name is Professor Jason Rivera. He prefers "Jason."

JASON: Hi, Luda. How are you?

LUDA: Fine. . . . This is Mark. He's a new student in English 2.

MARK: It's nice to meet you. When is class today? Is it time? Am I late?

JASON: Class is at 2:00. It's 1:30 now. Why are you so early?

MARK: Because I'm excited! . . . Are these the right books?

JASON: Yes, those are the right books. See you soon!

C UNDERSTANDING DETAILS Circle the correct answers.

1. Where is Mark's class?   **a.** In room 224.   **b.** In room 2.
2. Is Luda a returning student? **a.** Yes, she is.   **b.** No, she isn't.
3. Who is Mark's teacher?   **a.** Luda.   **b.** Jason.
4. When is Mark's class?   **a.** At 1:30.   **b.** At 2:00.

Grammar Focus 1 Simple present: *Yes / No* questions and short answers with *be*

Examples	Language notes
(1) **Am I** early? **Are you** a teacher? **Is he** a tutor? **Is she** a new student? **Is it** in room 224? **Are we** in the classroom? **Are you** new students here? **Are they** in the library?	*Yes / No* **questions** ask questions that have a yes / no answer. Begin with: **Be + subject** **Note:** *Be* matches the subject in form (singular or plural).
(2) **Q:** Is she late? **A: Yes,** she **is.**	For **affirmative short answers**, use: **Yes,** + subject + **be**
(3) **Q:** Are they here? **A: No,** they **are not.**	For **negative short answers**, use: **No,** + subject + **be** + **not**

(4) **Q:** Are they from Mexico?
  A: No, they**'re not.** / No, they **aren't.**
 	
  Incorrect: Yes, ~~they're~~.
	You can (and should) **contract negative short answers**.
	
	Note: You cannot contract affirmative short answers.

Questions	Short answers	
	affirmative	negative
Am I late?	Yes, you **are.**	No, you**'re not.** / No, you **aren't.**
Are you a student?	Yes, I **am.**	No, I**'m not.**
Is he from Mexico?	Yes, he **is.**	No, he**'s not.** / No, he **isn't.**
Is she a student?	Yes, she **is.**	No, she**'s not.** / No, she **isn't.**
Is it 10:00?	Yes, it **is.**	No, it**'s not.** / No, it **isn't.**
Are we in the computer lab?	Yes, we **are.**	No, we**'re not.** / No, we **aren't.**
Are you from here?	Yes, we **are.**	No, we**'re not.** / No, we **aren't.**
Are they old?	Yes, they **are.**	No, they**'re not.** / No, they **aren't.**

Grammar Practice

MyEnglishLab

Grammar Plus 1
Activities 1 and 2

A Look at the pictures. Complete the questions. Then write short answers.

1. Q: __*Is she*_____ a teacher?

   A: __*No, she isn't.*_____

2. Q: _____ 19 years old?

   A: _____

3. Q: _____ married?

   A: _____

4. Q: _____ happy?

   A: _____

student, 19 — single

5. Q: _____ students?

  A: _____

6. Q: _____ 52 and 50 years old?

  A: _____

7. Q: _____ single?

  A: _____

8. Q: _____ in class?

  A: _____

engineer, 52 teacher, 50 — married

B Read each answer. Write a *yes / no* question with *you*. Then stand up and talk with your classmates. Ask your questions. When someone says *yes*, write the person's name.

Questions	Answers
1. *Are you from South America?*	is from South America.
2.	a new student.
3.	is single.
4.	is married.
5.	is happy.

C Answer the questions. Write short answers.

1. Are you a student? *Yes, I am.* _____

2. Are you a returning student? _____

3. Are you married? _____

4. Are you and your classmates from interesting places? _____

5. Are your classmates friendly? _____

6. Is your classroom big? _____

7. Is your English book easy? _____

8. Is your teacher from the United States? _____

Grammar Focus 2 *This, that, these, those*

Examples	Language notes
(1) **This room** is 224. Are **those students** your classmates?	*This*, *that*, *these*, and *those* tell us how near something or someone is.
(2) **This class** is interesting. **These books** are new. **That teacher** is from Canada. **Those classrooms** are cold.	*This*, *that*, *these*, and *those* are called **demonstrative adjectives** when they are followed by a noun. They match the noun in form: singular or plural.
(3) **Q:** Is **this room** open? **A:** Yes. **This room** is open.	Use *this* with things that are **near** and **singular**.
(4) **Q:** Is **that room** closed? **A:** Yes. **That room** is closed.	Use *that* with things that are **far** and **singular**.
(5) **Q:** Are **these dictionaries** cheap? **A:** Yes. **These dictionaries** are cheap.	Use *these* with things that are **near** and **plural**.
(6) **Q:** Are **those dictionaries** expensive? **A:** Yes. **Those dictionaries** are expensive.	Use *those* with things that are **far** and **plural**.
(7) **This** is 224. *(This room)* Is **that** my classroom? *(that room)* **These** are cheap. *(These books)* **Those** are expensive. *(Those books)*	*This*, *that*, *these*, and *those* are called **demonstrative pronouns** when they replace a noun.

Grammar Practice

A Circle the correct words.

1. **This / These** room is open.

2. **Those / That** books are expensive.

3. **That / Those** students are new this year.

4. **These / This** classrooms are clean.

5. **That / Those** cell phone is on.

B Complete the sentences. Use *this, that, these,* or *those.* Use the correct form of *be* in the simple present.

Near

1. _____ _____ my notebooks.

2. _____ _____ Alex's teacher?

3. _____ _____ pencils new?

Not near

4. _____ _____ your dictionary.

5. _____ _____ her classmates?

C Practice with a partner. Put some things on your desk (pens, pencils, paper, notebook, dictionary, cell phone, etc.). Point and talk about the things. Use *this, that, these,* and *those.* Look at the model.

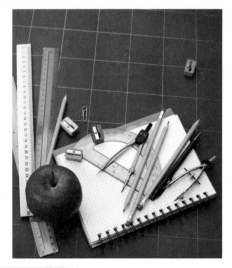

> This is a notebook. That is a cell phone.

> These are pens. Those are pencils.

D Now ask *yes / no* questions about the things on your desk. Use *this, that, these,* and *those.* Look at the model.

> Is this a book?

> Yes, that is a book.

The Class of 2016 **15**

Grammar Focus 3 Simple present: *Wh-* questions with *be*

Examples	Language notes
(1) **Q: Where am I?** **A:** You're in Building A. **Q: What is that book** about? **A:** It's about U.S. history. **Q: How are your parents?** **A:** They're fine, thanks.	*Wh-* **questions** ask for information. *Wh-* words include *Who, What, When, Where, Why,* and *How.* To form *wh-* questions with *be,* use: ***Wh-* word + *be* + subject** *Note: Be* matches the subject in form (singular or plural).
(2) **Q: Who** are they? **A:** They're my friends.	*Who* asks about people.
(3) **Q: What** is her name? **A:** Her name is Jill.	*What* asks about things.
(4) **Q: When** is class? **A:** It's at 11:00.	*When* asks about time.
(5) **Q: Where** are Tom and Marta? **A:** They're in class.	*Where* asks about place (location).
(6) **Q: Why** is she in the classroom? **A:** She's in the classroom **because** it is time for class.	*Why* asks for a reason. The answer often includes *because* + the reason.
(7) **Q: How** are you? **A:** I'm fine, thanks.	*How* asks about condition.
(8) **Q:** When is class? **A: It's on Tuesday. / Tuesday.**	Answer *wh-* questions with **complete sentences** or **short answers**.
(9) Who is → **Who's** What is → **What's** Where is → **Where's** How is → **How's**	We can make **contractions** with *wh-* words + *is.* *Note:* We usually only contract *wh-* words + *are* in speech—for example, *What're you doing?*

Grammar Practice

 Match the answers to the questions.

Questions	Answers
_____ 1. Where are they from?	**a.** Sonia Mato.
_____ 2. How are you?	**b.** Because we have a lesson.
_____ 3. When is the bookstore open?	**c.** They're from Canada.
_____ 4. Why are you here?	**d.** It's Thursday.
_____ 5. Who is your teacher?	**e.** I'm fine.
_____ 6. What is today?	**f.** It is open all day.

B Read the answers. Then use the words to write *wh-* questions.

1. Q: (Who) _____

   A: He's my classmate.

2. Q: (Where) _____

   A: The books are on the table.

3. Q: (How) _____

   A: I'm tired today.

4. Q: (When) _____

   A: Class is at 2:00.

5. Q: (What) _____

   A: Her name is Carmen.

C Write *wh-* questions for your partner. Then take turns asking and answering the questions. Look at the model.

> Where are you from?

> I'm from Brazil.

1. Q: _Where are you from?_ _____

2. Q: _____

3. Q: _____

4. Q: _____

5. Q: _____

Listening

A 🎧 UNDERSTANDING MAIN IDEAS Listen to a student journalist interview a new professor. Listen to the first half of the interview. Write the words you hear.

Luda: Hi. I'm Luda. _____ today?

John: Fine. Thank you. Please sit down. Not that chair. It has books on it. This chair.

Luda: Great, thank you. _____ ready?

John: Yes. _____ your first question?

Luda: _____ from here?

John: No, I'm not.

Luda: _____?

John: I'm from Cleveland.

Luda: _____ Cleveland? _____ in California?

John: _____. It's in Ohio.

Luda: Oh, . . . _____ cold in Ohio?

John: The winters are cold. The summers are nice: sunny and warm.

B 🎧 UNDERSTANDING DETAILS Listen to the second half of the interview. Answer the questions.

1. Is this John's first teaching job? _____

2. What is his favorite class to teach? _____

3. Is Luda a new student? _____

4. What is the interview for? _____

C AFTER LISTENING Work with a partner. Look at the world map on pages A8–9. Ask about places your partner knows. Use the questions to help you.

Questions: Where is your family from? How is the weather? Are the people friendly?

Speaking

A Write a *yes / no* question or a *wh-* question. Use the words.

Question	Example	Notes
1. (your name) *What's your name?*	*Su*	
2. (from)	*Vietnam*	
3. (old)	*20*	
4. (new student)	*No*	
5. (class in)	*English 2*	
6. (the class / interesting)	*Yes*	

B Interview a classmate. Take notes in the chart. Look at the model.

> What's your name?

> My name is Su.

C Now tell the class about your classmate. Look at the model.

> This is Su. She is from Vietnam. She is 20 years old. She is in English 2. She's not a new student. She's a returning student. She . . .

Writing

MyEnglishLab

▶ Linking Grammar to Writing

A Answer the questions about you.

1. What is interesting about you?

_____

2. Are you married? Are you a parent?

_____

3. Where is your favorite place to study? Why?

_____

4. What is your favorite movie?

_____

5. Who is your closest friend? Why?

_____

6. Are you a good cook?

_____

B Write a short online profile about you. Include the information on the list below. Add other information from Part A. Try to use the grammar from the chapter.

- Your name, age, and home country
- Your school status and major
- Your school's name
- Your class

My name is Marta Soto. I am from Peru. I'm 20 years old. I'm a new student at Atlantic College this year. I'm in English 2. Am I married? No, I'm not. I'm single. The café is my favorite place to study. What is your favorite "study spot"?

C Introduce yourself to the class. Listen as your classmates introduce themselves. Ask *yes / no* and *wh-* questions.

MyEnglishLab

▶ Diagnostic Test

Grammar Summary

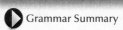

Nouns are people, places, and things. Nouns are singular or plural. **Subject pronouns** replace nouns. They are singular or plural. **Demonstratives adjectives** come before nouns and tell how near something or someone is. They match the noun in form: singular or plural. **Demonstrative pronouns** replace nouns.

	Singular	Plural (+ -s, -es, -ies)
Nouns	student, class, dictionary	students, classes, dictionaries
Subject pronouns	I You He / She / It	We You They
Demonstrative adjectives	**This** computer *(near)* **That** car *(not near)*	**These** notebooks *(near)* **Those** pencils *(not near)*

The verb *be* helps tell who, what, when, where, and how someone or something is. *Be* has singular and plural forms. We commonly use contractions with *be*.

Singular		Plural	
affirmative	**negative**	**affirmative**	**negative**
I am I'm You are You're } thirsty. She is She's He is He's	I'm not You're not OR aren't } hungry. She's not OR isn't He's not OR isn't	We are We're You are You're } ready. They are They're	We're not OR aren't You're not OR aren't } tired. They're not OR aren't
It is It's } hot.	It's not OR isn't } cold.		

Yes / No questions begin with a form of *be* and are answered with a short *yes / no* answer. **Wh- questions** begin with a *wh-* word and are answered with information.

Yes / No questions	Wh- questions
Q: Am I in Room C? **A:** Yes, you are. / No, you're not / you aren't.	**Q: Where** are you from? **A:** I'm from Nigeria. / Nigeria.
Q: Is she a teacher? **A:** Yes, she is. / No, she's not / she isn't.	**Q: Who** is he? **A:** He's Mario. / Mario.
Q: Are they students? **A:** Yes, they are. / No, they're not / they aren't.	

Self-Assessment

A (5 points) Correct the mistakes. Write the correct plural form.

1. dictionaryies _____
2. classs _____
3. studentes _____

4. wife's _____
5. countrys _____

B (6 points) Find and correct the mistake in each sentence.

1. We is students.
2. He are an engineer.
3. Shes' not tired today.

4. They are in these class.
5. You're aren't a new student.
6. This books are old.

C (6 points) Write sentences about the people. Use the information. Use the correct form of *be* and the simple present.

Luda

1. (a good student) _____
2. (from Ukraine) _____
3. (not married) _____

Rafa and Julia

4. (not new students) _____
5. (tired) _____
6. (late for class) _____

D (8 points) Look at the student ID. Answer the questions. Use short answers.

> **Atlantic College ID**   ☑ New student
>
> **Name:** Geidrus Lipkus
>
> **Email:** glipkus@mtn.com
>
> **Home country:** Belarus **Class:** English 2

1. What's the student's name? _____
2. Is he a student at Pacific College? _____
3. Is he from the United States? _____
4. Where's he from? _____
5. Is he in English 3? _____
6. What class is he in? _____
7. Is he a returning student? _____
8. Is he a new student? _____

Unit Project: Class newspaper

  A Work in groups of four (Partners A, B, C, and D). Create a class newspaper. Follow the steps.

1. Partners A and B: Write three more questions to ask a classmate. Then interview the classmate. Partner A asks the questions. Partner B takes notes.

Questions	
1. What's your name?	4.
2. Where are you from?	5.
3. Are you a new student?	6.

2. Partners C and D: Write three more questions to ask your teacher. Interview him or her. Partner C asks the questions. Partner D takes notes. Look at the model.

Questions	
1. Where are you from?	3.
2.	4.

Where are you from?

I'm from California.

B With your partners, write two articles. Write an article about your classmate. Write an article about your teacher. Use the information from Part A. Give your newspaper a name and date. Add pictures if possible.

The Daily Campus News — Spring

Meet the new students!
Daniel is from Mexico.
He's a new student . . .

Meet the teacher!
Our teacher Emma
is from California.
She . . .

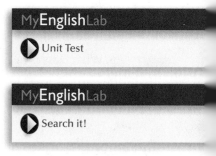

UNIT 2

7:00 A.M.

9:00 A.M.

7:00 P.M.

10:15 P.M.

11:00 P.M.

A Day in the Life

OUTCOMES

After completing this unit, I will be able to use these grammar points.

CHAPTER 3

Grammar Focus 1
Simple present: Statements

Grammar Focus 2
Third person singular: Irregular and other forms

Grammar Focus 3
Expressing frequency

CHAPTER 4

Grammar Focus 1
Simple present: Yes / No questions

Grammar Focus 2
Simple present: Wh- questions

MyEnglishLab

 What do you know?

Journal Writing

Getting Started

A Look at pictures. Read the weekend activities. Which of the statements are true for you?

> I always wake up at 9:00 A.M.
> I usually call my mom.
> I often do homework in the evening.
> I occasionally write in my journal.
> I sometimes exercise.

> We never get up early.
> We rarely go outside.
> Sometimes we have friends over.
> Usually we watch TV.

B Work with a partner. Talk about the pictures and your answer in Part A. Which of the statements about activities are true for you?

C Look back at the lists in Part A. Complete the tasks.

1. We express actions, habits, facts, thoughts, and emotions with **verbs** (*write, go*). Underline the verbs.

2. **Adverbs of frequency** tell *how often* someone does something. Circle the adverbs of frequency. What pattern do you notice about the order?

Reading

A WARM-UP Which of the activities do you and your friends do? Circle them.

check email	eat breakfast	hang out with friends	study at a café
cook a big dinner	exercise	pay bills	watch TV
do homework	go to class	read the newspaper	work

B SCANNING George is a new student at Atlantic College. Scan George's email. Circle his weekday activities. Underline his weekend activities. Then go back and read the whole email.

TO: amiga4@kazoo.com
FROM: georgem@kazoo.com
SUBJECT: My Life Now

Hi Gita,

I hope you are well. My English classes are good. I have a lot of friends from all over the world!

Every Monday, Wednesday, and Friday I wake up early and eat breakfast. I always review my class notes. I sometimes read the newspaper. I go to school at 8:00 A.M. My neighbor Yuliy and I walk to class together. We usually eat lunch after class. Sometimes I go to the computer lab after lunch. Yuliy never goes with me. He has a computer at home. I think he usually watches music videos, but he doesn't admit it.

On Tuesdays and Thursdays, I don't have class in the morning. I usually go to the gym and exercise. Yuliy doesn't like to go to the gym. He occasionally exercises at home. We meet in class, and then we usually go to the library. Our friends Mai and Mark often come, too. Mai does her homework, and Mark usually reads.

Every Saturday afternoon I work at a restaurant as an assistant server. I clean the tables and fill water glasses. It isn't an easy job, but I like it. It has some good parts, like the tips! I often go to parties after work on Saturdays. Usually the party is at a classmate's apartment. Everyone tries to bring something. Yuliy usually brings the music. I don't stay too late. On Sundays, I rarely leave my apartment. I usually study, watch TV, and go online. I check my email and write friends and family. My family writes every week.

Visit soon!

George

C UNDERSTANDING MAIN IDEAS AND DETAILS Circle the correct answers.

1. George **always / never** reviews his class notes in the morning.

2. He goes to **school / work** at 8:00 A.M.

3. He **has / doesn't have** class on Tuesday morning.

4. He **works / eats** at a restaurant every Saturday afternoon.

5. He **goes to a party / studies at the library** after work.

Grammar Focus 1 Simple present: Statements

Example	Language notes
(1) Past ———— **X** ————→ Future **Present** I **sleep** on Sunday. He **works** on Tuesday.	Use the simple present to talk about **regular actions** or **habits**.
(2) We **live** in a small apartment. The bookstore **opens** at 11:00.	Use it for **facts** (things that are true).
(3) You always **forget** your schedule. They **enjoy** school.	Use it to express **thoughts** and **emotions**.
(4) I **work** at the café. You **live** in a big city. We **study** on Sunday afternoon. They **open** in the fall.	To form **statements** with *I, you, we, they,* and plural subjects, use: subject + **base verb** (no *-s*)
(5) She **works** at the library. He **lives** in a small town. It **closes** in the summer.	To form **statements** with *he, she, it,* and singular subjects, use: subject + **base verb** + *-s* ***Note:*** See Grammar Focus 2 for other forms.
(6) I **do not work** on Tuesdays. You **do not order** pizza every Thursday.	To form **negative** statements with *I, you, we, they,* and plural subjects, use: subject + ***do not*** + base verb
(7) He **does not live** in a house. It **does not open** at 9:00.	To form **negative** statements with *he, she, it,* and singular subjects, use: subject + ***does not*** + base verb
(8) We **don't** have class on Friday. They **don't** enjoy city life. She **doesn't** work in a mall. That computer **doesn't** work.	It is common in speech and informal writing to use the **contraction** *doesn't* for *does not* and *don't* for *do not.*

See Appendix C on page A-2 for more examples of simple present verbs and for pronunciation and spelling rules for final -s.

Affirmative statements		Negative statements	
I You We They	**live** here.	I You We They	**don't live** here.
He She	**lives** here.	He She	**doesn't live** here.
It	**opens** at eight o'clock.	It	**doesn't open** at nine o'clock.

Grammar Practice

MyEnglishLab

▶ Grammar Plus 1
Activities 1 and 2

 Rewrite the sentences. Use the subjects and the correct verb form.

1. I wake up early on Wednesdays.

(He) *He wakes up early on Wednesdays.*

2. The students review the class notes.

(She) _____

3. We walk to school.

(They) _____

4. You eat lunch after class.

(I) _____

5. They don't work on Saturdays.

(Daniela) _____

6. She doesn't like Mondays.

(We) _____

7. They don't open on Sundays.

(It) _____

B Read Gita's email. Complete the sentences.
Use the simple present form of the verbs.

TO: georgem@kazoo.com
FROM: amiga4@kazoo.com
SUBJECT: RE: My Life Now

Hi George,

You sound busy! Everything here is good. Marta and I **1.** _____ (work) every Friday,

Saturday, and Sunday. We **2.** _____ (not / work) Mondays, Tuesdays,

Wednesdays, or Thursdays. Marta **3.** _____ (like) to study on her days off.

I **4.** _____ (prefer) to relax at the beach. Marta **5.** _____ (want) to go back to

school. I **6.** _____ (not / want) to go back.

   We **7.** _____ (not / hang out with) many of your old friends. They **8.** _____ (live)

in the city now. Marta **9.** _____ (not / enjoy) the city. She **10.** _____ (say)

that the city is too noisy. I **11.** _____ (hope) we can visit you soon.

Your friend, Gita

C Play "Round Robin." Follow the steps. Look at the model.

1. Sit in groups of four.
2. Listen as each partner says one activity he or she does and one activity he or she doesn't do.
3. Retell your partners' activities and add your own. Say different activities.

> *I wake up early. I don't eat breakfast.*

> *Kai wakes up early. She doesn't eat breakfast. I sleep late. I don't drink coffee.*

> *Kai wakes up early. She doesn't eat breakfast. Pierre sleeps late. He doesn't drink coffee. I . . .*

Grammar Focus 2 Third person singular: Irregular and other forms

Examples	Language notes
(1) **I do** homework every morning. **He does** homework every afternoon. **You have** class at 10:00 A.M. **She has** class at 9:00 A.M. **They go** slow. **It goes** fast.	The verbs **do**, **have**, and **go** have irregular forms with *he, she,* and *it* in the simple present: **do → does** **have → has** **go → goes**
(2) **try:** He **tries** to bring something interesting. **carry:** She **carries** books in her backpack. **fly:** It **flies** high.	For verbs that end in a **consonant + y**, change the *y* to *i* and add *-es*.
(3) **pass:** It **passes** quickly. **push:** The professor **pushes** the chairs under the desks. **watch:** She **watches** TV every night. **mix:** The class **mixes** history with language.	For verbs with *-s, -sh, -ch,* and *-x* endings, add *-es*.

Pronunciation of final -s	
The pronunciation of the final *-s* is /s/ if the last sound of the base verb is one of these *voiceless* sounds: /f/, /θ/, /p/, /t/, /k/.	sleeps writes walks
The pronunciation of the final *-s* is /z/ if the last sound of the base verb is one of these *voiced* sounds: /b/, /d/, /g/, /l/, /m/, /n/, /ŋ/, /r/, /v/, /ð/ or a vowel sound.	reads listens tries
The pronunciation of the final *-s* is /ɪz/ if the last sound of the base verb is one of these sounds: /s/, /z/, /ʃ/, /ʒ/, /tʃ/, /dʒ/.	mixes brushes watches

See Appendix C on page A-2 for more examples of simple present verbs and for pronunciation and spelling rules for final -s.

Grammar Practice

 A Complete the paragraph about Mai's regular activities. Use the simple present form of the verbs.

Every morning, Mai **1.** _____ (have) a cup of coffee. She takes a shower. But

she **2.** _____ (not / eat) breakfast. She **3.** _____ (not / have) time.

She gets on the bus and **4.** _____ (go) to school. She **5.** _____ (try)

to catch the early bus, but she often **6.** _____ (miss) it. But she

7. _____ (not / hurry) and take a taxi. She walks. After school, she

8. _____ (do) her homework, and she **9.** _____ (study) for

the next day. Mai prepares her dinner and **10.** _____ (try) to relax. She often

11. _____ (worry) about her busy schedule. At 10:00 P.M., she

12. _____ (brush) her teeth and **13.** _____ (wash) her face.

She **14.** _____ (not / watch) TV. She's too tired!

B Look at the pictures. Write sentences about the people's activities. Use the information. Use the simple present.

Cara

1. (study French) _Cara studies French._

2. (brush her hair) _____

3. (go to bed late) _____

Tom

4. (fix cars) _____

5. (go online) _____

6. (try to find a new job) _____

Samuel

7. (carry groceries home) _____

8. (have dinner) _____

9. (wash dishes) _____

Lucia

10. (teach yoga class) _____

11. (do her homework) _____

12. (watch TV) _____

Grammar Focus 3 Expressing frequency

Examples	Language notes
(1) I **always** review my class notes. We **usually** go to the library after class. She is **often** tired. He **sometimes** exercises at home. It **occasionally** snows in the spring. We **rarely** read the newspaper. They **never** ride their bikes to school.	**Adverbs of frequency** tell how often something happens. Common adverbs of frequency include *always, usually, often, sometimes, occasionally, rarely,* and *never.*
(2) I **am always** on time for school. It **is occasionally** cold in the spring. I **always wake up** early on Mondays. It **occasionally rains** in the summer.	Adverbs of frequency come **after be**. They come **before other verbs**.
(3) **Sometimes** he is bored. **Usually** you walk to school.	*Sometimes* and *Usually* can also come at the beginning of the sentence.
(4) I study **once a week**. **Twice a week** we go out for lunch. She sees her friends **three times a month**. We are late **every day**.	These **time signals** usually come at the beginning or end of the sentence: *once a* _____ (*week,* etc.) = one time *twice a* _____ (*year,* etc.) = two times *three* (*four,* etc.) *times a* _____ (*day,* etc.) *every* _____ (*morning, week,* etc.)

Adverbs of frequency	
100%	always
	usually
	often
50%	sometimes
	occasionally
	rarely
0%	never

Grammar Practice

 A Look at Devin's weekly calendar. Read the activities. Write one more. Mark (**X**) the frequency.

Activity	Sun.	Mon.	Tues.	Wed.	Thurs.	Fri.	Sat.
1. go to school		X		X		X	
2. work	X				X	X	X
3. practice the guitar at night	X	X	X	X	X	X	X
4. exercise in the morning	X			X	X	X		X
5. watch TV							
6. hang out with friends							X
7.							

30 Chapter 3

B Look at Devin's calendar again. Complete the sentences about Devin's week. Use the words from the box. For 7, use your own words.

always	never	occasionally	once	three times	usually

1. Devin goes to school _____ a week.

2. He _____ works during the week.

3. He _____ practices the guitar at night.

4. _____ he exercises in the morning.

5. He _____ watches TV.

6. He hangs out with friends _____ a week.

7. _____

C Complete your own activity chart. Choose activities from the list or use your own ideas. Then mark (✗) the days.

cook breakfast	go online	have dinner with friends
do homework	go to school	study
exercise	hang out with friends	watch TV

Activity	Sun.	Mon.	Tues.	Wed.	Thurs.	Fri.	Sat.
go to school							

D Write sentences about some of your weekly activities from Part C. Use adverbs of frequency and time signals.

1. _____

2. _____

3. _____

4. _____

E Read the paragraph about Chandra. There are five mistakes. Find and correct the mistakes.

   Chandra wakes up usually early. She takes a shower. She eats sometimes breakfast. She every morning leaves her house at 8:00 A.M., and she goes to school. She walks often to school. She is sometimes late to work. In her office, she occasionally meets other students. She rarely listens to music at work. Never she leaves her office early.

Listening

A 🎧 UNDERSTANDING MAIN IDEAS Listen to Nick and Keiko introduce themselves. Check (✓) the activities each student does.

1. goes to school	☐	☐
2. studies at the library	☐	☐
3. watches TV	☐	☐
4. goes online	☐	☐
5. listens to music	☐	☐
6. exercises	☐	☐
7. talks on the telephone	☐	☐
8. cleans house / apartment	☐	☐
9. hangs out with friends	☐	☐
10. cooks dinner	☐	☐

B 🎧 UNDERSTANDING DETAILS Listen again. Match the frequency words to the statements.

Statements	Frequency words
_____ 1. Nick goes to school ___.	**a.** usually
_____ 2. Nick watches TV ___.	**b.** every night
_____ 3. Nick's roommate ___ cleans the apartment.	**c.** once a week
_____ 4. Keiko ___ goes online in the evening.	**d.** every Sunday
_____ 5. Keiko cleans ___.	**e.** twice a week
_____ 6. Keiko hangs out with friends ___.	**f.** always

C AFTER LISTENING Who would you prefer as a roommate, Nick or Keiko? Why? Discuss with a partner.

Speaking

A Look at the list of activities. Which do you do? Circle them. Which activities don't you do? Cross them out.

cook	go shopping	relax	visit family
eat out	go to the library	stay home	watch TV
exercise	listen to music	study	work on the computer
finish homework	read	swim	write emails

B Fill in the calendar with your activities. Add notes about how often.

Su	M	T	W	Th	F	Sa

C Give a short presentation to the class. Tell about four activities you do and four you don't. Look at the model.

> *I always go to the supermarket on Mondays. I never go on Saturdays because it's crowded. I often study in the library. Sometimes I study in the cafeteria.*

Writing

A Read Alain's journal entry. What is it about? How does he organize the events?

September 24

I get up at 7:00 A.M. every morning. I make coffee, take a shower, and watch the news. I don't eat breakfast. I get dressed, and I walk to the bus stop. I take the bus to school. I go to three classes. After class, I often eat lunch in the cafeteria with my cousin. We usually go to the library to study after lunch. At 4:00, I take the bus home. I sometimes stop at the market to buy groceries. At home, I listen to music and call my family. Then I cook dinner. I usually have vegetables and rice. I don't eat meat. After dinner, I always do my homework. I sometimes check my email. I watch TV and go to bed.

B Write a journal entry about your daily activities. Try to use the grammar from the chapter.

C Exchange journal entries with a partner. Talk about your activities. Which of your partner's habits do you like? Why?

MyEnglishLab

Diagnostic Test

CHAPTER 4 Blogging

Getting Started

A Read the *yes / no* questions. Circle your answers. If you circle *Yes,* answer the *wh-* question.

Yes No **1.** Do you like to write? What do you like to write? _____

Yes No **2.** Do you write in a journal? When do you write in your journal? _____

Yes No **3.** Do you use online social networks? Who do you communicate with? _____

Yes No **4.** Do you read blogs (online journals)? How often do you read blogs? _____

Yes No **5.** Do you write a blog? Where do you blog from (a café, etc.)? _____

B Read the excerpt from an interview with blogger Patty Dawson.

INTERVIEWER:	How often do you blog?
PD:	I try to write every day.
INTERVIEWER:	What do you write about?
PD:	I write about my daily activities, thoughts, and ideas.
INTERVIEWER:	Who reads your blog? And who do you want to read your blog?
PD:	My family and friends read it. I hope others read it also.
INTERVIEWER:	Does it take a lot of time to write your blog?
PD:	No, it doesn't. It is like writing in a journal, but it's not private.
INTERVIEWER:	Do you write about personal things—for example, family things?
PD:	Sometimes. My parents don't love that!
INTERVIEWER:	Where do you usually write?
PD:	At a café in my neighborhood, usually.
INTERVIEWER:	When do you usually blog?
PD:	At night. However, I sometimes blog in the morning.

C Look back at Parts A and B. Complete the tasks.

1. Circle the *yes / no* **questions**. Underline the *wh-* **questions**.

2. How are these questions different from the *yes / no* questions and *wh-* questions you studied in Chapter 2?

Reading

A WARM-UP Look at the graphics. Which age group blogs the most? Who blogs more, men or women?

Bloggers: Age groups

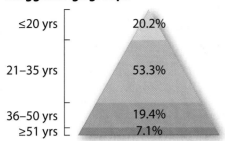

≤20 yrs	20.2%
21–35 yrs	53.3%
36–50 yrs	19.4%
≥51 yrs	7.1%

Bloggers: Men and women

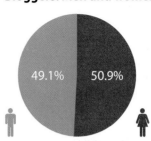

49.1%   50.9%

B SCANNING Scan the magazine article for the statistics (numbers that give detailed information) from Part A. Underline them. Then go back and read the whole article.

BLOG FAQs

Blogging is a daily activity for many people around the world. But many people don't understand blogging. Here are some common questions.

Who blogs? It is no surprise that people ages 21–35 blog the most. However, not far behind are the people 20 and under. Do women blog more? Not really. About the same number of men and women write blogs.

What do bloggers write about? Men write about work and other professional interests. Women write about personal interests and hobbies.

Where do bloggers live? The biggest percentage of bloggers live in the United States. The U.K. is second, and Japan is third. Does the average age change for each country? No, it doesn't. Adults in their 20s and 30s write the most blogs in any country.

How often do bloggers write? Many young bloggers write daily. However, bloggers in the 36-and-up age group write once or twice a week.

Why do people read blogs? One reason is to learn new things. What do people learn? A new recipe, a fashion tip, how to solve a problem.

How do you find a blog you like? You guessed it! Read a blog about blogs.

C UNDERSTANDING MAIN IDEAS AND DETAILS Match the answers to the questions.

Questions	Answers
_____ 1. Do men blog more than women?	**a.** To learn something new.
_____ 2. What age group blogs the most?	**b.** In the United States.
_____ 3. What do men blog about?	**c.** No, they don't.
_____ 4. What do women blog about?	**d.** People 21 to 35 years old.
_____ 5. Where do most bloggers live?	**e.** Yes, they do.
_____ 6. Do people in the U.K. and Japan blog?	**f.** Work and professional interests.
_____ 7. Why do people read blogs?	**g.** Personal interests.

Grammar Focus 1 Simple present: *Yes / No* questions

Examples	Language notes
(1) **Do** you **blog**? 　　**Do** we **write** journals? 　　**Do** they **read** blogs?	To form *yes / no* questions in the simple present with *I, you, we, they,* and plural subjects, use: ***Do*** + subject + **base verb**
(2) **Does** he **write** a blog? 　　**Does** she **blog** every day? 　　**Does** it **take** a long time to write? 　　*Incorrect:* **Does** it ~~takes~~ a long time to write?	To form *yes / no* questions in the simple present with *he, she, it,* and singular subjects, use: ***Does*** + subject + **base verb**
(3) **Q:** Do bloggers write every day? 　　**A:** **Yes, they do.** 　　**Q:** Does it take a long time to write? 　　**A:** **No, it doesn't.**	For **short answers**, use: **Yes,** + subject + ***do / does*** **No,** + subject + ***do / does*** + ***not***

Questions	Answers			
	affirmative		negative	
	short answers	long answers	short answers	long answers
Do you **blog**?	Yes, I **do**. Yes, we **do**.	Yes, I **blog**. Yes, we **blog**.	No, I **don't**. No, we **don't**.	No, I **don't blog**. No, we **don't blog**.
Does your friend **blog**?	Yes, he **does**.	Yes, he **blogs**.	No, he **doesn't**.	No, he **doesn't blog**.

Grammar Practice

MyEnglishLab

► Grammar Plus 1
Activities 1 and 2

A Complete the conversations. Write questions with *Do* or *Does*.

1. Q: *Does she work in an office?*

　A: Yes, she does. She works in an office.

2. Q: _____

　A: No, it doesn't. Blogging doesn't take a lot of time.

3. Q: _____

　A: Yes, he does. He goes online every day.

4. Q: _____

A: Yes, we do. We write journals in class.

5. Q: _____

A: No, they don't. They don't read blogs.

6. Q: _____

A: No, I don't. I don't send text messages every day.

B Work with a partner. Ask your partner a *yes / no* question. Use topics from the list below. Partner: Give a short answer. Take turns. Look at the model.

Partner A
go online every day
write in a journal
check email every day
want to blog
read a newspaper online

Partner B
like to communicate online
use a social network
write letters
do homework in the computer lab
think technology helps people

> *Do you go online every day?*

> *No, I don't.*

C Find the mistake in each question. Rewrite the questions.

1. Does she writes every day?

_____

2. Do you keeps a journal?

_____

3. Do he work at home?

_____

4. Do it take a long time?

_____

5. Does they like to read newspapers online?

_____

Grammar Focus 2 Simple present: *Wh-* questions

Examples	Language notes
(1) **Who do** news blogs **attract**? **What does** your blog **talk** about? **When does** she **write**? **Where do** most bloggers **come** from? **Why do** we **read** blogs? **How do** you **start** a blog? **How often** do you **write**?	As you learned in Chapter 2, the *wh-* words are *Who, What, When, Where, Why,* and *How.* To form *wh-* **questions** in the simple present, use: *Wh-* **word** + *do / does* + subject + **base verb** **Note:** The form of *do* agrees with the subject.
(2) **Q: Who reads** your blog? **A:** My friends.	When the *wh-* word is the **subject** of the question, use the third person singular form of the verb.
(3) **Q: How often** do bloggers **write**? **A:** Bloggers write **every day**.	**How often** asks about the frequency of something. Include **an adverb of frequency** or a **time signal** in the answer.

(4) **Q:** When does he blog?
    A: He blogs in the afternoon. / **In the afternoon.**
 	
    Q: Where do you write?
    A: I write in a café. / **In a café.**
	Wh- questions require answers with information. We often give **short answers**.

Wh- questions	Short answers	Long answers
Who does the blog attract?	People from around the world.	It attracts people from around the world.
What do we write about?	Our lives.	We write about our lives.
When do you write?	At night.	I write at night.
Where does he write?	In the library.	He writes in the library.
How do you find a good blog?	By asking friends.	You find a good blog by asking friends.
Why do you read blogs?	Because we like to learn new things. / To learn new things.	We read blogs because we like to learn new things.
How often do they post a blog entry?	Every week.	They usually post an entry every week.
Wh- word as subjects	Short answers	Long answers
Who writes this blog?	I do.	I write that blog.
What makes a blog interesting?	Good writing.	Good writing makes a blog interesting.

Grammar Practice

MyEnglishLab

Grammar Plus 2
Activities 1 and 2

 Write questions. Use the information. Add *do* or *does* when necessary.

1. (What / you / blog about) *What do you blog about?* _____

2. (What / it / mean) _____

3. (Where / she / write her blog) _____

4. (When / they / take classes) _____

5. (How often / you / use a computer) _____

6. (Why / they / journal online) _____

7. (Who / I / write this blog for) _____

8. (How / you / feel about online newspapers) _____

9. (Who / write / this blog) _____

10. (What / make / someone / a good blogger) _____

B Read the conversation. Complete the questions.

BLOGGER 1: I read your blog every day. I blog, too.

BLOGGER 2: Great. _____ you call your blog?

BLOGGER 1: The name is *Forever Student.*

BLOGGER 2: That's an interesting name. _____ you blog about?

BLOGGER 1: I blog about my student life. I have a busy life.

BLOGGER 2: Yes, I do, too. I rarely have time to blog. _____?

BLOGGER 1: I usually blog late at night. _____ often _____ blog?

BLOGGER 2: I blog twice a week. _____?

BLOGGER 1: I blog from any location, even the café!

BLOGGER 2: Me, too!

C Use the words to write a *yes / no* question or a *wh-* question. Then interview a classmate. Write the answers in the chart.

Questions	Classmate's answers
1. (What / like to read) *What do you like to read?*	
2. (Where / like to read)	
3. (When / read)	
4. (like to write)	
5. *If yes to #4* (When / like to write)	

Listening

A 🎧 LISTENING FOR MAIN IDEAS Listen to the conversation. Write a checkmark (✓) each time you hear a question that starts with a *wh-* word.

☐ ☐ ☐ **1.** Who   ☐ ☐ ☐ **3.** When   ☐ ☐ ☐ **5.** Why

☐ ☐ ☐ **2.** What   ☐ ☐ ☐ **4.** Where   ☐ ☐ ☐ **6.** How

B 🎧 LISTENING FOR DETAILS Listen again. Circle the correct answers.

1. What does Sara write about?
   a. Her friends' activities.   **b.** Her thoughts and experiences.

2. Where does Sara record her private thoughts?
   a. In a journal.   **b.** On a blog.

3. Who keeps a journal?
   a. Marcus.   **b.** Sara.

4. How does Sara know what Marcus does on Friday nights?
   a. She reads his blog.   **b.** She's part of his social network.

C AFTER LISTENING Ask a partner the questions. Circle *Yes* or *No*. Write short answers. Then compare your habits. Are your habits similar or different?

Yes   No   **1.** Do you belong to a social networking site? What's the name? _____

Yes   No   **2.** Do you post family pictures online? Why? / Why not? _____

Yes   No   **3.** Do you read a blog every day? When? _____

Yes   No   **4.** Do you check your email twice a day or more? Where? How? (at home, via computer, etc.) _____

Speaking

A Work with a partner. Look at and read about three well-known computer technology users. What else do you know about these people? Tell your partner.

Bill Gates
CEO and founder of Microsoft

Mark Zuckerberg
CEO and founder of Facebook

Shakira
singer and songwriter

B Work with a partner. Imagine you are a blogger. Your partner plays the role of someone from Part A. Write a conversation. Then role-play. Look at the model.

> Do you use the Internet?

> (Mark Zuckerberg) Yes, I do.

> Do you use Facebook?

> Yes, I do. It's a great social networking site!

> When do you have time?

> I usually check it in the morning. . . .

Yes / No questions	Answers
1. Q: _____	A: _____
2. Q: _____	A: _____
3. Q: _____	A: _____

Wh- questions	Answers
4. Q: _____	A: _____
5. Q: _____	A: _____
6. Q: _____	A: _____

Writing

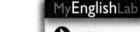
MyEnglishLab

Linking Grammar to Writing

 A Think about the questions in the list. Then read Malcolm's paragraph. Does his paragraph answer all of the questions?

- How do you communicate with your friends and family?
- Do you use social media?

- Do you post pictures?
- How often do you go online?
- What do you usually do online?

> I use the Internet to communicate with friends and family. Why? Because the Internet is a good way for us to stay in touch. Who disagrees with that? I often use social media and sometimes post pictures. My family never posts pictures. They are very busy. I go online every day. I like to check email, use social media, and do my homework online. But I don't shop online. Do I think it's convenient? Yes. But I don't trust it. . . .

B Now write about your online habits. Write a paragraph that answers the questions in Part A. Try to use the grammar from the chapter.

C Post your paragraph on a wall of the classroom. Read your classmates' paragraphs. Who has similar Internet habits?

MyEnglishLab

Diagnostic Test

Grammar Summary

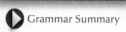

We use the **simple present** to talk about everyday activities, habits, and facts, and to express thoughts and feelings. To form the third person singular (*he, she, it*), add -*s* (or -*es*, or -*ies*) to the verb: *live – lives, catch – catches, try – tries*. The verbs *do, have,* and *go* are irregular in the third person singular. Form negative sentences by adding *do / does* + *not* + base verb.

Simple present affirmative	Simple present negative
I **write** every day.	I **don't write** on weekends.
You **read** the newspaper online.	You **don't read** magazines.
He **writes** a blog. *He **has** a blog.	He **doesn't write** a blog. He **doesn't have** an email account.
She **studies** in the morning. *She **does** her homework in the morning.	She **doesn't study** in the morning. She **doesn't do** her homework at night.
It **passes** quickly. *It **goes** fast.	It **doesn't pass** quickly. It **doesn't go** slowly.
We **surf** news sites.	We **don't surf** sports sites.
They **spend** a lot of time online.	They **don't spend** a lot of time outside.

Adverbs of frequency and **time signals** tell us how often something happens.

Frequency words			
100%	I **always** write in my journal.	about 20%	It **occasionally** rains in the fall.
about 90%	You **usually** read the newspaper online.	about 10%	We **rarely** do homework in the library.
about 70%	She **often** sends emails.	0%	They **never** come to class late.
about 50%	He **sometimes** eats breakfast.		

Time signals	
once a _____ (*day, week,* etc.) = one time	*number* + *times a* _____ (*day, week,* etc.)
twice a _____ (*day, year,* etc.) = two times	*every* _____ (*morning, week, month,* etc.)

Form **yes / no questions** with *Do / Does* + subject + base verb. Form **wh- questions** with *wh-* word + *do / does* + subject + base verb. When the *wh-* word is the subject, use the third person singular form of the verb. We often answer both forms with a short answer.

Yes / No questions with short answers	Wh- questions with long and short answers
Q: Do I **write** every day? **A:** Yes, you **do**. / No, you **don't**.	**Q: What do** I **write**? **A:** You write a blog. / A blog.
Q: Do you **read** the newspaper online? **A:** Yes, I **do**. / No, I **don't**.	**Q: Where do** you **read** the newspaper? **A:** I read it online. / Online.
Q: Does she **write** a blog? **A:** Yes, she **does**. / No, she **doesn't**.	**Q: When does** she **write**? **A:** She writes at night. / At night.
Q: Do we **surf** the Internet? **A:** Yes, we **do**. / No, we **don't**.	**Q: Where do** you **surf**? **A:** We surf new sites. / New sites.
Q: Do they **spend** a lot of time online? **A:** Yes, they **do**. / No, they **don't**.	**Q: Who write**s this blog? **A:** They write it. / They do.

Self-Assessment

A (10 points) Write sentences about the people's activities. Use the information. Use the simple present.

Mondi

1. (work / five days a week) _____

2. (rarely / cook) _____

3. (usually / study in the evening) _____

Ana

4. (go to school / every morning) _____

5. (always / surf the Internet) _____

6. (occasionally / watch TV) _____

7. (do homework / every Sunday night) _____

Lucy and Wade

8. (read the newspaper online / every day) _____

9. (sometimes / have dinner with friends) _____

10. (often / use social media) _____

B (5 points) Read each answer. Then write a *yes / no* question or a *wh-* question.

1. Q: _____

   A: Yes, she does. Amanda works in a restaurant.

2. Q: _____

   A: No, I don't. I don't take the bus to school.

3. Q: _____

   A: I go to school at City College.

4. Q: _____

   A: I study mathematics.

5. Q: _____

   A: I leave for class at 9:00 A.M.

C (10 points) Read Victor's blog. There are 10 mistakes. Find and correct the mistakes.

○ ○ ○

October 12

A Day in My Life

What does I do on Mondays? On Mondays, I do usually get up and turn on the computer. I takes a shower, and I do cook breakfast. I eat sometimes eggs and toast. I every day drink coffee. Then I brush my teeth, and I go to school. How I get to school? I often take the bus, or I walk sometimes with my friend Jana. At school, we studies English. The teacher does gives us a lot of homework.

Unit Project: Class blog

A Work as a class. Start a class blog about your everyday activities. Add something new to the blog every week. Follow the steps.

    1. What do you want to know about your classmates? In small groups, think of 10 questions (5 *yes / no* questions, 5 *wh-* questions).

        Example: **1.** _Do you use social media?_
                  2. _Do you work?_
                  3. _Where do you work?_

    2. As a class, agree on the 10 best questions. Write them in the chart.
    3. Write your answers.

10 best questions	Your answers
1.	
2.	
3.	
4.	
5.	
6.	
7.	
8.	
9.	
10.	

B Write a paragraph for the class blog. Use the questions and answers in Part A to help you write your paragraph.

My name is Na Lee. I'm a student at City College. What's my day like? Well, I'm a typical student, I think. I like technology, and I use it a lot every day. For example, I always read the news online and check my email in the morning. Who reads a newspaper these days? Before class, I usually text my friends. In class, I use a tablet and take notes. (Sometimes I surf the Internet—sorry, professors!). But in the evenings I turn off all technology and study. Do you want to read other students' blogs? Here's a link to the school's home page: www.citycollegeusa.edu.

D Post the class blog. Add pictures, links, and other class information to the blog.

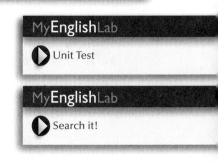

MyEnglishLab
▶ Unit Test

MyEnglishLab
▶ Search it!

UNIT 3

Where in the World?

OUTCOMES

After completing this unit, I will be able to use these grammar points.

CHAPTER 5

Grammar Focus 1
Simple present: *There is* and *There are*

Grammar Focus 2
Prepositions of place

CHAPTER 6

Grammar Focus 1
Simple past: *There + be* statements

Grammar Focus 2
Simple present and past: *Be + there* questions

CHAPTER 5 | Mapping It Out

Getting Started

A Look at the map. With a partner, talk about things you like to do when visiting a city.

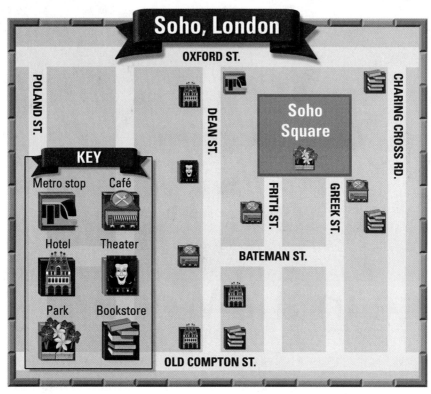

B Look at the map again. Write *T* for the true statements and *F* for the false statements.

_____ **1.** There is a theater on Dean Street.

_____ **2.** There are no parks in Soho.

_____ **3.** There is a café on Dean Street.

_____ **4.** There is a metro stop near Oxford Street.

_____ **5.** There are two bookstores between Old Compton and Bateman Streets.

C Look back at the statements in Part A. Complete the tasks.

1. We use **prepositions of place** (*on*, *between*, etc.) to describe location. Circle the examples.
2. We use *There is* and *There are* to tell about the existence or location of something. Complete the chart with the subjects that follow *There is* and *There are*.

There is	There are
a theater,	

Reading

A WARM-UP Work with a classmate. Describe a city or town that you know well. Answer the questions.

- What is the name of the town?
- What are some important places there?
- What are the important streets?

B SCANNING What does *GIS* mean? Scan the article and underline the answer. Then go back and read the whole article.

Where's Amy? A blog about travel and adventure

Saturday - 9:14 A.M.

My friend Erica and I are visiting London, England, for the first time. We plan to use a GIS (Geographic Information System) device to find places to visit. GIS devices are hand-held electronic gadgets that help people find the location of places.

On my device, there's an electronic map. On the map, there are "layers," or levels, of information. One layer shows the location of the streets in the neighborhood. Other layers show things such as restaurants, museums, hotels, and stores.

Our hotel is on the map, of course. The hotel is old. It's in Soho, a historic neighborhood in London. I'm interested in history and want to use my GIS device to find historic places in London. The GIS map shows many historical places near our hotel. For example, the poet William Blake lived at 28 Broadwick Street, the composer Mozart lived on Frith Street, and the poet Percy Shelley lived on Poland Street. There are not many interesting places like this back home!

Erica is not very interested in history. She likes to watch people, eat at restaurants, and relax. Soho is full of great places to eat and drink. The GIS map shows a layer of information about places to visit. There are several parks in the neighborhood. One is on Soho Square—that's between our hotel and Oxford Street. There are three good restaurants near the hotel. The bookstore Soho Books is on Dean Street. There aren't any big restaurants near our hotel, but there are a lot of nice, small places to eat. There are a lot of cafés in Soho, and people spend time talking there.

Erica and I have different interests, but we enjoy traveling together. There's no rain or wind today, so it's a good day to get out!

C UNDERSTANDING DETAILS Complete the sentences. Use the words from the box.

device	history	hotel	poets	restaurants

1. Amy and Erica plan to use a GIS _____.

2. Amy and Erica are staying in an old _____.

3. Amy is interested in _____.

4. There are houses of famous _____ in Soho.

5. Erica likes to visit _____.

Grammar Focus 1 Simple present: *There is* and *There are*

Examples	Language notes
(1) **There is** a lot of work to do.	We use *There is* and *There are* to say that things and places **exist**.
(2) **There are** some great restaurants on Dean Street.	We also use *There is* and *There are* to give **locations**.
(3) **There is one** grocery store on Main Street. **There are a few** students in the library. **There are many** fast food restaurants in this neighborhood.	We also use *There is* and *There are* to tell about **amounts**. We use **numbers** and words such as *a few* and *many*.
(4) **There is a subway stop** on Oxford Street.	With **singular** nouns, use: ***There is** + **singular noun***
(5) **There are two hotels** on this street.	With **plural** nouns, use: ***There are** + **plural noun***
(6) Look. **There's** the bus stop.	We often **contract** *There is*: *There's*. *Note:* We usually only use the contraction *There're* in speech.
(7) **There is not** a bus stop there. **There are not** many people here.	For **negative** statements, use: ***There is** + **not** + singular noun* ***There are** + **not** + plural noun*
(8) **There's not / There isn't** a bus stop there. **There aren't** many people here.	For **contracted negative** statements with *There is* or *There are*, use: ***There's not*** OR ***There isn't** + singular noun* ***There aren't** + plural noun*
(9) **There is no** bridge on North Street. **There are no** computers in the library.	We can also use *no* to form negative statements: ***There is no** + singular noun* ***There are no** + plural noun*
(10) There **are many stores** on this street. **There aren't any** large **hotels** in Soho.	To indicate a **large amount**, use: ***There are a lot of / many** + **plural noun*** To mean "**none**," use: ***There aren't any** + **plural noun***

Full forms	Contracted forms
There is	There's
There is not	There's not / There isn't
There are	There're [informal speech]
There are not	There aren't

Grammar Practice

A Notice the nouns in **bold**. Circle the correct form: *Singular* or *Plural*. Then look at the map. Complete the sentences with affirmative or negative forms of *be*.

1. There ___*is*___ a **hotel** on Dean Street.   (Singular) Plural

2. There _____ three **metro stops** between

    Oxford Street and Old Compton Street.   Singular   Plural

3. There _____ many **cafés** in Soho.   Singular   Plural

4. There _____ a **bookstore** on Charing Cross Road.   Singular   Plural

5. There _____ a **theater** on Poland Street.   Singular   Plural

6. There _____ a **metro stop** near Oxford Street.   Singular   Plural

B Look at the map in Part A. Complete the sentences. Use the information and words from the list. You may need to make some words plural.

bank	gas station	library	movie theater
café	grocery store	metro stop	taxi stand

1. __*There isn't a bank*_____ (There / not / a) on Dean Street.

2. _____ (There / no) between Oxford Street and Old

    Compton Street.

3. _____ (There / not / many) in Soho.

4. _____ (There / no) on Greek Street.

5. _____ (There / not / a) on the map.

6. _____ (There / not / any) near Oxford Street.

C Read the paragraph. There are four mistakes. Find and correct the mistakes

    Our hotel is cheap, but there no are restaurants near our hotel. Also, there isn't many

museums in the neighborhood, and there is no cafés on our street. But happily, there are any

bookstores in the area—20, according to the guidebook. Unfortunately, they aren't open today!

Grammar Focus 2 Prepositions of place

Examples	Language notes
(1) There is a nice park **in Soho**.	We use **prepositions of place** such as *in, on, at, near,* and *between* to **describe locations**.
(2) London is **in England**. We are staying **in London**. The hotel is **in Soho**. The library is **in Speakman Hall**. Our class meets **in this room**.	Use the preposition *in* for places you can find on a map (continents, countries, states, cities, and neighborhoods). Also use *in* for buildings and rooms.
(3) There is a restaurant **on Broad Street**. There isn't a library **on the first floor**. London is **on the Thames River**.	Use *on* for streets or roads. Also use *on* for floors of a building and for bodies of water such as rivers, lakes, and oceans.
(4) His house is **at 28 Broadwick Street**. I'm **at the restaurant**.	Use *at* for street addresses. Also use *at* to describe locations in a general way.
(5) There is a museum **near our school**.	Use *near* to describe short distances between locations.
(6) There is a theater **between Broad Street and the park**.	Use *between* to describe a location in the middle of two other locations.
(7) My GIS program shows many historical places **near our hotel**.	Prepositions come **before** nouns and noun phrases.
(8) There is a nice park **in this neighborhood**.	A **preposition + noun** is called a *prepositional phrase*.
(9) I am **at home**. *(in my house)* She keeps her phone **at work**. *(at the job site)* He's not **in school** this semester. *(taking classes)*	Some **preposition + noun** combinations have a different meaning than the words individually.

Grammar Practice

MyEnglishLab

Grammar Plus 2
Activities 1 and 2

 Complete the blog post. Use *in, on, at, near,* or *between*.

○○○

Erica and I are having a great time 1. _____ London. We are staying

2. _____ Soho. We have a room 3. _____ an old hotel. There are a

lot of great buildings 4. _____ our street. I want to spend the day tomorrow

5. _____ the neighborhood. I'm excited to see the home of some great writers.

I know that William Blake's house is 6. _____ Broad Street, and Washington

Irving's old house is 7. _____ 8 Argyll Street.

   I know that there are some nice restaurants 8. _____ our hotel—only one or

two blocks away. I hope to try them tomorrow. And our hotel is 9. _____ two

excellent cafés—one on the left, one on the right. Erica is reading about some other

places 10. _____ Bateman Street and Old Compton Street. I think we will stay

11. _____ our room tonight, and get up early to start our visit.

Amy

B Look at the Waterbury College campus map. Complete the sentences. Use prepositions.

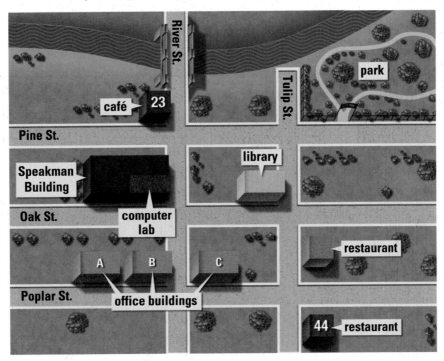

1. Oak Street is _between_ Pine Street and Poplar Street.

2. There is a library _____ Pine Street and Oak Street.

3. There are three office buildings _____ Poplar Street.

4. There is a café _____ 23 River Street.

5. There is a computer lab _____ the Speakman Building.

6. The park is _____ the library.

7. There is a restaurant _____ 44 Tulip Street.

8. There is a river _____ the college.

Listening

A BEFORE LISTENING Look at the map. Find the places in the list.

Broadwick Street   Foyle's Books   Poland Street   Soho Theater

Café Soho   John Snow Pub   Soho Square   William Blake's house

Dog and Duck Pub   Percy Shelley's house

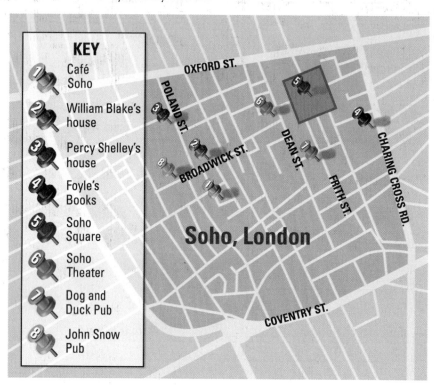

KEY
1. Café Soho
2. William Blake's house
3. Percy Shelley's house
4. Foyle's Books
5. Soho Square
6. Soho Theater
7. Dog and Duck Pub
8. John Snow Pub

Soho, London

B 🎧 UNDERSTANDING MAIN IDEAS Listen to the conversation. Check (✓) the places Amy and Erica talk about.

☐ Café Soho   ☐ Poet's Café   ☐ Soho Square
☐ William Blake's house   ☐ Golden Square   ☐ Soho Theater
☐ Italian restaurant   ☐ Soho Books   ☐ John Snow Pub
☐ Percy Shelley's house   ☐ Foyle's Books   ☐ Dog and Duck Pub

C 🎧 UNDERSTANDING DETAILS Listen again. Write the locations of the following places.

1. Café Soho: _____

2. Percy Shelley's house: _____

3. Foyle's Books: _____

4. Dog and Duck Pub: _____

Speaking

A. Work with a partner. Study the map of the city of Las Mesas for two minutes.

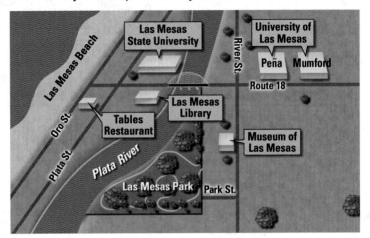

B. Work with a partner. Cover the map. Take turns asking about places and locations. Look at the model.

> What schools are in Las Mesas?

> There are two universities in Las Mesas. . . .

Writing

A. Think about places on and around your campus. Take notes.

Places to study: _____

Places to take visitors: _____

B. Read the postcard. Then write a postcard to a friend. Write about places on campus and around your school. Try to use the grammar from the chapter.

Dear Jen,

How are you? How is school? Life in Las Mesas is good. I get coffee every morning before class. The café is between my apartment and campus. There are always a lot of people in line! Our English classroom is in the Peña Building on River Street. Some of my classes are in the Mumford Building. It's near the gym. The computer lab is also in the Mumford Building. Luckily, there isn't any waiting—there are 100 computers available.

Write soon,

Becky

Jen Stills
1401 Ellis Ave.
Portland, ME 04105

C. Exchange postcards with a classmate. Did you write about the same places?

CHAPTER 6

Traveling Through Time

Getting Started

A Think about the town where you live. Cross out the statements that aren't true. Then talk about your answers with a partner.

Today in my town . . .

there are many good **restaurants**.   there is **a college**.
there are many young **people**.   there is **a library** near my house.
there are many **students**.

B Look at the map. Write *T* for the true statements and *F* for the false statements.

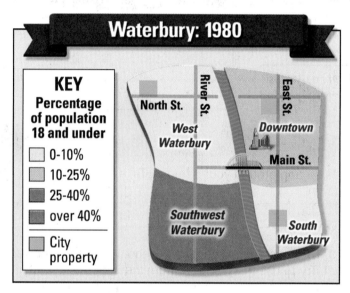

Waterbury: 1980

KEY
Percentage of population 18 and under
☐ 0-10%
☐ 10-25%
☐ 25-40%
☐ over 40%

☐ City property

North St.
River St.
East St.
West Waterbury
Downtown
Main St.
Southwest Waterbury
South Waterbury

In 1980 . . .

_____ **1.** there was city **property** in West Waterbury.

_____ **2.** there were many young **people** in West Waterbury.

_____ **3.** there was a **college** in the city of Waterbury.

_____ **4.** there were many **bridges** from Downtown to West Waterbury.

C Look back at Parts A and B. Complete the tasks.

1. Notice the words in **bold** in Part A. Then circle the simple present forms of *be*.
2. Notice the words in **bold** in Part B. Then circle the **simple past** forms of *be*.
3. Complete the chart with the forms of *be* in Parts A and B.

	Present	Past
Singular		
Plural		

Reading

A WARM-UP What was life like in England in the 1800s?
Check (✓) the things you think existed.

☐ computers   ☐ antibiotics   ☐ doctors   ☐ GIS devices

☐ pollution   ☐ disease   ☐ electricity   ☐ maps

B SCANNING Scan the conversation. Who is the topic of Amy and Erica's conversation?
Circle each occurrence of the name. Then go back and read the whole conversation.

AMY: Hey, here we are. This is the John Snow Pub. It's named after Dr. John Snow, a famous Soho doctor in the mid-1800s. See that old pump across the street? It honors Dr. Snow.

ERICA: Was there a hospital here at that time?

AMY: No, there wasn't. But there was a famous use of GIS right here, back in 1854. And some people say that Dr. Snow was the inventor.

ERICA: In 1854? Were there computers in Soho in 1854?

AMY: No, there were no computers then. There weren't even houses with electricity! But remember: GIS stands for "geographic information system." Here's the story. It's the 1850s, and Dr. Snow lives here in Soho. At that time, there was a very bad disease called cholera, but there wasn't any information about the real cause.

ERICA: Wow. That sounds terrible. Were there any medicines for cholera?

AMY: No, there weren't. So this disease is really serious. Dr. Snow believes the water pump is the cause of the disease. He doesn't know the term "GIS," but he uses GIS to prove his theory. He makes a map of all the households in Soho with cholera. He marks the location of each with a dot. Then he marks the location of each water pump in the neighborhood with an "x." There were many pumps like this all over the city. He talks to neighbors to get information about the pumps and the users. When he finishes, his map shows the answer: there were pollution problems near the water pump on Broadwick Street. So Dr. Snow is the father of GIS!

C UNDERSTANDING MAIN IDEAS AND DETAILS Circle the correct answers.

1. It's the 1850s, and John Snow is a famous _____.
   a. computer scientist   **b.** doctor   **c.** pub owner

2. Snow puts information about cholera on a _____.
   a. computer   **b.** map   **c.** website

3. Snow thinks the cause of cholera was polluted _____.
   a. water   **b.** air   **c.** clothes

Grammar Focus 1 Simple past: *There* + *be* statements

Examples	Language notes
(1) Present **Past** —— X —— | ————► Future **There was** a pump on Broadwick Street. **There were** two major problems with the project.	As with the present form, we use the past form of ***There*** + ***be*** to say something exists and to talk about location and amounts.
(2) **There was** a bridge over the river.	To form **statements** with **singular** nouns, use: ***There was*** + singular noun
(3) **There were** two hotels on this street.	To form **statements** with **plural** nouns, use: ***There were*** + plural noun
(4) **There was not** a bus stop on Dean Street. **There were not** any good medicines.	To form **negative** statements, use: ***There was*** + ***not*** + singular noun ***There were*** + ***not*** + plural noun
(5) **There wasn't** a bus stop on Dean Street. **There weren't** many people there.	To form **contracted negative** statements, use: ***There wasn't*** + singular noun ***There weren't*** + plural noun
(6) **There was no** hospital. **There were no** computers. *Incorrect:* **There ~~wasn't no~~** computers.	We can also use ***no*** to form negative statements: ***There was no*** + singular noun ***There were no*** + plural noun
(7) **There were many hotels** on this street. **There weren't any banks** in Soho.	To indicate a **large amount**, use: ***There were a lot of / many*** + **plural noun** To mean "**none**," use: ***There weren't any*** + **plural noun**

	Affirmative	Negative	Contractions
Singular	There was	There was not	There wasn't
Plural	There were	There were not	There weren't

Grammar Practice

A Notice the words in **bold**. Then complete the sentences. Use the correct simple past form of *be*.

1. There _____ many **bridges** over the river.

2. There _____ no **college** in 1980.

3. There _____ not many **doctors** in the neighborhood.

4. There _____ some young **people** in downtown Waterbury.

5. There _____ a **house** on Poland Street.

B Rewrite the sentences. Use the simple past.

1. There are many sick people in London.

_____

2. There isn't a good hospital in Soho.

_____

3. There is an historic house on Dean Street.

_____

4. There aren't any young people there.

_____

5. There are two theaters near the square.

_____

6. There are no houses with electricity.

_____

C Find and correct the mistake in each sentence.

1. There were a restaurant on the corner many years ago.

2. There no were antibiotics in 1850.

3. There was sick people in London at that time.

4. There wasn't no bridge on North Street in 1980.

5. No there were many doctors in the 1850s.

D Look at the map of Waterbury in 1980 on page 54. Use the words to write affirmative and negative sentences. Use *There was (not)* or *There were (not)*.

1. (city property / North Street)   *There was city property on North Street.*

2. (bridges / River Street)   _____

3. (a college / Watertown)   _____

4. (a bridge / Main Street)   _____

5. (many young people / West Waterbury)   _____

Grammar Focus 2 Simple present and past: *Be* + *there* questions

Examples	Language notes
(1) **Is there** a college in Waterbury? **Are there** restaurants in Collegetown?	For **questions** with *Be* + *there* in the **present**, use: *Is there* + singular noun *Are there* + plural noun
(2) **Was there** a hospital in Soho? **Were there** good doctors at that time?	For **questions** with *Be* + *there* in the **past**, use: *Was there* + singular noun *Were there* + plural noun
(3) **Are there any** bookstores in Soho? **Are there many** bookstores in Soho?	To ask about **amounts** in the **present**, use: *Are there any / many / a lot of* + plural noun
(4) **Were there any** cafés on your block? **Were there many** cafés on your block?	To ask about **amounts** in the **past**, use: *Were there any / many / a lot of* + plural noun

(5) **Q:** Is there a library in this building?
   A: Yes, there is.
 	
Q: Are there good restaurants in Waterbury?
   A: Yes, there are.
	For **affirmative short answers** in the **present**, use:
	
	Singular: *Yes,* ***there is.***
	
	Plural: *Yes,* ***there are.***

(6) **Q:** Was there a good bookstore in the area?
   A: Yes, there was.
 	
Q: Were there any tourists?
   A: Yes, there were.
	For **affirmative short answers** in the **past**, use:
	
	Singular: *Yes,* ***there was.***
	
	Plural: *Yes,* ***there were.***

(7) **Q:** Is there a bathroom on this floor?
   A: No, there isn't. / No, there's not.
 	
Q: Are there Indian restaurants in Pacific City?
   A: No, there aren't.
	For **negative short answers** in the **present**, use:
	
	Singular: *No,* ***there isn't.*** OR *No,* ***there's not.***
	
	Plural: *No,* ***there aren't.***

(8) **Q:** Was there a college in Soho?
   A: No, there wasn't.
 	
Q: Were there any good doctors in the city?
   A: No, there weren't.
	For **negative short answers** in the **past**, use:
	
	Singular: *No,* ***there wasn't.***
	
	Plural: *No,* ***there weren't.***

Grammar Practice

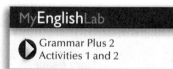

MyEnglishLab

Grammar Plus 2
Activities 1 and 2

 A Complete the conversation. Use *there* and the correct form of *be*.

A: I fly to London next week. **1.** _____ any good restaurants in Soho?

B: Yes, **2.** _____ a lot of them! **3.** _____ a famous one
   on Frith Street called the Dog and Duck Pub.

A: 4. _____ a good bookstore?

B: Yes, 5. _____ two good ones. One of them has a great café.

A: 6. _____ a park in Soho?

B: Yes, Soho Square has a park.

① 1804
Locomotive trains
in England

② 1878
Electricity in
English houses

④ 1932
Antibiotics

1800   1850   1900   1950

③ 1928
Women's suffrage
(right to vote) in England

⑤ 1941
Computers

B   Look at the timeline. Write questions about the events and inventions. Use *Was there* and *Were there*.

1. _____ in the early 1800s?

2. _____ in the late 1800s?

3. _____ in the early 20th century?

4. _____ before 1932?

5. _____ in 1950?

C   Work with a partner. Take turns asking and answering the questions you wrote in Part B. Look at the model.

> Were there locomotive trains in England in the early 1800s?

> Yes, there were.

D   Look at the map of Waterbury in 1980 on page 54. Write *be + there* questions with the information. Then take turns with a partner asking and answering the questions. Give short answers.

1. (a lot of people over age 18 / in West Waterbury)

    Q: _____

2. (a bridge / on Main Street)

    Q: _____

3. (a lot of young people / in South Waterbury)

    Q: _____

4. (a bridge / on North Street)

    Q: _____

5. (city property / in Downtown)

    Q: _____

6. (a college / in Southwest Waterbury)

    Q: _____

Listening

A BEFORE LISTENING Find these places on the map: Collegetown, South Waterbury, Downtown, West Waterbury.

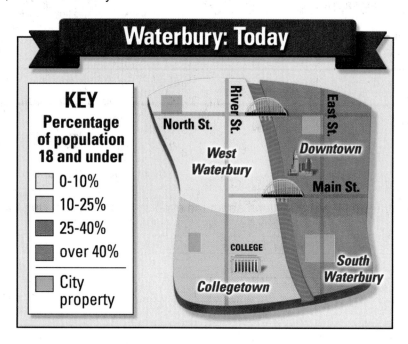

Waterbury: Today

KEY
Percentage
of population
18 and under

☐ 0-10%
☐ 10-25%
☐ 25-40%
☐ over 40%

☐ City
   property

River St. · North St. · West Waterbury · East St. · Downtown · Main St. · COLLEGE · Collegetown · South Waterbury

B 🎧 UNDERSTANDING MAIN IDEAS Listen to the conversation. Then match the main ideas to the sentences.

Sentences

_____ 1. Kwame has _____ for _____ class.

_____ 2. The city of Waterbury wants to build _____ and _____.

_____ 3. There are a lot of _____ in West Waterbury. It's the best place for _____.

_____ 4. There are a lot of _____ in South Waterbury. It's the best place for _____.

Main ideas

a. a playground / a senior center
b. a project / his GIS class
c. kids / a playground
d. seniors / a senior center

C 🎧 UNDERSTANDING DETAILS Listen again. Cover the map and write *T* for the true statements and *F* for the false statements. Then look at the map to help check your answers.

_____ 1. There's city property in four neighborhoods.

_____ 2. There are a lot of seniors in South Waterbury.

_____ 3. There are a lot of seniors in West Waterbury.

_____ 4. There is a bridge on North Street.

_____ 5. There are a lot of young people in South Waterbury.

_____ 6. There is city property in South Waterbury.

_____ 7. There is a college in Waterbury.

Speaking

A Work as a class. Transform your classroom into a town. Label objects as places around a town. For example, label one chair "Hotel," another "Bookstore," etc. Name the streets.

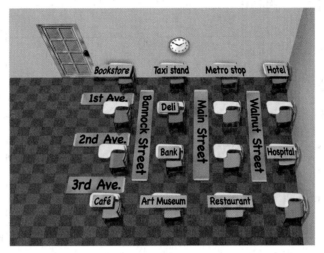

B Work in groups of three. Two students are tourists, one student is a concierge at a hotel. (A concierge is a hotel employee who gives guests information about a city.) The tourists ask questions about places around town. The concierge gives short answers. Look at the model.

> Is there a good bookstore near the hotel?

> Yes, there is. There's one at 1st Avenue and Bannock Street.

Writing

A Draw a map of the town where you grew up. In your map, include the important natural features such as rivers and mountains. Also, include important streets and buildings, such as your house and your school.

B Now write a letter to your future grandchildren. In the first paragraph, describe the town where you grew up. In the second paragraph, describe what it's like today. Try to use the grammar from the chapter.

> Dear Grandchildren:
>
> My hometown of Springfield was a small city in the 1980s. There weren't many businesses. There was only one school. . . .
>
> Today Springfield is a big city. There are many people in the city. . . .

C Work with a partner. Take turns reading your letters. Is you partner's hometown similar to or different from yours? How?

Grammar Summary

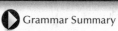
MyEnglishLab
▶ Grammar Summary

Use *There + be* to explain something's existence or location or to tell about an amount. We often contract *There is* to *There's*. Use *a lot of* and *many* to mean a large amount. Use *not, not any,* and *no* in negative sentences.

Simple present	
singular	**plural**
There's a hotel downtown. **There isn't** a bus stop on Dean Street. **There isn't any** time. **There is no** hotel on Pine Street.	**There are many** bookstores on this street. **There aren't a lot of** rooms available. **There aren't any** rooms available. **There are no** restaurants on Tulip Street.
Simple past	
singular	**plural**
There was a cholera problem. **There wasn't** a metro in the 1800s. **There wasn't any** entertainment. **There was no** bridge on North Street.	**There were many** guests at the hotel. **There weren't** answers to our questions. **There weren't any** young people. **There were no** computers.

We use some **prepositions** to describe **location**. Use *in* with countries, cities, neighborhoods, and for buildings and rooms. Use *on* for streets, floors of a building, and bodies of water. Use *at* for addresses and to describe locations in a general way. Use *near* to describe short distances between locations. Use *between* when referring to things on either side.

Prepositions of place	
in	The college is **in Waterbury**. / Our class meets **in this room**.
on	There is a playground **on East Street**. / The library is **on the first floor**. / Waterbury is **on a river**.
at	He lives **at 15 Poland Street**. / I'm **at the restaurant**.
near	There is a **museum near our school**.
between	The **library** is **between** the **Kazar Science Building** and the **Lemon Theater**.

Use *Be + there* to form a **question**. Use *any, many,* and *a lot of* with plural nouns. We often reply with **short answers**.

Questions	Short answers
Is there a park in Waterbury?	Yes, **there is**. No, **there is not**. / No, **there isn't** / **there's not**.
Are there public restrooms? **Are there any** good bookstores on the campus?	Yes, **there are**. No, **there are not**. / No, **there aren't**.
Was there a hospital in Soho?	Yes, **there was**. No, **there was not**. / No, **there wasn't**.
Were there good medicines in 1853? **Were there many** people there?	Yes, **there were**. No, **there were not**. / No, **there weren't**.

Self-Assessment

A (5 points) Complete the sentences. Use the correct form of *there + be*.

1. Now _____ a college in Southwest Waterbury.

2. In 1980, _____ not a bridge on North Street

3. Now _____ a lot of young people in South Waterbury.

4. In 1850, _____ a water pump on Broadwick Street

5. In 1980, _____ a lot of seniors in West Waterbury.

B (6 points) Complete the sentences. Use prepositions.

1. There are a lot of parks _____ London.

2. He lives _____ Dean Street.

3. The bookstore is _____ 749 Main Street

4. My class is _____ the first floor.

5. Is there a gas station _____ here? I don't want to drive far.

6. My house is _____ the community garden on the left and the bank on the right.

C (4 points) Read the answers. Then write questions with *be + there*.

1. Q: _____

   A: Yes, there's a nice restaurant on Tulip Street.

2. Q: _____

   A: No, there weren't many young people.

3. Q: _____

   A: Yes, there are a lot of good doctors in Waterbury.

4. Q: _____

   A: Yes, there was a college in Soho.

D (10 points) Read the story. There are 10 mistakes. Find and correct the mistakes.

Dear Anh:

London is great! Our hotel is at the Soho neighborhood. It is in Dean Street. There is many things to do. There is many old houses. There's no many children in the city. There a lot of interesting sites. There are some really nice cafés. They are beautiful parks. To London, people sit in the park and watch other people. Yesterday there was a lot of people in the park. There not were problems!

Your friend,

Erica

Unit Project: City council presentation

A Help a city develop a new facility. You'll present your ideas to the city council. Work in groups of four. Follow the steps.

1. Read the project background:

   The City of Waterbury has funds to build a new facility on its property. You and your partners are on the planning committee. What kind of facility does the city of Waterbury need? Where is the best location?

2. Study the map. Discuss these questions:
   • Where is city property available?
   • What kinds of people live in the different neighborhoods?
   • What kinds of facilities make sense for the city and the citizens? Consider the list of possibilities below. Add your own ideas.

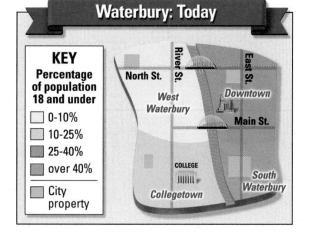

Waterbury: Today

KEY
Percentage of population 18 and under
☐ 0-10%
☐ 10-25%
☐ 25-40%
☐ over 40%
☐ City property

North St. | River St. | East St.
West Waterbury | Downtown
Main St.
COLLEGE
Collegetown | South Waterbury

animal shelter	park / playground	senior center	swimming pool
community college	prison	soup kitchen	_____
library	recycling center	sports stadium	_____

3. Now decide what kind of facility to build and where to build it.

B Present your ideas to the class. Describe the facility. Describe the locations. Explain your decisions. Look at the model.

> We think that a recycling center is the perfect new facility for Waterbury. And we think Collegetown is the best place for it. Why a recycling center? First, there is a large population of young people in Collegetown . . .

MyEnglishLab
▶ Unit Test

MyEnglishLab
▶ Search it!

Time is Money

UNIT 4

English Fun

OUTCOMES

After completing this unit, I will be able to use these grammar points.

CHAPTER 7

Grammar Focus 1
Parts of speech: Nouns, pronouns, verbs, prepositions, and adjectives

Grammar Focus 2
Sentences: Subjects, verbs, and objects

Grammar Focus 3
Question forms

CHAPTER 8

Grammar Focus 1
Sentence patterns with *be*

Grammar Focus 2
Prepositional phrases / Object pronouns

MyEnglishLab

 What do you know?

CHAPTER 7   Proverbs

Getting Started

A   Look at the pictures and read the captions. Then read the proverbs. Match the pictures to the proverbs.

A   **They accomplish things!**

B   **This student eats nutritious foods.**

C   **Tarima is unhappy.**

Proverbs

_____ **1.** An apple a day keeps the doctor away.

_____ **2.** I woke up on the wrong side of the bed.

_____ **3.** The early bird gets the worm.

B   Discuss the questions with a partner.

    1. What do you eat to stay healthy?

    2. How do you wake up: happy or unhappy?

    3. When do you get up?

C   Look at the captions in Part A. Complete the tasks.

    1. The noun or pronoun that starts a sentence is the **subject**. Circle the subjects.

    2. Words that express a state of being or action are **verbs**. Underline the verbs.

    3. Words that describe nouns are **adjectives**. Draw a square around the adjectives.

    4. Words that receive the action of the verb are **objects**. Double underline the objects.

Reading

A WARM-UP What do you think these proverbs mean? Discuss them with a classmate.

Time is money.   *Money talks.*   *The best things in life are free.*

B SCANNING Scan Bastien's notes. Find and circle the three proverbs from Part A. Were your predictions about meaning correct? Then go back and read all of the notes.

English 1   April 15   Class topic: Proverbs
What is a proverb?
A proverb is a short traditional saying. Proverbs give advice. Proverbs don't change over time.

Proverbs about money
Time is money. = Time is important.
Money talks. = People pay attention to money.
Money doesn't grow on trees. = You have to work hard for money.
The best things in life are free. = Friends and family are important.

Proverbs about life
All clouds don't bring rain. = Problems look bad. Not all problems are bad.
You can't judge a book by its cover. = You don't know a person by the way he / she looks.
Too many cooks spoil the stew. = A lot of ideas or people aren't always helpful.
Good things come in small packages. = The size of something doesn't equal its quality.

Homework: Do you have proverbs in your first language? What do they mean?

C APPLYING INFORMATION Read each scenario. Then write the proverb from Part B.

1. A mother and child are shopping. Again and again, the child asks the mother for things (toys, games, candy). "No," the mother says, "We don't have the money."

   What else could she say? _____

2. Kobe and his friends are fixing Kobe's car. Everyone has a different idea of how to fix it. One friend thinks the problem is the engine. Another friend thinks it's the brakes.

   What is Kobe probably thinking? _____

3. Hafiza is very busy. She's a student and works two jobs. She works overtime when she can.

   How does Hafiza feel about time? _____

Grammar Focus 1 Parts of speech: Nouns, pronouns, verbs, prepositions, and adjectives

Examples	Language notes
(1) An **apple** a **day** keeps the **doctor** away. **Proverbs** give **advice**.	As you learned in Unit 1, **nouns** represent people, places, things, and ideas.
(2) **Singular** **Plural** apple → apples day → days doctor → doctors time – money – advice – *Incorrect:* advice → ~~advices~~	Some nouns have **singular** and **plural** forms. Other nouns have only a singular form.
(3) <u>The boy</u> likes apples. → **He** likes apples. <u>Good things</u> come in small packages. → **They** come in small packages.	As you learned in Unit 1, **pronouns** take the place of <u>nouns</u>. **Subject pronouns** are *I, you, he, she, it, we,* and *they.*
(4) Time **is** money. She **feels** unhappy. You **wake** up early. He **doesn't eat** nutritious foods.	As you learned in Units 1 and 2, **verbs** tell about a state of being (*feel, seem*) and describe action (*grow, work, eat*). We make verbs negative by adding a helping verb—also called auxiliary verb— + *not*.
(5) Good things come **in small packages**. Money doesn't grow **on trees**. I get up **at 7:00** A.M. I accomplish a lot **in the morning**.	As you learned in Unit 3, **prepositions** and **prepositional phrases** often answer the questions *Where?* and *When?*
(6) The **best things** in life **are free**. **Good things** come in **small packages**. *Incorrect:* ~~Goods~~ **things** come in small packages.	**Adjectives** describe people, places, and things. They often come before the thing they describe (**nouns**) or after **be**. **Note:** Adjectives **do not change form** to match the thing they modify.

Adjectives	
for people	for things
tall, short, nice, friendly, beautiful, handsome, tired, returning	little, big, square, round, hot, cold, soft, new, old
for places	for situations
far, near, interesting, beautiful, warm, historic	interesting, boring, confusing, easy, difficult, good, bad

Grammar Practice

A Read the proverbs. Follow the instructions.

Instruction	Proverbs
1. *Underline the verb.*	Money talks.
2. *Circle the nouns.*	The early bird gets the worm.
3. *Underline the preposition.*	Too many cooks spoil the stew.
4. *Circle the pronoun.*	You are never too old to learn.
5. *Underline the adjectives.*	Good things come in small packages.

B Read the sentences. Then complete the chart. Put the words in the correct columns.

1. Proverbs give good advice.
2. He thinks proverbs are difficult.
3. They like English class.
4. Class is in Room B.
5. Proverbs have new vocabulary.

Nouns	Pronouns	Verbs	Prepositions	Adjectives
1. *Proverbs, advice*		*give*		*good*
2.				
3.				
4.				
5.				

C Work with a partner. Complete the proverbs. Use the words from the box. (The clues tell you the part of speech.) There are four extra words.

at	door	I	is	isn't	key	old	~~with~~	you	young

1. You can't take it _____*with*_____ you (when you die).
                preposition

2. The grass _____ always greener on the other side of the fence.
           verb

3. A golden _____ opens any door.
           noun

4. You're never too _____ to learn.
           adjective

5. Charity begins _____ home.
           preposition

6. _____ never know what you have until it's gone.
        pronoun

Grammar Focus 2 Sentences: Subjects, verbs, and objects

Examples	Language notes
(1) **Money talks.** **Proverbs give good advice.**	A **sentence** is a group of words that expresses an idea. We form sentences with: **subject + verb (+ object)**
(2) **Time** flies. **You**'re never too old to learn. **A golden key** opens any door.	A **subject** is the person, place, thing, or idea (noun or pronoun) that performs the action. It's usually at the beginning of the sentence.
(3) **Time is** money. **Good things come** in small packages.	The **verb** is the main action of the sentence. The verb must agree in number with the subject. This means: **singular subject + singular verb** **plural subject + plural verb**
(4) The early bird **gets the worm.** You can't **judge a book** by its cover.	Some verbs are followed by an **object**. An object is the person, place, or thing that receives the action—it's affected by the **verb**.

Subject	Verb	Object
All clouds	don't bring	rain.
Proverbs	give	advice.
The early bird	gets	the worm.
An apple a day	keeps	the doctor away.

Grammar Practice

A Underline and label the sentence parts *S* (subject), *V* (verb), and *O* (object).

MyEnglishLab

Grammar Plus 2
Activities 1 and 2

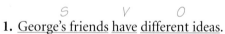

        S   *V*   *O*

1. George's friends have different ideas.

2. All proverbs give advice.

3. Her mother doesn't have extra money.

4. The early bird gets the worm.

5. Children like candy and toys.

6. Professor Winter teaches English.

7. All clouds don't bring rain.

8. Sam and Emma learn English.

B Complete the sentences. Use the words from the box.

Subject	Verb	Object
She	have	a computer
~~The students~~	is	~~Professor Winter's class~~
We	speak	

1. _The students_ like _Professor Winter's class_ .

2. Languages _____ different proverbs.

3. A proverb _____ an expression.

4. _____ speaks English.

5. They _____ English and Spanish.

6. I use _____ to write my papers.

7. _____ are Malaysian.

C Work in groups of three. Partner A says a subject. Partner B adds a verb, using the correct form. Partner C adds an object. Use words from the list. Add your own ideas. Look at the model.

We . . .

We speak . . .

We speak English.

Subjects: I, our teacher, we, our classmates, some people

_____

Verbs: like, play, study, speak, know, enjoy, don't like

_____

Objects: English, Spanish, Chinese, computer, basketball, ping-pong, soccer, school, homework

_____

Grammar Focus 3 Question forms

Examples	Language notes
(1) **I am** a cook. → **Am I** a cook? **He works** here. → **Where does he work?**	A **question** has the same parts as a sentence: a **subject** and a **verb**. There are two kinds of questions: *yes / no* questions and *wh-* questions.
(2) **Is** this expression clear? **Are** proverbs helpful? **Do** they **explain** ideas? **Does** he **need** help?	*Yes / No* questions in the simple present begin with *Is / Are* or *Do / Does* and require a *yes* or a *no* answer. They do not ask for any new information.
(3) **What** are proverbs? **Where** do they come from?	*Wh-* questions ask for information. They start with *Who, What, When, Where, Why,* or *How.*
(4) **Am** I late? **Is** it cold today? **Is** the weather cold today? **Are** they early birds? **Are** your parents early birds?	To form *yes / no* questions with *be,* start with: *Am + I* *Is + he, she, it,* singular subjects *Are + you, we, they,* plural subjects
(5) **Do** you **know** that proverb? **Do** you and Ira **know** that proverb? **Does** he **understand** the proverb? **Does** Yves **understand** the proverb?	To form *yes / no* questions with **other verbs,** start with: *Do + I, you, we, they,* plural subjects + **base verb** *Does + he, she, it,* singular subjects + **base verb**
(6) **Why am** I here? **Where is** class? **Who are** the English 2 teachers?	To form *wh-* questions with *be,* use: *Wh-* word + *am* + *I* *Wh-* word + *is* + *he, she, it,* singular subjects *Wh-* word + *are* + *you, we, they,* plural subjects
(7) **What do** you **mean?** **How does** he **teach** proverbs? **Who likes** proverbs?	To form *wh-* questions with **other verbs,** use: *Wh-* word + *do* + *I, you, we, they,* plural subjects + **base verb** *Wh-* word + *does* + *he, she, it,* singular subjects + **base verb** **Note:** When the *wh-* word is the subject, use the third person singular form of the verb.
(8) Do too many cooks **spoil** <u>the stew</u>? Why do you **judge** <u>people</u>?	*Yes / no* and *wh-* questions often have <u>**objects**</u>. Objects receive the action of the verb and often come directly after the **verb.**
(9) **Q:** Are proverbs helpful? **A: Yes, they are.** **Q:** Do proverbs explain ideas? **A: Yes, they do.** **Q:** What are proverbs? **A: Expressions.**	For **short answers** to *yes / no* questions with *be,* use *be.* For **short answers** to *yes / no* questions with **other verbs,** use *do / does.* For **short answers** to *wh-* questions, give information.

Grammar Practice

A Circle the correct word to complete each sentence. Then work with a partner. Take turns asking and answering the questions. Write your partner's answers.

Questions   **Partner's answers**

1. Are / Is you a student? _____

2. When / Are do you speak your first language? _____

3. Who / What is your favorite proverb? _____

4. Are / Where proverbs easy or difficult? _____

5. Do / Why you want to learn other proverbs? _____

B Find and correct the mistake in each question.

1. What language does we speak?

2. Money does grow on trees?

3. Who the worm gets?

4. What does proverbs teach?

5. What they are?

6. Proverbs are helpful?

C Read each incomplete statement in the chart. Below, write a *yes / no* question with *you.* Then interview your classmates. Who says *yes*? Complete the statements with your classmates' names.

Names	Statements
1.	thinks some proverbs are funny.
2.	believes proverbs are difficult.
3.	likes proverbs.
4.	knows many proverbs.
5.	is tired of proverbs.

Questions

1. *Do you think some proverbs are funny?* _____

2. _____

3. _____

4. _____

5. _____

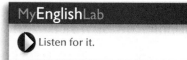
Speaking

A Think of a proverb in your first language. Tell a partner about the proverb. Use the list of questions to help you. Look at the model.

- What is the proverb?
- Who uses it?
- What does it mean?

- Do you agree with the proverb? Why or why not?
- Is there a similar proverb in English?

> What is your proverb?

> It's "The branch never falls far from the tree."

> What does it mean?

> It means children are often like their parents.

B Tell the class about your proverb. Do your classmates know similar proverbs in their languages?

Listening

A BEFORE LISTENING Look at the world map on pages A-8–9. Find countries where people speak Chinese, Korean, Spanish, Arabic, and Japanese. Do you know any proverbs from these languages?

B UNDERSTANDING MAIN IDEAS Listen to the conversation. Then match the languages to the proverbs.

Proverb	Language
_____ **1.** One hand cannot clap.	**a.** Chinese
_____ **2.** A tree that is twisted never grows straight.	**b.** Korean
_____ **3.** Misfortune doesn't come alone.	**c.** Spanish
_____ **4.** Even monkeys fall from trees.	**d.** Arabic
_____ **5.** Barking dogs rarely bite.	**e.** Japanese

C UNDERSTANDING DETAILS Listen again. Complete the meaning of each proverb.

Proverb

1. One and one make 11.

2. You can't teach an old dog new tricks.

3. When it rains, it pours.

4. Even monkeys fall from trees.

5. Barking dogs rarely bite.

Meaning

One _____ cannot do something alone.

It's difficult to break _____ habits.

Problems _____ problems.

Even experts _____ mistakes.

Don't be _____ of mean-looking people. They rarely act.

Writing

A Look at the pictures. Choose one and think of a proverb that fits the image. Or create your own proverb.

A

B

C

D

B Read about the picture and proverb Regina chose. Then write your proverb and what it means. Try to use the grammar from the chapter.

> I chose Picture A, of the woman with the hairless cat.
> **Proverb:** Love is blind.
> **Meaning:** Love makes a person not care what something or someone looks like.

Proverb: _____

Meaning: _____

C Share your proverb with the class. Are any proverb meanings the same?

CHAPTER 8 | Changing Language

Getting Started

A Read the blog entry. What language is it about?

English is interesting. Many words in English have more than one meaning. For example, the adjective *funny* means *amusing* and *strange*. A word's meaning often changes over time. For example, *text* is from the French language. It means "book." Today it also describes a message or action on a cell phone. Also, English is now a world language. Not surprisingly, people use different words to mean the same thing. For example, in the U.K., people say *lorry* to mean *truck*. Language fascinates me!

B Discuss the questions with a partner.

1. Do all words in English have only one meaning?
2. What does *text* mean in French? In English?
3. What does "world language" mean?
4. Do you agree that English is interesting?

C Look back at the blog entry in Part A. Complete the tasks.

1. In sentences with *be*, *be* is often followed by an **adjective**, a **noun phrase**, or a **prepositional phrase**. Underline and label the sentences with *be*.

2. **Object pronouns** receive the action of the verb and replace noun objects. Circle the object pronoun in the last sentence of the blog post. Who or what does it refer to?

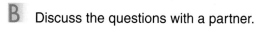

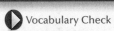

Reading

A WARM-UP "Changing Language" is the title of the chapter. What do you think that means? Is your first language changing? Discuss the question with a partner.

B SKIMMING What is Professor Winter's class about? Skim the conversation to get an idea. Then go back and read the conversation again.

PROF. WINTER:	Today our topic is language changes. Is language dynamic? Does it change?
ALI:	No, it isn't dynamic.
ZAINIB:	Yes, it is.
ALI:	Really? What are the changes?
PROF. WINTER:	Zainib is right. Language is dynamic. *Text, post* . . . What do you think of when you hear these words? Do you think of the Internet? Do you think of technology? Well, starting in the late 20th century, these words started to have technological meanings. A *text* is a piece of writing—and an electronic message. A *post* is a part of a fence, a place of work—and something published on a website. These words have new meanings. Language changes. Now, tell me this: Why does language change?
ALI:	People change language.
ZAINIB:	I think it's because we use each other's words. *Karate* is from the Japanese language, and now we use it in English.
LUCIO:	I think technology changes language.
PROF. WINTER:	You are all right. Language changes because people change. Young people try to use old words in new ways. They want to be independent and different. The word *bad* often means *good*. Also, we borrow words. We use words from other languages. You can find *dollar* in a German dictionary—it's a German word. English borrows it. Many languages use *dollar*. Are there words in your first languages that we use in English?
ZAINIB:	*Guitar* and *bronco* are examples. They use them in Spanish.
LUCIO:	In Italy, we say *opera*. Is it the same in English?
PROF. WINTER:	Yes, it is. Lucio is right about technology and language change. Technology grows. Old words get new definitions. *Web* is something a spider makes. But now, it is also a system that connects computers around the world. There is more to discuss, but we are out of time today.

C UNDERSTANDING MAIN IDEAS AND DETAILS Circle the correct answers.

1. Language ___.
   a. stays the same
   b. changes

2. ___ and technology change ___.
   a. People / language
   b. Language / computers

3. We get new words ___.
   a. from our language
   b. from other languages

4. The new meaning of the word *web* is ___.
   a. something a spider makes
   b. a system of connected computers

Grammar Focus 1 Sentence patterns with *be*

Examples	Language notes
(1) Language **is** fun and dynamic. *Dollar* **is** a German word. We **are** in the classroom.	Most sentences with *be* follow one of three patterns.
(2) They **are independent**.	One common pattern is: subject + *be* + **adjective**
(3) Our topic **is language and language change**.	Another common pattern is: subject + *be* + **noun (phrase)**
(4) Borrowed words **are from other languages**.	Another common pattern is: subject + *be* + **prepositional phrase** A **prepositional phrase** is a preposition + other information (often about place or time).
(5) **There's** my book. **There are** many words with similar meanings.	As you learned in Unit 3, another common sentence pattern with *be* is: **There** + *be* + subject

Subject	Be	
They	**are**	independent. [adjective]
Karate	**is**	a Japanese word. [noun phrase]
The English word *fest*	**is**	from the German language. [prepositional phrase]

Grammar Practice

MyEnglishLab

Grammar Plus 1
Activities 1 and 2

 A Read the sentences and think about the sentence parts. Then label the words in **bold**: *N* (noun phrase), *A* (adjective), or *P* (prepositional phrase).

1. This text is **important**.

2. The textbooks are **on the bookshelf**.

3. The words *text* and *post* are **two examples**.

4. This online post is **interesting**.

5. There are fence posts **around the ranch**.

B Complete the sentences with words from the lists or use your own words. Then identify the sentence patterns. Write *SVN* (subject + verb + noun phrase); *SVA* (subject + verb + adjective); or *SVP* (subject + verb + prepositional phrase). Write three sentences of your own. Follow the pattern.

Subject	+	*Be*	+	Noun phrase	OR	Adjective	OR	Prepositional phrase
A sentence		~~am~~		a language		difficult		around the corner
English class		are		a student		friendly		down the hall
Languages		aren't		a good friend		helpful		near campus
They		is						
We		isn't						

SVN **1.** I _am_ _____ a student.

_____ **2.** English is _____.

_____ **3.** Our classroom _____ on the second floor.

_____ **4.** _____ are my classmates.

_____ **5.** My teacher is _____.

_____ **6.** The bookstore isn't _____.

_____ **7.** Language learning _____ fun.

_____ **8.** Julia is _____.

_____ **9.** _____ aren't teachers.

_____ **10.** _____ is a group of words.

SVA **11.** _____

SVN **12.** _____

SVP **13.** _____

C Unscramble the words to make sentences. Use the correct form of *be*.

1. interesting / be / this book _This book is interesting._____

2. be / all languages / different _____

3. not / be / serious students / they _____

4. the school / near my house / be _____

5. language learning / easy / not / be _____

6. English class / in room 224 / be _____

Grammar Focus 2 Prepositional phrases / Object pronouns

Examples	Language notes
(1) **Q:** Where is the English 1 classroom? **A:** It's **in room 224**. **Q:** When is your class? **A:** It's **at 11:00** A.M.	**Prepositional phrases** often tell us *where* or *when*. To form a prepositional phrase, use: **preposition + noun or noun phrase**
(2) People speak English **around the world**.	The word or words that follow the **preposition** are called the **object of the preposition**.
(3) Who can answer **the question?** → Who can answer **it?** I trust **the students.** → I trust **them.**	**Object pronouns** are the pronouns *me, you, him, her, it, us, them*. They take the place of an **object**.
(4) We study language **with him.** We **study it** in Professor Martin's class.	**Object pronouns** often follow **prepositions** and **verbs**.
(5) I called **Brandon.** But I didn't speak to **him.** English borrows **words** but uses **them** differently.	After the **first reference**, we often use **object pronouns**.

Subject pronouns	Object pronouns
I	me
you	you
he	him
she	her
it	it
we	us
they	them

Grammar Practice

 Write the words from each sentence in the correct category.

MyEnglishLab

Grammar Plus 2
Activities 1 and 2

1. Professor Martin teaches English class in room 224.

   subject: _Professor Martin_

   verb: _teaches_

   object: _English class_

   preposition: _in_

   object of the preposition: _room 224_

2. We borrow words from other languages.

   subject: _____

   verb: _____

   object: _____

   preposition: _____

   object of the preposition: _____

3. Technology creates new words in English.

   subject: _____

   verb: _____

   object: _____

   preposition: _____

   object of the preposition: _____

4. The students study proverbs and language change in class.

   subject: _____

   verb: _____

   object: _____

   preposition: _____

   object of the preposition: _____

B Complete the follow-up questions. Use object pronouns. (Hint: Notice the words in **bold**.) Then ask a partner the questions.

1. Do you use **email**? When do you use _____?

2. Do you study with **friends**? When do you study with _____?

3. Do you understand **Mr. Klein**? Do you like _____?

4. Do you use your **computer** every day? Why do you use _____?

5. Do you use a bilingual **dictionary**? How often do you use _____?

C Circle the objects. Then rewrite the sentences. Change the objects to object pronouns.

1. I study (English) every day.

    I study it every day. _____

2. We know Luisa.

    _____

3. John likes computers and languages.

    _____

4. My class enjoys the listening lab.

    _____

5. Tomas sometimes helps me and my roommate.

    _____

D Unscramble the sentences. Use the correct form of *be*.

1. write / homework / a notebook / we / in

    We write homework in a notebook. _____

2. from / different countries / the students / be

    _____

3. be / the Internet / a *post* / a message / on

    _____

4. a fence / part of / be / a *post*

    _____

5. from / other languages / use / we / words

    _____

Listening

A BEFORE LISTENING Look at the map. Work with a partner. Try to label the states and regions with the words from the box. Write the letters in the circles.

| A. Alaska | B. Northeast | C. Midwest | D. South | E. West | F. Hawaii |

B 🎧 UNDERSTANDING MAIN IDEAS Listen to the lecture. Circle the things the professor talks about.

C 🎧 UNDERSTANDING DETAILS Listen again. Write the words from the box in the correct blanks on the map in Part A. Some words are used more than once.

| bucket | pail | snow machine | soda |
| faucet | pop | snow mobile | spigot |

Speaking

A Work with a partner. Think about your first language. Do people from different places use different words? Make a list.

carro – Dominican Republic
coche – Mexico
auto – other Spanish-speaking places

B Tell your class about your first language. Are words different in different places? Look at the model.

There are many words for car *in Spanish. In the Dominican Republic we say* carro. *In Mexico, the people say* coche. *And in other places, they say* auto. *But we use them the same.*

Writing

MyEnglishLab

▶ Linking Grammar to Writing

A Interview a partner about his or her first language. Take notes.

Questions	Notes
1. What is your name?	
2. Where are you from?	
3. What language(s) do you speak?	
4. In your first language, are words different in different places?	
5. What are some examples?	
6. In your first language, is there more than one word for something?	
7. What are some examples?	

B Write a short article about your partner's first language. Try to use the grammar from the chapter.

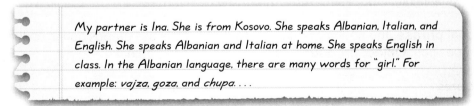

My partner is Ina. She is from Kosovo. She speaks Albanian, Italian, and English. She speaks Albanian and Italian at home. She speaks English in class. In the Albanian language, there are many words for "girl." For example: vajza, goza, and chupa....

C Share your writing with your partner. Read your partner's paragraph about you. Is the information correct? Share ideas about how to improve your paragraphs.

MyEnglishLab

▶ Diagnostic Test

Grammar Summary

Use **nouns** to refer to people, places, things, and ideas. They are singular and plural. **Subject pronouns** replace nouns. **Object pronouns** replace objects. **Verbs** express a state of being or an action. **Prepositions** often tell where and when. **Adjectives** describe nouns.

Parts of speech				
Nouns	singular	student	**Verbs**	be, learn study, change
	plural	students		
Pronouns	subject pronouns	I, you, she, he, it, we, they	**Prepositions**	**in** the house, **at** night
	object pronouns	me, you, her, him, it, us, them	**Adjectives**	**good** idea, **small** classroom

A **sentence** is a group of words that expresses an idea. A **subject** is the noun or pronoun that performs the action. The **verb** must agree with the subject. An **object** is the person, place, or thing that receives the action. The object usually follows the verb.

Parts of a sentence		
subject + verb	subject + <u>verb</u> + object	subject + <u>verb</u> + object pronoun
Language changes.	The early bird <u>gets</u> the worm.	The early bird <u>gets</u> it.

A question has the same parts as a sentence: a subject and a verb. There are two kinds of questions: *yes / no* **questions** and *wh-* **questions**. *Yes / No* questions require a *yes* or a *no* answer. *Wh-* questions ask for information about *Who, What, When, Where, Why,* or *How*.

Yes / No questions	*Wh-* questions
be + subject	*wh-* word + *be* + subject
Are we there?	What are proverbs?
do / does + subject + verb + object	*wh-* word + *do / does* + subject + verb + object
Q: Do too many cooks spoil the stew? **A:** Yes, they do. / No, they don't.	**Q:** When do you study English? **A:** At night.

Most sentences with *be* follow one of three **patterns**: *be* + adjectives, noun phrases, or prepositional phrases. Another common sentence pattern with *be* is *There is* or *There are*.

Sentence patterns with *be*	
Subject + *be* + adjective	Class is interesting.
Subject + *be* + noun (phrase)	Our topic is language and language change.
Subject + *be* + prepositional phrase	Borrowed words are from other languages.

In a **prepositional phrase**, the noun or noun phrase that follows the preposition is called an object of the preposition. **Object pronouns** can take the place of objects.

Prepositional phrases	Object pronouns	
in the evening from other languages at 3:00 P.M.	me you him, her, it	us you them

Self-Assessment

A (7 points) Find and correct the mistake in each sentence.

1. Words change. Them get new meanings.

2. Proverbs are traditional sayings. We study it.

3. My favorite proverb is "Money grows for trees."

4. Mario and Luisa are in my class. They study with I.

5. We have class today on 11:30 A.M.

6. When they do study?

7. Do you understands that proverb?

B (11 points) Complete the categories. Use the words from the box.

all the best things	goes	in the classroom	the language lab instructor
at 12:00	he	nice	them
easy	her	talks	

1. subject pronoun: _____

2. verbs: _____

3. adjectives: _____

4. object pronouns: _____

5. prepositional phrases: _____

6. noun phrases: _____

C (7 points) Create sentences. Use words from the list or your own words. Use the simple present. Follow the pattern. More than one correct answer is possible.

at home	change	fun	in the classroom	proverbs	teach
at noon	easy	I	like	she	work
books	English	interesting	my friend	study	you

Statements

1. (subject + *be* + noun phrase) _____

2. (subject + *be* + prepositional phrase) _____

3. (subject + *be* + adjective) _____

Questions

4. (*Be* + subject + adjective) _____

5. (*Do / Does* + subject + verb + object) _____

6. (*Wh-* word + *be* + subject) _____

7. (*Wh-* word + *do / does* + subject + verb) _____

Unit Project: Proverb poster

A Work with a partner. Create a proverb poster. Follow the steps.

1. Choose a proverb from the bulletin board.

Don't count your chickens before they hatch.

You win some, you lose some.

Absence makes the heart grow fonder.

Two heads are better than one.

Old habits die hard.

Opportunity seldom knocks twice.

Look before you leap.

Love is blind.

Laughter is the best medicine.

Blood is thicker than water.

Silence is golden.

Two wrongs don't make a right.

2. Research the proverb's meaning.
3. Create a poster that shows the proverb's meaning. Use pictures, words, art—anything that helps you explain the expression.

B With your partner, present your poster to the class. Answer any questions. Look at the model.

We drew a picture to represent our proverb. Look at our poster. Who can guess what the proverb is?

Is it "No news is good news"?

That's right! It means that hearing nothing probably means everything is fine.

MyEnglishLab

Unit Test

MyEnglishLab

Search it!

Generations

OUTCOMES

After completing this unit, I will be able to use these grammar points.

CHAPTER 9

Grammar Focus 1
Expressing advice: *Should*

Grammar Focus 2
Infinitives

CHAPTER 10

Grammar Focus 1
Possessive nouns and adjectives

Grammar Focus 2
Gerunds

Different Points of View

Getting Started

A Read the statements to a partner. What is his or her opinion? Check (✓) your partner's answers.

Statements	Agree	Disagree
1. A young child should decide his or her bedtime.	☐	☐
2. Parents should choose their children's friends.	☐	☐
3. Parents should pay for their children's college education.	☐	☐
4. Children should be quiet when around adults.	☐	☐
5. Parents should help their children with homework.	☐	☐
6. A young child should have a job.	☐	☐

B Write *T* for the true statements and *F* for the false statements. Report your answers to the class.

_____ **1.** I plan to send my children to college.

_____ **2.** I need to live near my family in order to be happy.

_____ **3.** I like to listen to others' opinions.

_____ **4.** I hope to visit my family's homeland someday.

C Look back at Parts A and B. Complete the tasks.

1. We use *should* + verb to give advice. In Part A, circle the verbs that follow *should*.
2. Infinitives (*to* + verb) often follow the main verb. In Part B, circle the infinitives.
3. Look at the verbs you circled. What do you notice about their form?

Reading

A WARM-UP A person's "point of view" is the way the person sees things. It's the opinion the person has. Do children and parents usually have the same point of view? What about immigrant parents and their children? What about you and your parents? Discuss the questions with a partner.

B SCANNING Scan Jin-woo's letter to his sister. Underline what is important to him. Circle what is important to his parents. Then go back and read the whole letter.

Dear Jin-sook,

How are you? How are the kids? Everything with me is fine. School is good. Actually, that's not true. I don't like engineering very much. I don't like to study, and I don't think grades are very important. I'm writing because I need your advice.

When you were a student, did Mom and Dad want you to come home every weekend? I go, but it's stressful. They always ask about my grades, and they tell me to study hard. They want me to make different friends. I should have more friends from Korea, they say. I shouldn't spend a lot of time having fun, in their opinion. They don't encourage me to become "Americanized."

They care about me and want me to be successful. They think I should get a good job and earn a lot of money. I don't agree with them. They're from a different generation. My friends and I try to be different. Our ideas, our clothes, and our hair are different. We don't care about money.

I want to please Mom and Dad. But I also want my freedom. I need to control my life. What's your advice? Should I think about my happiness? Or should I follow Mom and Dad's wishes?

Jin-woo

C UNDERSTANDING OPINIONS Which of these statements are Jin-woo's point of view? Which are his parents'? Check (✓) your answers.

Statements	Jin-woo	Parents
1. Grades are very important.	☐	☐
2. Jin-woo should not become "Americanized."	☐	☐
3. Jin-woo should earn a lot of money.	☐	☐
4. Being different is important.	☐	☐
5. Jin-woo should control his life.	☐	☐

Grammar Focus 1 Expressing advice: *Should*

Example	Language notes
(1) Children **should** follow their parents. When **should** children get their first job?	We use **should** to give or ask for **advice**. If we *should* do something, it is good or right to do that thing.
(2) He **should pay** for it.	*Should* is a **modal** verb. A modal verb is a helping verb that changes the meaning of the **main verb**.
(3) She **should call** her parents.	To form **statements**, use: subject + **should** + base verb
(4) Children **should not work** for money.	To form **negative** statements, use: subject + **should** + *not* + base verb
(5) We **shouldn't** go.	The **contraction** of *should* + *not* is **shouldn't**.
(6) **I should** get a job. **She should** get a job.	*Should* does **not change forms** with the subject.
(7) **Should** children **work** for money? **Shouldn't** he **be** here?	To form **yes / no questions**, use: **Should** + subject + **base verb** **Note:** Add *not* when you think you know the answer.
(8) **Q:** Should children work for money? **A: Yes, they should. / No, they shouldn't.**	For **short answers** to *yes / no* questions, use *should* or *shouldn't*.
(9) **What should** we **do?** **When should** I **tell** them? *Incorrect:* When ~~I should~~ tell them?	To form **wh- questions**, use: **Wh- word** + **should** + subject + **base verb**

Grammar Practice

MyEnglishLab

Grammar Plus 1
Activities 1 and 2

A Read each answer. Then write a *yes / no* question or a *wh-* question with *should*.

1. **Q:** *Should young children stay up late at night?*

   A: No, young children shouldn't stay up late at night.

2. **Q:** _____

   A: Yes, parents should listen to their children's opinions.

3. **Q:** _____

   A: Children should get a job by age 18.

4. **Q:** _____

   A: College students should eat healthy foods, not fast foods.

5. **Q:** _____

   A: Adult children should live near their parents.

6. **Q:** _____

   A: Grandchildren should call their grandparents once a week.

B Should young teenagers (13–15 years old) do these things? Complete the sentences with your opinion. Use *should* or *shouldn't*. If using *shouldn't*, add affirmative advice.

Young teenagers . . .

1. (drive) *shouldn't drive. They should walk or take the bus.* _____

2. (get married) _____

3. (choose their friends) _____

4. (have a variety of friends) _____

5. (work) _____

C Work with a partner. Use the list to think of situations and questions with *Should*. Then ask your partner for an opinion. Take turns. Give short answers. Look at the model.

> I'm a math major, but I don't like math. Should I change my major?

> No, you shouldn't. You should take other classes, like art, for one semester. Then decide.

Topic ideas

Family: call your mother?
get married?
have children?

School: change your major?
go to summer school?
get a tutor?

Work: get a job?
quit your job?
ask for a raise?

Grammar Focus 2 Infinitives

Examples	Language notes
(1) I want **to live** by myself.	Infinitives often act as objects in a sentence.
(2) I like **to study**.	To form **statements**, use: subject + main verb + **infinitive** (*to* + **base verb**)
(3) **She** needs **to do** it. **They** need **to do** it.	The main verb changes form to match the **subject**. The **infinitive** does not.
(4) **I agree to help** you. We **hope to hear** something soon. They **plan to get** married. He **seems to think** he is the boss. They **try to understand** their parents.	Some verbs, such as *agree, hope, plan, seem,* and *try,* **never have an object before the infinitive**: **main verb + infinitive**
(5) The instructor **encourages** Lara **to study**. They always **invite** us **to go** to the beach. I should **teach** you **to make** kimchi. Our parents **tell** us **to be** honest.	Some verbs, such as *encourage, invite, teach,* and *tell,* **always have an object before the infinitive**: **main verb** + object + **infinitive**
(6) Ross **needs** you **to move** your car. She **likes** him **to sing** to her. We **want** Junko **to come**. He **needs to park** there. She **likes to listen** to jazz, too. We **want to live** alone.	*Need, like,* and *want* **sometimes have an object** before the infinitive, and **sometimes do not**: **main verb** + object + **infinitive** **main verb + infinitive**
(7) She **doesn't** like **to read** aloud. She **doesn't** like you **to read** aloud.	To form **negative** statements, use: subject + *do / does* + *not* + base verb (+ object) + **infinitive**
(8) **Do** you **plan to stay**? **Does** he **want** me **to leave**?	To form **yes / no questions**, use: *Do / Does* + subject + base verb (+ object) + **infinitive**
(9) **Q:** Do they want to come? **A: Yes, they do. / No, they don't.**	For **short answers** to *yes / no* questions, use: **Yes,** + subject + *do / does* **No,** + subject + *do / does* + *not*
(10) **Where do** you hope **to go** to college? **Why does** she invite us **to come**? She knows we're busy.	To form *wh-* **questions**, use: *Wh-* **word** + *do / does* + subject + base verb (+ object) + **infinitive**

My**English**Lab

▶ Grammar Plus 2
Activities 1 and 2

Grammar Practice

A Complete the sentences. Use the information and infinitives.

1. He _____ (plan / get married) this summer.

2. We _____ (need / buy) some food for the weekend.

3. She _____ (not / like / read) books in her first language.

4. I _____ (hope / see) you during the summer.

5. They _____ (want / Lisa / live) with them.

6. Our teacher _____ (encourage / us / study) in a group.

B Read each answer. Then write a *yes / no* question or a *wh-* question.

1. Q: _____

   A: No, she doesn't want to be in class today.

2. Q: _____

   A: Yes, the teacher tries to be fair.

3. Q: _____

   A: He wants to live in New York.

4. Q: _____

   A: No, the students don't agree to turn off their phones.

5. Q: _____

   A: Her brother plans to get married this summer.

6. Q: _____

   A: You need to call 911 in an emergency.

7. Q: _____

   A: Her roommate likes to read fashion magazines.

8. Q: _____

   A: Yes, Lin's parents hope to see her this weekend.

9. Q: _____

   A: No, the library doesn't seem to be busy today.

C Read the story. There are nine mistakes. Find and correct the mistakes.

Jin-woo likes listen to music. He plans to goes to Pacific City with his friends. They want to hear some music at a club. But Jin-woo has two problems. First, he needs save some money for the trip. Second, his parents want him come home for the weekend.

Jin-woo hopes have fun this weekend. He also hopes to makes his parents happy. Jin-woo tries understand his parents' feelings. He agrees of finish his schoolwork before the trip. Now his parents seem feel a little better about the trip.

Speaking

A Take the survey. Do you agree or disagree with the statements? Imagine your parents' answers. Write *A* (Agree) or *D* (Disagree).

Statements	You	Your parents
It's important to sleep 8 hours every night.		
It's important to be on time to things.		
Surfing the Internet is dangerous.		
Parents should choose their children's major.		
Children should live at home until marriage.		
Adult children should visit their parents often.		
Teachers should give homework for the weekend.		

B Work with a partner. Talk about the differences between your generation and your parents' generation. Look at the model.

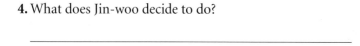

My parents think everyone needs to sleep for eight hours. I disagree. I like to go to bed late and get up early.

Listening

A BEFORE LISTENING Some schools offer counseling for students. Counseling helps students make decisions about school, family, and friends. What things can you imagine speaking to a counselor about?

B 🎧 UNDERSTANDING MAIN IDEAS Listen to the conversations between Jin-woo and his counselor. Answer the questions. Write complete sentences.

1. What are Jin-woo's friends' plans?

_____

2. What does Jin-woo hope to do this weekend?

_____

3. What do Jin-woo's parents want?

_____

_____

4. What does Jin-woo decide to do?

_____

_____

C 🎧 UNDERSTANDING DETAILS **Listen again. Write *T* for the true statements and *F* for the false statements.**

_____ 1. Jin-woo is upset.

_____ 2. Jin-woo plans to study this weekend.

_____ 3. Jin-woo tries to make his friends happy.

_____ 4. Jin-woo doesn't like to make his parents happy.

_____ 5. The counselor wants Jin-woo to stay home.

Writing

MyEnglishLab

▶ Linking Grammar to Writing

A Students often have stress. Consider the list of common problems. Write more problems. Think about advice.

Classes are difficult.   It is hard to understand the teachers.

There is no time to rest.   _____

Parents expect good grades.   _____

It is hard to work and study.   _____

B Think of a friend with one of the problems in Part A. Write your friend an email. Give advice. Try to use the grammar from the chapter.

○ ○ ○

Dear Johan,
How's it going? I know you are stressed by your busy schedule. I have some advice for you. First, you need to quit one of your jobs. I encourage you to . . .

C Work with a partner. Read your partner's advice. Do you agree or disagree? Why?

MyEnglishLab

▶ Diagnostic Test

CHAPTER 10 | Generational Differences

Getting Started

A How important are these things to you? Check (✓) your answers.

	Not important	Somewhat important	Very important
1. Having fun	☐	☐	☐
2. Getting good grades	☐	☐	☐
3. Following cultural traditions	☐	☐	☐
4. Being successful	☐	☐	☐
5. Pleasing your family	☐	☐	☐
6. Feeling happy	☐	☐	☐

B Answer the questions. Circle your answers.

1. What is important to your parents? **a.** Their friends. **b.** Their children.
2. Who helps you more? **a.** My parents. **b.** My friends.
3. What is important to your family? **a.** What our neighbors think. **b.** Our time together.
4. What is important to your teacher? **a.** His or her students. **b.** His or her vacation.

C Look back at Parts A and B. Complete the tasks.

1. **Gerunds** are base verbs + *-ing* (*traveling*). Use the gerunds from Part A to complete the chart. What do you notice about spelling?

Base verb	Gerund	Base verb	Gerund
1. have	*having*	4. be	
2. get		5. please	
3. follow		6. feel	

2. Try to match the subject pronouns to the **possessive adjectives**. Use Part B to help you.

Subject pronouns: I   you   he   she   it   we   they

Possessive adjectives: its   her   our   my   your   his   their

Reading

A WARM-UP Work with a partner. Do you agree with the statements? Write *A* (Agree) or *D* (Disagree). Discuss your answers.

_____ **1.** Immigrants should keep their cultural traditions.

_____ **2.** Young adults should follow their parents' advice.

_____ **3.** Parents should help choose their children's partners.

B SCANNING Scan the article about immigrant families. What's important to immigrant parents? Underline the information. Then go back and read the whole article.

Understanding immigrant families and their challenges
———— by Howard Kerns ————

We social scientists study groups of people. Our main focus is society and human behavior. We enjoy studying interactions. Immigrants is my specialty. This is a very interesting area.

All families have disagreements. Immigrants and their children sometimes disagree about traditions. Keeping traditions is very important to the parents. For the children, fitting in is important. Having freedom and making personal decisions are also important. These children live between cultures. They understand the old culture and its values, but they live in the new culture. They are their parents' children. But sometimes they do not share their parents' values.

Here is an example of a young person with these challenges. We can call him "J." J and his parents disagree about many things. J is like other young people who grow up in the United States. Not having freedom is stressful to him. He often says to his parents, "It's not your decision."

J's parents have different ideas. They think parents should always be the leaders of the family. They often say to J and his sister, "This is our way. Why is respecting our culture difficult for you?" They value the family. They want all members of the family to work together. They think J should listen to them. J's sister should also follow their advice, they believe. They want her to go to college. They also want her to get married, and they are very interested in choosing her husband.

There's good news: there are solutions for conflicts between generations. Talking and listening are good tools. Is communicating a quick solution? No. But it is the first step down the road to peace.

C UNDERSTANDING DETAILS Which things are important to immigrant parents (P)? Which are important to their children (C)? Write *P* or *C*.

_____ **1.** Keeping traditions

_____ **2.** Fitting in

_____ **3.** Having freedom

_____ **4.** Making personal decisions

Grammar Focus 1 Possessive nouns and adjectives

Examples	Language notes
(1) **Jin-woo's** father is an engineer. **Her** office is closed.	**Possessive nouns** and **possessive adjectives** show ownership or possession of something or a close connection to someone or something.
(2) The **teacher's** name is Janet. I'm in **Janet's** class.	To form the **possessive of a singular noun**, add: **apostrophe (') + -s**
(3) The **books'** covers are red. Those **boxes'** labels are all wrong.	To form the possessive of **a plural noun that ends in -s or -es**, add: **apostrophe (')** *Note:* The pronunciation does not change.
(4) Our **children's** lives are different. **People's** opinions change over time.	To form the possessive of an **irregular plural noun**, add: **apostrophe (') + -s**
(5) **Stephen's** hair is dark. But **his** beard is white. **Melissa and Tom's** father is quiet. But **their** mother is talkative.	We use **possessive adjectives** in place of possessive nouns. We use them after the first reference to the noun.
(6) **My daughter** is good at math. **My daughters** are good at math.	Possessive adjectives **do not change form** to match the word they modify.

Subject pronouns	Possessive adjectives
I	**My** parents understand the situation.
you	**Your** son is a good student.
he	**His** hair is dark.
she	**Her** class starts at 1:00 P.M.
it	**Its** capital is Carson City.
we	**Our** teacher has the summer off.
they	**Their** parents are still young.

See Appendix D on page A-3 for a list of subject pronouns, object pronouns, and possessive adjectives.

Grammar Practice

MyEnglishLab

Grammar Plus 1
Activities 1 and 2

 A Notice the possessive adjectives in **bold**. Then match the possessive nouns to the sentences.

Sentences	Possessive nouns
_____ 1. It's **her** idea.	**a.** Miguel's
_____ 2. Those are **their** backpacks.	**b.** the new café's
_____ 3. Mrs. Lee is **his** counselor.	**c.** Tina's
_____ 4. **Its** tables are small.	**d.** the Brazilian students'

B Make the nouns possessive.

1. teacher   *teacher's*   6. Rafael   _____

2. students _____   7. men   _____

3. children _____   8. churches _____

4. women _____   9. classes _____

5. chef   _____   10. parents _____

C Complete the story. Circle the correct words.

I want to get a job this semester. **1. My / Me** parents think it is a bad idea. They want me to study. They say, **2. "You / Your** job is to study!" They do not want **3. they / their** daughter to quit school.

4. I / My brother is also a student. He has a job. **5. He / His** job is at a restaurant. He works late. He does not have much time to do **6. his / he's** homework. He studies in the morning.
7. His / Their grades are not very good. **8. Us / Our** parents are not happy about that.

9. My / My's friend Andrea has a job. **10. She's / Her** job is at a clothing store. She gets very good grades. **11. Her / She** parents let her make her own decisions. **12. My / Their** parents do not do that.

D Complete each sentence with the correct possessive adjective. (The possessive nouns are hints.)

1. Olga plans to go shopping with

    *her*_____ mother.
            Olga's

2. Stefan wants to visit

    _____ grandparents.
        Stefan's

3. Stefan says, "I plan to save

    _____ money."
        Stefan's

4. Olga needs to do

    _____ homework.
        Olga's

5. Stefan and Olga study at _____ favorite café.
                      Stefan and Olga's

6. Olga lives in _____ parents' house.
             Olga's

7. Thomas and Sara say, "This is _____ culture."
                   Thomas and Sara's

8. Jose and Stefan spend the weekend with _____ friends.
                          Jose and Stefan's

9. Olga says to Stefan, "I like _____ idea."
                   Stefan's

Grammar Focus 2 Gerunds

Examples	Language notes
(1) **Talking** is good. **Communicating** helps families live in peace.	A **gerund** is a base verb + -ing. We use gerunds as nouns.
(2) **Listening is** important. **Exercising makes** you feel good.	Gerunds can be the **subject** of a sentence. When the gerund is the subject, use: **gerund + third person singular verb form**
(3) We **enjoy cooking**. Counselors **suggest listening**.	Gerunds can be the **object** of certain verbs, such as *like, enjoy, suggest,* and *(don't) mind.* Use: subject + **verb** + **gerund**
(4) **Earning good grades** is important. I suggest **getting some exercise**.	In either case, gerunds can be part of a **noun phrase**.
(5) The story is **about believing**. She is **good at solving** problems. I **don't believe in dieting**.	**Prepositions** often come before gerunds: **preposition + gerund** **adjective + preposition + gerund** **verb + preposition + gerund**
(6) **Not having** freedom is stressful. Most retirees enjoy **not working**.	To form **negative** gerunds, use: *not* + gerund
(7) **Is changing** majors difficult?	To form *yes / no* **questions**, use: *Is* + gerund + other information
(8) **Why is listening** hard for you?	To form *wh-* **questions**, use: *Wh-* word + *is* + gerund
(9) They **go dancing** with their friends. She **goes shopping** on Saturday.	The verb *go* + **gerund** makes up many expressions.

Spelling of -ing endings
For verbs that end in a consonant + -e, drop the -e and add -ing.   dance: **Dancing** is fun.   write: **Writing** is difficult.   make: **Making** friends is easy.
For short verbs that end in a consonant + vowel + consonant, double the consonant and add -ing.   plan: **Planning** is helpful.   swim: **Swimming** is good exercise.   shop: She doesn't enjoy **shopping**.
Note: Don't double the last consonant if it is a *w, x,* or *y*.   sew: **Sewing** is a great skill.   fix: **Fixing** cars is his hobby.   I don't believe in **paying** in cash.
For most other verbs, just add -ing   talk: **Talking** is a good idea.   sleep: Who doesn't like **sleeping** in?   learn: **Learning** is exciting.

See Appendix E on page A-3 for more examples and for spelling rules for -ing endings.

Grammar Practice

A Complete the sentences. Use the gerund form of the words in **bold**.

1. I like to **sing**.   _Singing_ is fun.

2. They don't like to **drive** at night.   _____ at night is dangerous.

3. It's not hard to **get** tickets.   _____ tickets is easy.

4. He likes to **sleep** late.   _____ late is great.

5. I need to **study** grammar.   _____ grammar is necessary.

6. We want to **help** our parents.   _____ our parents is important to us.

7. She likes to **play** soccer.   _____ soccer is good exercise.

8. She **understands** her parents.   _____ her parents makes her happy.

B Complete the sentences. Use the words from the box. Use the gerund form.

listen	live	review	sit	study

1. She enjoys _____ to music.

2. We don't like _____ in the library.

3. They don't mind _____ on the floor.

4. He likes _____ in his own apartment.

5. Our professor suggests _____ our notes before the test.

C Find and correct the mistake in each sentence.

1. Stay awake in English class is hard.

2. She enjoys practices the piano.

3. The lecture is about be open-minded.

4. We don't believe in eat meat.

5. I'm sometimes guilty of not make my bed.

D Work with a partner. Use the words in the lists to form questions. Use the correct form of the words in **bold**. Take turns. Look at the model.

Is writing an essay hard?

No. It's easy.

Yes / No **questions**
Be / write an essay / hard
Be / work and **be** a student / easy

Wh- **questions**
When / **be** / **be** honest / important
Why / **be** / **get** good grades / important

Listening

A BEFORE LISTENING Look at the pictures. Which activities do you enjoy? Which do your parents (or older people) enjoy? Discuss the pictures with a partner.

B 🎧 UNDERSTANDING MAIN IDEAS Listen to the conversation. Write *T* for the true statements and *F* for the false statements.

_____ **1.** Jin-woo wants to go on a trip with his friends.

_____ **2.** His parents want Jin-woo to visit the family.

_____ **3.** His parents are upset at first.

_____ **4.** Living in two cultures is easy.

_____ **5.** Jin-woo changes his mind.

C 🎧 UNDERSTANDING DETAILS Listen again. Circle the correct answers.

1. Jin-woo's trip is ___.	**a.** to Pacific City	**b.** to his grandparents'
2. His parents plan ___.	**a.** a trip for the weekend	**b.** a family dinner
3. Jin-woo lives ___.	**a.** in two cultures	**b.** with his parents
4. Jin-woo's mother wants him to ___.	**a.** call her	**b.** get a job

Speaking

A A student club is conducting a survey. Complete the form.

Cultural Crossroads Survey
Please give us your opinion: 1 = Disagree 2 = I don't know 3 = Agree

A. Parents should pay for their children's college education.		1 2 3
B. Parents should choose their children's major in college.		1 2 3
C. Parents shouldn't allow their adult children to live at home.		1 2 3
D. Children of immigrants should continue to practice cultural traditions (language, holidays, etc.).		1 2 3
E. International students should pay higher tuition.		1 2 3

B Work with a partner. Talk about the survey. Share opinions. Give reasons. Use the phrases in the list. Give examples. Look at the model.

Opinion phrases

I agree with . . .   I disagree with . . .   In my opinion . . .   I think . . .

> I disagree with Statement A.

> Why?

> I think paying for something makes you appreciate it more. . . .

Writing

MyEnglishLab

▶ Linking Grammar to Writing

A Read the list of topics. Add others. Which one do you have an opinion about? Choose one and take notes. Include examples.

Topics

Learning the language of a new culture   Respecting traditional practices

Adopting the dress of a new culture   _____

Trying the food of a new culture   _____

B Write a paragraph about the topic you chose. Express your opinion. Is your parents' point of view different? How? Try to use the grammar from the chapter.

> I am 18 years old. My parents are immigrants. We usually agree, but sometimes we have different points of view. For example, my parents know some English. However, they prefer to speak Arabic. In my opinion, speaking English is better. Why? . . .

C Work in small groups. Pass your paragraph to the left. Read your classmate's paragraph. Add your opinion below the paragraph. Then pass the paper to the left and read another paragraph. Continue until your paragraph returns. Read the opinions.

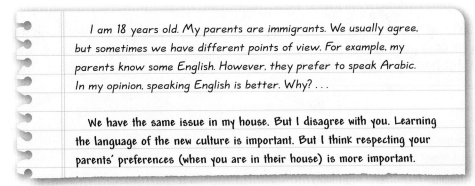

> I am 18 years old. My parents are immigrants. We usually agree, but sometimes we have different points of view. For example, my parents know some English. However, they prefer to speak Arabic. In my opinion, speaking English is better. Why? . . .
>
> We have the same issue in my house. But I disagree with you. Learning the language of the new culture is important. But I think respecting your parents' preferences (when you are in their house) is more important.

MyEnglishLab

▶ Diagnostic Test

Grammar Summary

We use **should** to give or ask for advice. *Should* is a modal verb. A modal verb is a helping verb that changes the meaning of the main verb. *Should* does not change forms with the subject. For short answers, use *should* or *shouldn't*.

Statements	Questions and short answers
People **should** follow the rules. We **should** talk to our children. You **shouldn't** live with your parents.	**Q: Should** children **work?** **A:** Yes, they **should.** / No, they **shouldn't.** **Q:** What **should** we **tell** them? **A:** The truth.

An **infinitive** is **to + base verb**. Infinitives often act as objects in a sentence. (A) Some verbs, such as *agree, hope, plan, seem,* and *try,* never have an object before the infinitive. (B) Some verbs, such as *encourage, invite, teach,* and *tell,* always have an <u>object</u> before the infinitive. (C) *Need, like,* and *want* sometimes have an <u>object</u> before the infinitive, and sometimes do not.

Infinitives	
(A)	I **plan to call** you tomorrow. You **seem to be** upset.
(B)	They **invited <u>us</u> to attend** their wedding. We **encourage <u>our son</u> to be** honest.
(C)	What do you **need <u>me</u> to do?** Do you **want to live** alone?

Possessive nouns and **possessive adjectives** show ownership or possession of something or a close connection to someone or something. We use possessive adjectives in place of possessive nouns. We use them when we already know the person or thing that the possessive adjective refers to. Possessive adjectives do not change form with the word they modify.

Possessive nouns		Possessive adjectives	
singular	Mike's, my team's	my	our
plural	the boxes', six families'	your	your
		his / her	their
plural (irregular)	women's, children's	its	

A **gerund** is a base verb + *-ing*. (A) We use gerunds as nouns—both as subjects and as objects. As an object, a gerund can follow certain verbs such as *like, enjoy, suggest,* and *(don't) mind*. (B) Prepositions often come before gerunds. (C) The verb **go** + **gerund** makes up many expressions.

Gerunds	
(A)	**Cooking** is fun. Do you enjoy **cooking?**
(B)	The article is **about making** lifestyle changes. What are you **good at doing?** We **believe in respecting** tradition.
(C)	He **goes skiing** in the winter. We **go shopping** on Saturday.

Self-Assessment

A (5 points) Complete the sentences. Use the correct form of the verb.

1. Sheila wants _____ (learn) Latin dancing.

2. I hope _____ (go) back home to Russia this month.

3. My parents enjoy _____ (hear) about my job.

4. My friend's family doesn't mind _____ (eat) late.

5. She doesn't encourage us _____ (study) and work.

B (4 points) Read each answer. Then write a *yes / no* question or a *wh-* question.

1. Q: _____

   A: Yes, parents should know their children's teachers.

2. Q: _____

   A: She should leave at 4:00.

3. Q: _____

   A: Yes, surfing is fun.

4. Q: _____

   A: She hopes to graduate.

C (6 points) Complete the sentences. Use possessive adjectives. (The possessive nouns are hints.)

1. Sam wants to help _____ parents.

Sam's

2. Eva says, "I don't want to waste _____ time."

Eva's

3. Tilly and Mia live in _____ parents' house.

Tilly and Mia's

4. Rhea rents a room in _____ friends' basement.

Rhea's

5. Dee says to Joe, "I remember _____ brother."

Joe's

6. Kelly and Bo say, "These are _____ friends."

Kelly and Bo's

D (10 points) Read the story. There are 10 mistakes. Find and correct the mistakes.

I want get a good job after college. Live in a nice house is important to me. I hope to get married. I hope me family is very big. Families should are big, in my opinion. Make money is not important to me. Be happy is very important.

I want my children to haves everything. I want living with my wife and her parents. They not should live alone or in a nursing home. The family should to stay together. Living together is important.

Unit Project: Magazine article

A Work in small groups. Research a cultural challenge and write a magazine article giving tips.

1. As a group, research one of the cross-cultural topics or think of your own. (Each group in the class should choose a different topic.)

Handling culture shock
Marrying someone from another culture
Parenting: Tips for immigrant parents

Learning a new language
Socializing: How to become a local
Dealing with traditional parents

2. With your group, create a survey. Write five to ten items about your topic.

Culture Shock Survey

	Agree	Disagree	Details
1. Immigrants who don't speak the local language should hire a language tutor.			
2. Immigrants should dress like everyone else.			
3. Immigrants shouldn't make their children practice cultural traditions.			
4. Immigrants should make friends with their neighbors.			

3. Each group member interviews two people and writes their answers.

4. Share your survey results with your group. As a group, combine the results. Use the following questions and your findings to write a presentation.
   • What tips did you learn from the people you interviewed?
   • Did you notice any patterns in the answers from certain people? For example, did women give different answers than men?

5. Add visual aids to your article—for example, pie charts and photos.

B Present the main points of your article to the class. Answer any questions. Look at the model.

Our article is called "Handling Culture Shock: You should find a language tutor." Based on our research, we have eight tips. . . . Our article also includes a pie chart. It shows . . .

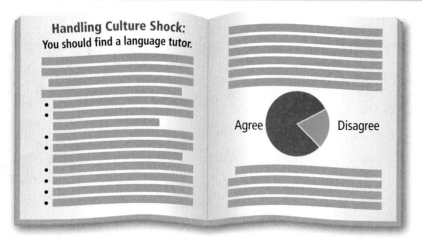

MyEnglishLab
▶ Unit Test

MyEnglishLab
▶ Search it!

UNIT 6

We're Cooking Now

OUTCOMES

After completing this unit, I will be able to use these grammar points.

CHAPTER 11

Grammar Focus 1
Present progressive: Statements

Grammar Focus 2
Present progressive: Questions

Grammar Focus 3
Simple present vs. present progressive

CHAPTER 12

Grammar Focus 1
Count and noncount nouns

Grammar Focus 2
How many . . . ? How much . . . ? /
Quantifiers

MyEnglishLab

 What do you know?

CHAPTER 11   Culinary Science

Getting Started

A What are the people's roles? Label the pictures. Write the letter.

| **a.** baker | **b.** chef | **c.** consumer | **d.** farmer | **e.** health inspector | **f.** server |

B Complete the sentences. Use the words from Part A.

1. The _____ is planting seeds now. He plants them every spring.

2. The _____ takes orders every day at work. He is taking a food order now.

3. The _____ is looking around a restaurant kitchen now. He often looks around restaurants.

4. The _____ and _____ always prepare food at work. They are preparing food right now.

5. The _____ is shopping for produce at this moment. She usually goes shopping on Saturday.

C Look back at the sentences in Part B. Complete the tasks.

1. We use the simple present to tell about habits, facts, and general truths. Circle the simple present verb forms.

2. We use the **present progressive** (*be* [+ *not*] + **verb** + *-ing*) to talk about actions happening now and longer events in progress (*talking, sleeping*). Underline the present progressive verb forms.

Reading

A WARM-UP Where do you get your food today? What about in the future? Check (✓) the best possible future source(s) of food.

☐ Pills from the pharmacy   ☐ Food factories on the moon

☐ Gardens on top of skyscrapers   ☐ Farms in the deserts and mountains

☐ "Virtual" food from the Internet   ☐ Special drinks from a science lab

B SCANNING Scan the article for your guess(es) in Part A. Underline the information. Then go back and read the whole article.

Garden in the Sky

Farms produce a lot of food. But the world population is growing. As a result, the need for food is increasing now. What are we doing about it? Agriculture is changing. Scientists and farmers are trying to meet the planet's needs. For example, they're using new techniques to produce more food. One technique is vertical farming, a new and exciting approach to producing food.

When you think of the word *vertical*, you probably think of something tall, like a skyscraper. That's exactly what vertical farming is! In urban areas, there usually isn't extra land for farming. Vertical farming uses tall buildings, such as city skyscrapers, to farm. Imagine you are living in an urban area. You and a friend are walking down a city street. You see a tall green building. Employees aren't wearing suits and ties. They're not typing on computers. They are planting, harvesting, and producing food at this moment. They plant, harvest, and produce food every day. That building is growing strawberries on one level, and tomatoes on another level. People are harvesting lettuce on another level. Recycled water is providing irrigation to the crops. Employees ship healthy foods every day to places all over the world. Are you sleepwalking in the year 2025? No, this is happening now. This is vertical farming. Vertical farming is the creation of a Columbia University professor in New York. He believes vertical farming is possibly the answer to the world's land shortage. Many people agree with him. What do you think?

C UNDERSTANDING MAIN IDEAS AND DETAILS Write *T* for the true statements and *F* for the false statements.

_____ 1. The world population is growing.

_____ 2. Vertical farming uses tall buildings, such as skyscrapers, to grow food.

_____ 3. In cities, there is usually a lot of land to farm.

_____ 4. Vertical farm workers wear suits and ties.

_____ 5. Vertical farming is the answer to the population growth problem.

Grammar Focus 1 Present progressive: Statements

Examples	Language notes
(1) **Present** Past ———— XXX ————→ Future The farmers **are working** in the field. She**'s washing** the vegetables in the sink.	We use the **present progressive** to talk about an **action happening now**.
(2) The world population **is growing**. We **are trying** new seeds this year.	We also use the present progressive to talk about a **longer event in progress**.
(3) Agriculture **is changing**. You **are living** in an urban area. **They're harvesting** potatoes.	To form **statements**, use: subject + **be** + base verb + **-ing** *Note:* We often **contract** subject pronouns with *be*.
(4) **type:** Employees **aren't typing** on computers. **ship:** Employees are **shipping** healthy foods. **try:** We're **trying** to grow strawberries. *Incorrect:* We're ~~tryying~~ to grow strawberries. **plant:** We are **planting** seeds.	The spelling rules for gerunds also apply to verbs in the present progressive: • For verbs that end in a **consonant** + **-e**, drop the -e and add **-ing**. • For short verbs that end in a **consonant** + **vowel** + **consonant**, double the last consonant and add -*ing*. Exceptions: Don't double *w, x,* or *y*. • For most other verbs, just add -*ing*.
(5) I'm **not living** in the country. Employees **aren't wearing** suits and ties.	To form **negative** statements, use: subject + **be** + **not** + base verb + **-ing**
(6) The need for food is becoming greater **now**. You are reading about vertical farming **at this moment**.	**Time signals** help us know when an action is happening. We often use time signals with the present progressive. Examples include *now, right now,* and *at this moment*.

See Appendix E on page A-3 for more examples and for spelling rules for -ing endings.

Grammar Practice

MyEnglishLab
Grammar Plus 1
Activities 1 and 2

A Look at the pictures. Write sentences about the activities. Use the information, subject pronouns, and the present progressive.

Raj

1. (sit in cafeteria) _____

_____

2. (consider career in agriculture) _____

_____

Jamie

3. (shop at a supermarket) _____

_____

4. (watch the family budget) _____

_____

Marcel and Tony

5. (prepare a meal) _____

_____

6. (run a successful restaurant) _____

_____

B Work with a partner. Partner A: Read a sentence. Partner B: Look at the picture and correct Partner A's sentence. Take turns. Look at the model.

> She's fixing a car.

> No. She's not fixing a car. She's fixing breakfast.

She's fixing a car.

1. He's reading a book.

2. She's harvesting lettuce.

3. We're working in a factory.

4. They're eating fast food.

C Find and correct the mistake in each sentence.

1. The world population grows.

2. We planting our garden today.

3. I'm harvesting not carrots. I'm harvesting potatoes.

4. Your shopping in the market right now.

Grammar Focus 2 Present progressive: Questions

Examples	Language notes
(1) **Are** you **preparing** a grocery list? **Are** they **cleaning** the tools?	We use the **present progressive** to ask questions about an **action happening now**.
(2) What **are** we **doing** about the food shortage? How **are** farms **changing**?	We also use the present progressive to ask about a **longer event in progress**.
(3) **Is** he **farming** in a skyscraper? **Are** you **living** in an urban area?	To form **yes / no questions**, use: **Be** + subject + **base verb** + **-ing**
(4) **How is** she **farming** in a city? **Who is** **harvesting** lettuce?	To form **wh- questions**, use: **Wh- word** + **be** (+ subject) + **base verb** + **-ing**
(5) **Q:** Is she farming now? **A: Yes, she is. / No, she isn't.** **Q:** Are they working? **A: Yes, they are. / No, they aren't.** **Q:** What are we doing about the problem? **A: Building vertical farms.**	For **short answers** to **yes / no questions**, use **be**. For **short answers** to **wh- questions**, give information.

Grammar Practice

MyEnglishLab

Grammar Plus 2
Activities 1 and 2

A Use the words to write a *yes / no* question or a *wh-* question. Then answer the questions. Write long answers.

1. (What / they / celebrate) Q: _____

                                        A: _____ their grandmother's birthday.

2. (he / study English / right now) Q: _____

                                        A: No, _____.

3. (Where / you / live / now) Q: _____

                                        A: _____

4. (it / work / now) Q: _____

                                          A: Yes, _____.

5. (they / eat dinner / at this moment) Q: _____

                                          A: No, _____.

6. (you / farm / now) Q: _____

                                          A: Yes, _____.

B Read each answer. Then write a *yes / no* question or a *wh-* question.

1.Q: *What are they doing?*

   A: They are cooking.

2.Q: _____

   A: Yes. She is preparing lunch.

3.Q: _____

   A: No. He isn't pushing a shopping cart.

4.Q: _____

   A: They are cooking because they are hungry.

5.Q: _____

   A: I'm reading a recipe.

6.Q: _____

   A: No. We aren't planting seeds right now.

C Think of an activity and act it out for the class. The class guesses. Look at the model.

It's three words. What am I doing?

Are you dancing?

No. Guess again.

Are you harvesting vegetables?

Yes! I'm harvesting vegetables. Carrots!

Grammar Focus 3 Simple present vs. present progressive

Examples	Language notes

(1)   **Present**
     Habits, facts, truths
Past ————— **X** ————→ Future
   She **prepares** dinner. [habit]
   Apples **grow**. [fact]
   He **is** a difficult person. [general truth]
	Use the **simple present** to tell about **habits**, **facts**, and **general truths**.

(2)   **Present**
  Actions now or longer events
Past ————— **XXX** ————→ Future
   She**'s preparing** dinner. [action now]
   These apples **are growing** fast. [longer events]
	Use the **present progressive**, on the other hand, to suggest **actions**—often **change**—**happening now** or **a longer event in progress**.

(3) The farmers **always** <u>harvest</u> lettuce in the
    afternoon.
   We **often** <u>eat</u> vegetables for dinner.
   Incorrect: The world population ~~often~~ is growing.
	We often use **adverbs of frequency** and **time signals** such as *every day, always, often, sometimes, rarely, never, generally,* and *normally* with the <u>simple present</u>, but not with the present progressive.
	
	Note: See Chapter 2 for rules about placement.

(4) We <u>are eating</u> food from the garden **now**.
   The need for food <u>is growing</u> **right now**.
   Incorrect: The need for food ~~grows~~ **right now**.
	We often use the **time signals** *now, right now,* and *at this moment* with the <u>present progressive</u>, but not with the simple present.
	
	Note: Time signal words can go before or after the verb + *-ing* form.

(5) There **isn't** land to farm.
   Do you **see** that tall building?
   Incorrect: ~~Are~~ you ~~seeing~~ that tall building?
	Use the simple present—not the present progressive—with most **non-action verbs**.

Non-action verbs	
used to describe	examples
Possession	belong, have
Senses	feel, hear, see, smell, taste, touch
Emotions	feel, hate, hope, like, love, prefer, regret, want, wish
Mental activities	believe, forget, know, think, remember, understand
States of being	be, look, seem

See Appendix F on page A-4 for more non-action verbs.

Grammar Practice

A Read the sentences. Check (✓) the form of the underlined verbs.

	Simple present	Present progressive
1. She<u>'s working</u> in the supermarket.	☐	☑
2. He <u>works</u> on a farm every day.	☐	☐
3. They <u>are studying</u> farming techniques.	☐	☐
4. We <u>are</u> in a skyscraper.	☐	☐
5. She <u>sees</u> the farm.	☐	☐
6. I<u>'m growing</u> tomatoes.	☐	☐

B Complete the sentences. Use the simple present or present progressive form of the words.

1. Marta often _goes_____ (go) to the supermarket on Saturdays.

2. We _____ (visit) a vertical farm now.

3. I _____ (learn) about farming now.

4. **Q:** What do your parents do?

   A: They _____ (work) on a farm.

5. He sometimes _____ (plant) vegetables in his garden.

6. You _____ (watch) a movie about food production right now.

C Interview your classmates. Write their answers in the chart.

Classmate's name	What do you do every day?	What are you doing right now?
Sianna	I study English.	I'm sitting in English class.
	I send my friends text messages.	I'm interviewing a classmate.
1.		
2.		
3.		
4.		
5.		

Listening

A 🎧 UNDERSTANDING MAIN IDEAS Listen to the newscast. Answer the question.

What is Professor Dennis Varty doing to bring attention to farming?

_____

B 🎧 UNDERSTANDING DETAILS Listen again. Complete the sentences.

1. Dennis Varty _____ a professor of agriculture.

2. He _____ to bring attention to farmers, agriculture, and food production.

3. He _____ across Canada on a tractor.

4. The farmers _____ their experiences, and the professor _____.

5. The professor _____ a lot from the people of Canada.

6. He _____ in hotels.

7. He _____ to write a book.

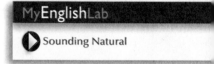

C AFTER LISTENING Work with a partner. Answer the questions.

• What does "raise awareness" mean?
• How does an act like driving a tractor across the country raise awareness?

Speaking

A Look at the picture. What is the person doing? What is her job?

B Work with a partner. Each person circles four different jobs from the list. Follow the steps on page 117. Look at the model.

architect	doctor	health inspector	restaurant server
baker	farmer	mechanic	scientist
chef	fitness instructor	professor	supermarket clerk

1. Draw stick figures of the four jobs you circled.
2. Show your partner one of your drawings. Ask, "What is the person doing?" Your partner tries to guess the activity, then the job.
3. Take turns.

> *(Shows stick figure.) What is she doing?*

> *Is she examining a patient?*

> *Yes, she is. What is she?*

> *Is she a nurse?*

> *No, she isn't. She's a doctor.*

Writing

MyEnglishLab

▶ Linking Grammar to Writing

A Think about activities that happen every day in class. Write them. Then look around at your classmates. What are people doing? Write the actions you see.

Everyday activities	Actions now

B Use the chart in Part A to write two paragraphs. In the first paragraph, write what you do in class every day. In the second paragraph, write about what you and your classmates are doing now. Try to use the grammar from the chapter.

> Every day we learn a new idiom. We always have a conversation about expressions in our first language. . . .
> At this moment Marta is reading a book. Juan and George are talking . . .

C Share paragraphs with a partner. Do you have the same actions and activities? Does your partner use the simple present and present progressive correctly?

MyEnglishLab

▶ Diagnostic Test

CHAPTER 12 Around the Global Dinner Table

Getting Started

A Imagine that you are going grocery shopping. Look at the top half of your list. How many do you want? Write a number. Underline the correct word form.

_____ tomato(es)		_____ orange(s)	
_____ banana(s)		_____ apple(s)	
_____ red pepper(s)		_____ egg(s)	

B Now look at the bottom half of your list. How much do you want? Write a number. Underline the correct word form.

sugar	_____ cup(s) of . . .		soap	_____ bar(s) of . . .	
milk	_____ carton(s) of . . .		rice	_____ bag(s) of . . .	
chicken	_____ pound(s) of . . .		yogurt	_____ container(s) of . . .	

C Look back at Parts A and B. Complete the tasks.

1. Things we can count one by one are called **count nouns**. We usually make them plural by adding -*s* or -*es*. Write the food count nouns. Write the plural forms:

_____tomatoes_____, _____, _____, _____,

_____, _____.

2. Things we can't count—for example, liquids or solids—are called **noncount nouns**. They never change form. Write the noncount nouns:

_____, _____, _____, _____,

_____, _____.

3. We use units of measure (*a can, a pound*) to express a quantity with noncount nouns. Write the units of measure from Part B. Write the plural forms:

_____, _____, _____, _____,

_____, _____.

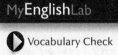

Reading

A WARM-UP Work with a partner. Guess where the foods come from.

1. naan   3. perogi   5. spring rolls   7. spaghetti

2. fish and chips 4. tacos   6. sushi   8. hamburgers

Answers: 1. India 2. the U.K. 3. Poland 4. Mexico 5. China 6. Japan 7. Italy 8. the U.S.

B PREDICTING Look at the title of the article. Look at the pictures. What's the article about? Tell a partner. Then go back and read the article. Was your prediction correct?

The Global Table Project

A blogger in Tulsa, Oklahoma, is cooking dishes from all the countries in the world, from Afghanistan to Zimbabwe. Each week she gives a little information about a country and its cuisine. She tells how many people live there and what they consume. She also writes about some customs. Next, she prepares three to four recipes. Recipes answer questions such as "How much milk do I need?" They also tell if you need an egg or two. The blogger takes pictures of a few of the ingredients. She also photographs the steps she follows and the final dish. She posts many photos on her blog. Here are some of her recipes.

Coconut Ice Cream from Honduras

2 ½ cups of milk   1 ½ cups of coconut milk
1 ½ cups of condensed milk   a tablespoon of shredded coconut

Cold Cherry Soup from Hungary

1 jar of cherries   1 cinnamon stick
⅓ cup of sugar

Jollof (Rice with Vegetables) from Nigeria

2 cups of peas   1 can of tomato sauce
1 tablespoon of oil   2 cups of white rice
1 onion   1 head of cabbage
2 cloves of garlic   1 quart of water
a sprinkle of ginger, cinnamon, some salt and pepper to taste
  and cayenne pepper

These recipes are just a few of the many recipes on The Global Table website. People around the world are logging on and trying them. How many are you planning to try?

C UNDERSTANDING DETAILS Complete the recipes. Find the information in Part B.

1. Coconut ice cream

2 ½ _____ of milk

_____ cups of condensed milk

1 ½ cups _____ coconut milk

a _____ of shredded coconut

2. Cold cherry soup

1 _____ of cherries

⅓ cup of _____

_____ cinnamon stick

Grammar Focus 1 Count and noncount nouns

Examples	Language notes
(1) **Singular** **Plural** meal → meals ingredient → ingredients woman → women	Count nouns are **people, places,** or **things that we can count**, one by one. They can be singular or plural.
(2) **a** country **an** hour **one** cinnamon stick	A **singular count noun** can have *a, an,* or *one* before it. For nouns starting with a consonant sound, use *a* + noun. For nouns starting with a vowel sound, use *an* + noun.
(3) This **recipe is** from Hungary. That **orange smells** nice.	Use the **singular** form of **verbs** with **singular count nouns.**
(4) apple → appl**es** tomato → tomato**es**	A **plural count noun** is a count noun + -s or -es. *Note:* See Unit 1 for plural noun spelling rules.
(5) **Tomatoes are** good for you. **People read** her blog.	Use the **plural** form of **verbs** with **plural count nouns.**
(6) We need **milk, sugar,** and **flour.** *Incorrect:* We need ~~milks, sugars,~~ and ~~flours.~~ *Incorrect:* ~~one~~ salt, ~~one~~ oil	**Noncount nouns** are things that cannot be counted one by one. They do not have a plural form. Do not use *a, an,* or numbers with noncount nouns.
(7) The **salt is** on the table. The **water feels** warm.	Use the **singular** form of **verbs** with **noncount nouns.**
(8) She is posting **the recipe.** We are taking pictures of **the pies!** We forgot **the cinnamon!**	*The* can be used with **singular count, plural count,** and **noncount nouns.** Use *the* when an item is familiar to both the speaker and the listener.

See Appendix G on page A-4 for more noncount nouns.

Units of measure		
We use **units of measure** to talk about amounts of noncount nouns. A **partitive** measurement describes how something is packaged or sold. **Volume** measure tells the amount of a product. **Weight** tells how heavy it is.		
Partitives	a bag of, a bar of, a bottle of, a bowl of, a box of, a bunch of, a can of, a carton of, a cup of, a glass of, a head of, a jar of, a loaf of, a tube of	
Volume	a pint of, a quart of, a liter of, a gallon of	
Weight	a milligram of, a gram of, a kilogram of, an ounce of, a pound of	
We make most **units of measure** plural the same way as other nouns (by adding -s or -es: *two bags of, three boxes of,* etc.). *Note:* The **noncount noun** doesn't change form: *a **bag** of rice* → *two **bags** of rice*; *an **ounce** of fish* → *two **ounces** of fish*.		
We can also use **units of measure** with **count nouns:** *a **bunch** of **bananas**, a **pound** of **tomatoes**.*		

Grammar Practice

A Look at the shopping lists for the recipes. Mark the ingredients *C* (count) or *N* (noncount).

Blueberry ice cream, Iceland

_C_ 1. blueberries

_____ 2. heavy cream

_____ 3. milk

_____ 4. sugar

_____ 5. water

Empanadas, Argentina

_____ 6. butter   _____ 10. garlic

_____ 7. broth   _____ 11. onions

_____ 8. cheese   _____ 12. pepper

_____ 9. eggs   _____ 13. salt

B Look at the shopping list. Mark the ingredients *SC* (singular count), *PC* (plural count), or *N* (noncount).

Um ali, Egypt

_____ 1. a coconut

_____ 2. almonds

_____ 3. milk

_____ 4. puff pastry

_____ 5. raisins

_____ 6. sugar

Potato and pickle soup, Czech Republic

_____ 7. flour

_____ 8. gherkin pickles

_____ 9. one potato

_____ 10. salt

_____ 11. sour cream

_____ 12. water

C Complete the sentences. Circle the correct verb.

1. Cherries **is / are** an ingredient in the soup from Hungary.

2. Milk **is / are** good for your bones.

3. Salt and pepper **is / are** popular in many countries.

4. There **is / are** garlic in this recipe.

5. The apples **is / are** in the bowl.

D Read the list. Add units of measure. More than one correct answer may be possible.

1. _a jar of_ jelly

2. _____ ice cream

3. _____ bread

4. _____ yogurt

5. _____ soup

6. _____ lettuce

7. _____ hamburger

8. _____ olive oil

9. _____ bananas

10. _____ pasta

11. _____ peanut butter

12. _____ rice

Grammar Focus 2 How many . . . ? How much . . . ? / Quantifiers

Examples	Language notes
(1) **How many countries** are in the world? **Incorrect:** How many ~~country~~ are in the world?	To ask about amounts of **count nouns**, use: **How many** + plural count noun
(2) **How much sugar** do you need?	To ask about amounts of **noncount nouns**, use: **How much** + noncount noun
(3) **Q:** How many recipes are on her blog? **A:** She posts **two recipes** a week. / There are **several recipes** on her blog.	Talk about **plural count nouns** with **numbers** and **quantifiers** such as *a few, some, several, many,* and *a lot of.*
(4) **Q:** How much information is on her blog? **A:** She gives **a little information** about each country.	Talk about **noncount nouns** with **quantifiers** such as *not much, a little (bit of), some,* and *a lot of.*
(5) **Q:** **How much** coffee do we have? **A:** **None.** **Q:** **How many** cookies do you want? **A:** **None.**	We can use the quantifier **none** to answer both *How much . . . ?* and *How many . . . ?* questions when the answer is zero.
(6) **Q:** Does she have **a bowl**? **A:** Yes, she does. **Q:** Do you have **an egg**? **A:** No, I don't.	To ask **yes / no questions** about **singular count nouns**, use *a* or *an.*
(7) **Q:** Do we have **any oranges**? **A:** No, we don't have **any** (oranges). **Q:** Do you have **any butter**? **A:** No, we don't have **any** (butter).	To ask **yes / no questions** about **plural count nouns** and **noncount nouns**, use *any.* Use *any* in **negative** long answers. **Note:** We can drop the noun and use just the quantifier in the answer.

Grammar Practice

MyEnglishLab

Grammar Plus 2
Activities 1 and 2

A Complete the questions. Add *much* or *many*.

1. How _____ chips are in the bag?

2. How _____ water do you need?

3. How _____ coffee is in the coffee pot?

4. How _____ glasses of milk do you drink each day?

5. How _____ tubes of toothpaste do we have?

B Complete the sentences. Add *a few* or *a little*.

1. Oh, crackers! Can I have _____?

2. That cake looks great. I want to try _____.

3. Do you want _____ tea? It's fresh.

4. This Romanian soup is delicious. I need _____ more, please.

5. She loves cookies. It's difficult for her to eat only _____.

Chapter 12

C Complete the questions. Use words from the list. Then interview a classmate about eating and drinking habits. Write complete answers.

cans of soda   pieces of fruit

cheese   rice

chicken   salads

chocolate   sandwiches

cookies   soup

cups of coffee tea

ice cream   water

milk   yogurt

1. Q. How many _____ do you eat in one day?

   A: _____

2. Q. How many _____ do you drink in one day?

   A: _____

3. Q. How many _____ do you eat in one week?

   A: _____

4. Q. How many _____ do you drink in one week?

   A: _____

5. Q. How much _____ do you eat in one weekend?

   A: _____

6. Q. How much _____ do you drink in one weekend?

   A: _____

7. Q. How much _____ do you eat in one month?

   A: _____

8. Q. How much _____ do you drink in one month?

   A: _____

Listening

A BEFORE LISTENING Look at the picture of ratatouille with a side of French bread. Which ingredients are needed to make these foods? Underline your guesses.

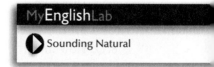

☐ olive oil   ☐ sugar   ☐ yeast

☐ onion   ☐ garlic   ☐ tomatoes

☐ flour   ☐ zucchini   ☐ rosemary

☐ red pepper   ☐ salt   ☐ thyme

☐ yellow pepper   ☐ eggplant   ☐ water

B 🎧 UNDERSTANDING MAIN IDEAS Listen to the podcast. Check (✓) the ingredients in the list in Part A that you hear. Were your guesses correct?

C 🎧 UNDERSTANDING DETAILS Listen again. Write the missing information.

1. Ratatouille
_____ olive oil
1 large _____
1 red _____
_____ pepper
6 cloves of _____
_____ zucchini
1 small _____
4 _____
_____ rosemary
1 teaspoon of _____

2. Artisan French bread
5 cups of _____
_____ water
1 1/8 teaspoons of _____
_____ salt

Speaking

A Think of a dish you love. List the main ingredients.

Ingredients

B Work with a partner. Imagine that you are roommates. You are going shopping for groceries. Create a short conversation. Include things from your list in Part A. Perform your conversation for your class. Look at the model.

> Do we need anything from the supermarket?

> Yes. I want to make my mother's bread recipe.

> What do you need?

> I need some flour, a little bit of yeast, and two eggs.

Writing

MyEnglishLab

▶ Linking Grammar to Writing

A What is a famous dish from your home country? Answer the questions.

1. What is the name of the dish? _____

2. Why is it famous? Do people usually make it for a special occasion? _____

3. What are the ingredients? _____

4. How much or how many of each ingredient do you need? _____

B Write about your home country's famous dish. Use the information in Part A. Try to use the grammar from the chapter.

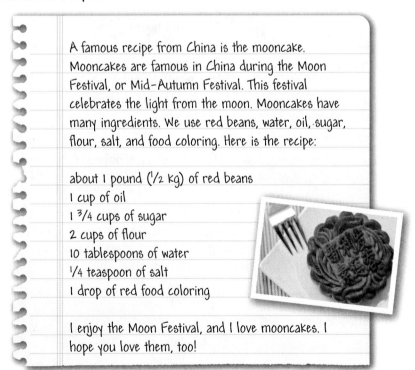

A famous recipe from China is the mooncake. Mooncakes are famous in China during the Moon Festival, or Mid-Autumn Festival. This festival celebrates the light from the moon. Mooncakes have many ingredients. We use red beans, water, oil, sugar, flour, salt, and food coloring. Here is the recipe:

about 1 pound (½ kg) of red beans
1 cup of oil
1 ¾ cups of sugar
2 cups of flour
10 tablespoons of water
¼ teaspoon of salt
1 drop of red food coloring

I enjoy the Moon Festival, and I love mooncakes. I hope you love them, too!

C Share your recipe your classmates. Read your classmates' recipes. Which recipes do you want to make?

MyEnglishLab

▶ Diagnostic Test

Grammar Summary

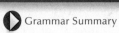
We use the **present progressive** to talk and ask about an action happening now. We also use it to talk and ask about a longer event in progress. We often use the **time signals** *now, right now,* and *at this moment* with the present progressive. The **simple present**, on the other hand, feels less "active." We use it to tell habits, facts, and general truths. We often use **adverbs of frequency** and **time signals** such as *every day, always, often, sometimes, rarely, never, generally,* and *normally* with the simple present. Use the simple present with most **non-action verbs** (*have, see, feel, think, be,* etc.).

Present progressive	Simple present
These trees **are growing** fast. [now] **Are** you **gardening** this summer? [longer event]	Trees grow. [fact] Do you garden? [habit]
Time signals	
The farmers aren't harvesting the greens **right now**.	The farmers **rarely** harvest greens in the afternoon.
Non-action verbs	
Incorrect: ~~Are~~ you ~~hearing~~ that bird?	**Do** you **hear** that bird?

Count nouns are people, places, or things that we can count, one by one. They can be singular or plural. A singular count noun can have *a, an,* or *one* before it. **Noncount nouns** are things that cannot be counted one by one. They do not have a plural form. Use a singular verb form with noncount nouns. *The* can be used with singular count, plural count, and noncount nouns. Use **units of measure** to talk about amounts of noncount nouns. A partitive measurement describes how something is packaged or sold. Volume measure tells the amount of a product. Weight tells how heavy it is.

Count nouns		Noncount nouns
A fresh **peach** smells great. **People** read her blog. She is posting **the pictures** now.		We need bottled **water** and **butter**. **Pepper** is on the table We forgot **the milk**!
Partitives	a bag of, a bar of, a bottle of, a bowl of, a box of, a bunch of, a can of, a carton of, a cup of, a glass of, a head of, a jar of, a loaf of, a tube of	
Volume	a pint of, a quart of, a liter of, a gallon of	
Weight	a milligram of, a gram of, a kilogram of, an ounce of, a pound of	
Note: For two or more, add -s or -es: *two glasses of, three liters of,* etc.		

To ask **questions** about count nouns, use: *How many* + plural form of count noun. To ask about noncount nouns, use: *How much* + noncount noun. Use *none* when the answer is zero. To ask *yes / no* questions about singular count nouns, use *a* or *an*. To ask *yes / no* questions about plural count nouns and noncount nouns, use *any*.

Questions	Answers
How many cups of sugar are in that recipe?	Two. / None.
How much coffee do we have?	A little. / None.
Do you have **an egg**?	No, I don't.
Do you have **any apples**?	No, we don't have any.
Do you have **any milk**?	

Self-Assessment

A (9 points) Write sentences about the people's activities. Use the information. Use the subject pronouns and the present progressive.

Two farmers

1. (buy new seeds) _____

2. (plant tomatoes) _____

3. (pick vegetables) _____

George

4. (sit in the classroom) _____

5. (write an email to his friend) _____

6. (do his homework) _____

Tomas and I

7. (visit a vertical farm) _____

8. (listen to a tour guide) _____

9. (read about the food shortage) _____

B (6 points) Complete the conversations. Use *much, many, a little,* or *a few*.

1.Q: How _____ sugar do you like in your coffee?

  A: Just _____, please.

2.Q: How _____ cookies are you buying?

  A: Only _____.

3.Q: How _____ vegetables do you eat every day?

  A: Well, I don't like _____ vegetables. But I eat a lot of fruit!

C (10 points) Read the paragraph. There are 10 mistakes. Find and correct the mistakes.

    Today I'm making a new recipe. We call it *avena* in Spanish. It's a cold drink with sugars. It's tasting so good. You need one cup of oatmeal, four cups of milks, one-half cup of brown sugar, and a few cinnamon. Let's get started. First, I get out a large pot. Next, I put the milk in the pot and bring it to a boil. Now, I adding the oatmeal. It smells so good. Now I add a few brown sugar and a sprinkle of cinnamon. I love the cinnamon smell. Next, I'm pour the ingredients in the blender and blend them. Now, I'm puting it in the fridge for one hour. After one hours, you can enjoy a tall glass of *avena*!

Unit Project: Class cookbook

A Work in a group. Create a class cookbook. Follow the steps.

1. Write a recipe from your home country. Ask a family member to tell you the ingredients and secrets for making it. Be sure to include the correct ingredients and units of measure.
2. Follow the recipe and prepare the dish. Bring the dish in to share with your class.
3. Have one student be the photographer and take a picture of each dish and the "chef" who made it.

B Create a class website with the recipes and pictures. (Option: Create a handout with the recipes and pictures. Make copies for everyone in the class.) Try to make one of your classmate's recipes!

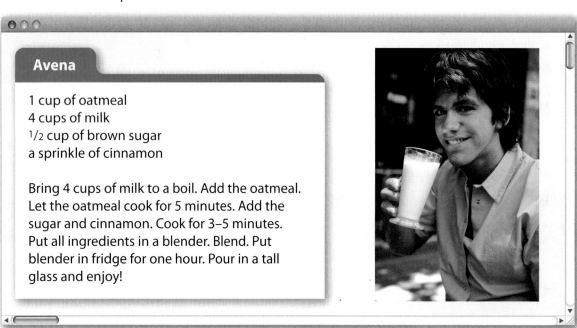

Avena

1 cup of oatmeal
4 cups of milk
1/2 cup of brown sugar
a sprinkle of cinnamon

Bring 4 cups of milk to a boil. Add the oatmeal. Let the oatmeal cook for 5 minutes. Add the sugar and cinnamon. Cook for 3–5 minutes. Put all ingredients in a blender. Blend. Put blender in fridge for one hour. Pour in a tall glass and enjoy!

My**English**Lab

▶ Unit Test

My**English**Lab

▶ Search it!

UNIT 7

The Future Is Coming Soon

OUTCOMES

After completing this unit, I will be able to use these grammar points.

CHAPTER 13

Grammar Focus 1
Future: *Be going to*

Grammar Focus 2
Future: Present progressive

CHAPTER 14

Grammar Focus 1
Future: *Will*

Grammar Focus 2
Quantifiers: Comparisons

My**English**Lab

 What do you know?

CHAPTER 13   My Future

Getting Started

A Think about your future. Check (✓) your answers.

In five years . . .

☐ **1.** I'm going to have a good job.

☐ **2.** I'm going to be married.

☐ **3.** I'm going to run my own business.

☐ **4.** I am going to finish my degree.

☐ **5.** I am going to own a house.

☐ **6.** I'm going to have children.

B What are your future plans? Circle *Yes* or *No*.

1. I'm visiting a friend tomorrow.	**Yes**	**No**
2. I am having lunch with a classmate next week.	**Yes**	**No**
3. I'm sleeping late on Sunday.	**Yes**	**No**
4. I am eating dinner at a restaurant tonight.	**Yes**	**No**
5. I'm going to English class at 2:00 P.M. tomorrow.	**Yes**	**No**

C Look back at Parts A and B. Complete the tasks.

1. We use *be going to* + verb to talk about the future. Underline the verbs after *be going to*. What form are they?

2. Circle the **present progressive** verbs in Part B. Do the sentences refer to the past, present, or future?

3. What do the sentences in Parts A and B tell about? Circle your answers.

habits   plans

past experiences   predictions

Reading

A

WARM-UP **Make predictions about your future. Check (✓) the events in your life. Then compare answers with a partner.**

I'm going to . . .

☐ invent something.   ☐ be famous.   ☐ cure a disease.   ☐ have children.

☐ start a business.   ☐ finish college.   ☐ travel the world.   ☐ live near family.

B

SCANNING **Scan Aditi's story. Underline her plans for this year. Then go back and read the whole story.**

My future: School, work, family

Our teacher wants us to write about our plans. Her first question is "What are you doing this semester?" This question is easy for me. I'm taking mid-terms next month, in March. I'm not doing any coursework over spring break in April. I'm going on a trip on April 24. I'm visiting my friends in Texas. After that, I'm coming back to school and finishing the semester. I'm enrolling in an English writing class this summer. Then I'm signing up for math and science classes next fall.

Our teacher also wants us to write about the distant future. Her question is, "Describe your life 10 years from now. For example, where are you going to be?" I'm going to return to India after school. I'm going to be a photojournalist. I'm going to photograph important world events. But I'm not going to work too much—I want time for family. I'm going to get married, and we're going to have two or three children. My children are going to be happy. They're not going to worry about anything. And, they're going to get good grades in school.

C

UNDERSTANDING DETAILS **Answer the questions.**

1. What is Aditi doing next month? _____

2. What is she doing this summer? _____

3. When is she taking math? _____

4. In the future, where is Aditi going to live? _____

5. Is Aditi going to have a career? a family? _____

_____

Grammar Focus 1 Future: *Be going to*

Examples	Language notes

(1)   Present
Past ——————— | ——— X ——→ **Future**
 	
    We **are going to** buy a new house.
    She has a good education. She **is going to** get a good job.
	Use **be going to** to talk about **future plans** and to **make predictions**.

(2) She **is going to start** school soon. They **are going to open** a restaurant.	To form **statements**, use: subject + **be going to** + base verb
(3) **She's** going to get married. **They're** going to work in a hospital.	In speech we usually **contract** the subject pronoun + **be**.

(4) I **am not going to study** tonight.
    She **is not going to get married**.
    We **are not going to take** courses this summer.
	For **negative** statements, use:
	
	subject + **be** + **not** + **going to** + base verb

(5) She's **not going to** get married.
    She **isn't going to** get married.
 	
    We're **not going to** take courses this summer.
    We **aren't going to** take courses this summer.
	In speech we often **contract** *be* OR *not* before *going to*.
	
	is not → **'s not** OR **isn't**
	
	are not → **'re not** OR **aren't**

(6) **Is** she **going to stay**? **Are** they **going to work** in a hospital?	To form **yes / no questions**, use: **Be** + subject + **going to** + base verb
(7) **When are** you **going to get** your degree? **Who is going to graduate?**	To form **wh- questions**, use: **Wh- word** + **be** + subject + **going to** + base verb *Note:* When the *wh-* word is the subject, use *is going to* + base verb.

(8) **Q:** Are you going to go to India?
    A: Yes, we are. / No, we aren't.
 	
    Q: Where are you going to stay?
    A: With my cousins.
	For **short answers** to **yes / no questions**, use **be**.
	
	For **short answers** to **wh- questions**, give information.

(9) They're going to arrive **at 10:00** A.M.
 	
    She's going to get married **in May**.
 	
    What are you going to do **this summer**?
 	
    Are you going to be home **tonight**?
 	
    On Wednesday we're going to have a test.
 	
    Next year I'm going to start graduate school.
	We often use **time signals** with *be going to*. They usually come at the end of sentences but can also come at the beginning with statements. Examples include:
	
	at + time
	
	in + month / year
	
	this _____ (afternoon, summer, etc.)
	
	tonight, tomorrow
	
	on + day of the week
	
	next _____ (month, year, etc.)

Grammar Practice

A Complete the sentences. Use the correct form of *be going to* and the verbs.

1. Rashid _____ (start) a new business.

2. You _____ (be) late!

3. Cynthia and Stephanie _____ (get) college degrees.

4. We _____ (have) children.

5. I _____ (learn) a new language.

B Find the mistake in each sentence. Then rewrite the sentence. Add a time signal.

1. She going to get up early. _____

2. My friends are going to goes home. _____

3. Our teacher is going to retiring. _____

4. Cynthia no is going to finish her paper. _____

5. We're going remember this story. _____

6. Her mom isn't go to come to the play. _____

C Read each sentence. Then write a *yes / no* question and a *wh-* question about the sentence. Use *be going to*. Use the *wh-* words.

1. He is going to finish the course.

   Q: *Is he going to finish the course?*

   Q: (When) *When is he going to finish the course?*

2. She is going to go to law school.

   Q: _____

   Q: (Why) _____

3. We are going to text.

   Q: _____

   Q: (How often) _____

4. Pete and Nigel are going to relax.

   Q: _____

   Q: (Where) _____

5. The Mahana family is going to move.

   Q: _____

   Q: (Who) _____

6. Aditi is going to finish her degree.

   Q: _____

   Q: (How) _____

Grammar Focus 2 Future: Present progressive

Examples	Language notes
(1) I'm **taking** skiing lessons next winter. Her flight **is leaving** tomorrow.	We use the **present progressive** to talk about **future plans** and **schedules**.
(2) She**'s going to go** to Texas for a visit. She**'s going** to Texas for a visit.	With future plans, the present progressive is similar in meaning to **be going to**.
(3) The next bus is coming **at 6:30**. **On Monday**, we're having a test.	We often add **time signals**. Examples include: **at** + time **in** + month / year **this** _____ (afternoon, summer, etc.) **tonight, tomorrow** **on** + day of the week **next** _____ (month, year, etc.)
(4) They**'re coming** this week. I**'m not staying** home tonight.	As you learned in Chapter 11, to form present progressive **statements**, use: subject + **be** (+ **not**) + **base verb** + **-ing**
(5) **Are** you **working** this summer?	To form **yes / no questions**, use: **Be** + subject + **base verb** + **-ing** (+ time signal)
(6) **When are** you **leaving?** **What is** she **doing** tomorrow? _Incorrect:_ **What ~~she is~~ doing** tomorrow? **Who's coming?**	To form **wh- questions**, use: **Wh- word** + **be** + subject + **base verb** + **-ing** (+ time signal) **Note:** When the wh- word is the subject, use _is_ + base verb + -_ing_.

See Appendix E on page A-3 for more examples and for spelling rules for -ing endings.

 ## Grammar Practice

MyEnglishLab

Grammar Plus 2
Activities 1 and 2

A Complete the sentences. Use the present progressive form of the words. Use contractions with subject pronouns.

1. My parents _are staying_____ (stay) home this weekend.

2. Our teacher _____ (give) a test on Monday.

3. She _____ (not / work) on Sunday morning.

4. He _____ (finish) his report on Thursday.

5. We _____ (go) to class on Tuesday.

6. They _____ (not / have) dinner with friends on Saturday.

B Look at Kim's schedule. Then answer the questions. Use the present progressive.

Sunday	Monday	Tuesday	Wednesday	Thursday	Friday	Saturday
Study for exam	10:15 A.M.: Take science exam	Have lunch with John	10:15 A.M.: Go to science class	DON'T GO TO THE LIBRARY – it's closed	10:30 A.M.: English tutor	
		Work: 3:00– 7:00 P.M.	1:30 P.M.: Turn in English essay		See a movie with Gene 5:00– 10:00 P.M.	Go home: Dinner with the family

1. What are Kim's plans on Monday?

_____

2. What is her plan for Tuesday afternoon?

_____

3. What does she plan to do on Wednesday afternoon?

_____

4. What isn't she doing on Thursday?

_____

5. What is her plan for Friday night?

_____

6. What is she going to do on Saturday?

_____

7. What is her plan for Sunday?

_____

C Read each answer. Then write a *yes / no* question or a *wh-* question. Use the present progressive.

1. Q: _____

   A: Yes, he's getting a new job.

2. Q: _____

   A: Yes, they're going on vacation next week.

3. Q: _____

   A: No, our class is not having a test next week.

4. Q: _____

   A: They're staying at a hotel.

5. Q: _____

   A: They're arriving in the afternoon.

6. Q: _____

   A: I'm going to bed because I have a headache.

Listening

A 🎧 UNDERSTANDING MAIN IDEAS Listen to the conversation between two college friends. Check (✓) each person's plans.

	Ron	Paula
1. Get married	☐	☑
2. Stay in school	☐	☐
3. Buy house	☐	☐
4. Take over family business	☐	☐
5. Work	☐	☐
6. Save money	☐	☐
7. Finish English courses	☐	☐
8. Take one course in the fall	☐	☐

B 🎧 UNDERSTANDING DETAILS Listen again. Circle the sentence you hear.

1. **PAULA:**   **a.** I'm getting married.   **b.** I'm getting worried.

2. **PAULA:**   **a.** Things are going to change.   **b.** Things aren't going to change.

3. **RON:**   **a.** Are you coming back to school?   **b.** Are they coming back to school?

4. **PAULA:**   **a.** I'm staying in school.   **b.** I'm not staying in school.

5. **PAULA:**   **a.** We're not buying a house.   **b.** We're buying a house.

6. **RON:**   **a.** I'm not getting married.   **b.** I'm getting married.

7. **RON:**   **a.** I'm finishing my English courses.   **b.** I'm finishing my major courses.

8. **PAULA:**   **a.** I'm going to give up the family business.   **b.** I'm not going to give up the family business.

C AFTER LISTENING Discuss the questions with a partner.

- What do you think Paula's life is going to be like next fall?
- What do you think about working and going to school at the same time?

Speaking

A   Work with a partner. Use the chart to ask about your partner's plans. Ask your partner to make predictions. Take notes.

Time	Partner's answer
Tomorrow	
Next weekend	
Next summer	
5 years from now	
20 years from now	

B   With your partner, join another pair. Share your plans and predictions. How are your futures similar? Different? Look at the model.

> Mika, what are you and Halim doing tomorrow?

> In the morning, we're both going to class. I'm going to math, and Halim is going to biology. In the afternoon . . .

Writing

A   Complete the calendar. Write notes about your upcoming week.

	Sunday	Monday	Tuesday	Wednesday	Thursday	Friday	Saturday
Morning							
Afternoon							
Evening							

B   Write a paragraph about your upcoming plans. Use your notes from Part A. Try to use the grammar from the chapter.

> On Monday I'm going to get up early. I'm going to go to class at 8:00 in the morning. After class I'm meeting my friends at the library. . . .

C   Exchange paragraphs with a partner. Are your schedules similar? Different? How?

CHAPTER 14   Our Future

Getting Started

A   Take the survey.

SURVEY: In the Distant Future . . .

I. Check (✓) the statement(s) you agree with.
- ☐ **1.** Most of the world will be peaceful.
- ☐ **2.** Many people will live to be 150 years old.
- ☐ **3.** We will move to other planets.
- ☐ **4.** Global warming will cause flooding.

II. Circle your guesses.

5. There will be **more / fewer** people on Earth.

6. There will be **more / less** clean water for drinking.

7. There will be **more / fewer** problems with health.

8. There will be **more / less** technology in our lives.

B   Compare answers with a partner. Who has a more positive outlook?

C   Look back at the survey in Part A. Complete the tasks.

    1. We use *will* + verb to make predictions and promises. Are the statements predictions or promises? _____

    2. What verb form always follows *will*? _____

    3. Complete the chart with the **quantifiers** *more, fewer,* and *less.* Look at Part II of the survey for help.

	Count nouns	Noncount nouns
more	people, problems	water, technology
	people, problems	—
	—	water, technology

Reading

A WARM-UP Look at the pictures. Which energy source(s) will support us in the future? Make a prediction. Circle your prediction.

Sun

Wind

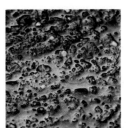
Oil

B SCANNING Is your prediction in Part A correct? Scan the article for answers. Then go back and read the whole article.

Futurists at Work: How will the future be different?
by Margo Steves

"Futurists" are people who study the future. They try to picture the world in 10 years—or 50 years.

ENERGY One area futurists study is energy. They predict that the world will use new kinds of energy in the future. They say that we will use more wind power and more solar power. These kinds of power are less expensive, and they won't run out.

HEALTH Futurists also study the future of health. Many believe that healthcare will improve in the future. For example, doctors will reach people around world. How? With advanced communication devices. The result? More people will get information, and fewer people will travel for treatment.

JOBS Another area futurists study is jobs. Workers will still make things, but more people will work with information. More people will work from home, too. This will save time and energy.

POPULATION Finally, futurists study changes in population. According to futurists, there will be more people on Earth in 50 years.

Will these predictions come true in 10 years? Will these predictions change our future? Dear Reader, I'll answer that . . . in a future post. Promise!

C UNDERSTANDING MAIN IDEAS AND DETAILS Circle the correct answers.

1. Futurists try to understand how the world ___.
   a. is **b.** will be **c.** should be

2. In the future, the world will use more power from ___.
   a. sickness **b.** universities **c.** the sun

3. Futurists say that doctors will ___.
   a. reach more people **b.** use less technology **c.** make more money

4. Fewer people will ___, according to futurists.
   a. travel for treatment **b.** save time **c.** work from home

Grammar Focus 1 Future: *Will*

Examples	Language notes
(1) People **will** use wind power. I **will** help you later today.	We use *will* to make **predictions** and **promises**.
(2) He **will** be a great student. He**'s going to** be a great student.	For predictions, *will* is more **formal** than *be going to*.
(3) Doctors **will cure** diseases.	To form **statements**, use: subject + ***will*** + **base verb**
(4) **She will** find new sources of energy. **We will** find new sources of energy.	*Will* **does not change form** with the subject.
(5) **I'll** finish my paper tonight. **She'll** have a good job. **We'll** use new kinds of energy. **They'll** cure more diseases.	In speaking, we often **contract** *will* after subject pronouns: *I will → I'll* *we will → we'll* *you will → you'll* *they will → they'll* *he will → he'll* *she will → she'll* *it will → it'll*
(6) People **will not work** more.	For **negative** statements, use: subject + ***will*** + ***not*** + **base verb**
(7) People **won't** work more.	The contraction of *will* + *not* is **won't**.
(8) I won't be here **next week**.	We often use **time signals** with *will*. Examples include: ***at*** + time ***in*** + month / year ***this*** _____ (*afternoon, summer, etc.*) ***tonight, tomorrow*** ***on*** + day of the week ***next*** _____ (*month, year, etc.*)
(9) **Will** you turn on the heater, please? **How will** we find new kinds of energy?	We use *will* in **questions** to **make requests** and to ask about **predictions**.
(10) **Will** they **make** energy from the wind?	To form ***yes / no* questions**, use: ***Will*** + subject + **base verb**
(11) **How old will** you **be** in 2025? **Who will be** here tomorrow?	To form ***wh-* questions**, use: ***Wh-* word** + *will* + subject + **base verb** *Note:* When the *wh-* word is the subject, use *will* + base verb.
(12) **Q:** Will you finish your degree? **A: Yes, I will. / No, I won't.** **Q:** When will he be available? **A: Tomorrow.**	For **short answers** to ***yes / no* questions**, use: **Yes,** + subject + ***will*** **No,** + subject + ***won't*** For ***wh-* questions**, give information.

Grammar Practice

A Rewrite the sentences as predictions. Use *will*.

1. We use energy from the sun.

   _____

2. They don't work at home.

   _____

3. There is a new kind of energy.

   _____

4. The doctor gets in at 8:30 A.M.

   _____

5. My friend helps me with my grammar homework.

   _____

B Match the sentence parts.

A	B
_____ 1. What kinds	**a.** we run out of water?
_____ 2. How much	**b.** energy will we need?
_____ 3. When	**c.** will we visit the doctor?
_____ 4. Will	**d.** will be the world's leaders?
_____ 5. Who	**e.** of houses will people live in?

C Read the story. There are five mistakes. Find and correct the mistakes.

Jurgen enjoys thinking about his life in the future. Here are his predictions: He will gets a degree in engineering in five years. He will moving out of his parents' basement. When he will get married? He doesn't know. But there willing be more people on Earth in the future. So his chances wills get better every year!

Grammar Focus 2 Quantifiers: Comparisons

Examples	Language notes
(1) There are **more** students this year. *(compared to last year)* Some people have **less** energy. *(compared to other people)* We get **fewer** hours of sleep now. *(compared to before)*	Use the quantifiers **more**, **less**, and **fewer** with count and noncount nouns to make **comparisons** about amounts.
(2) We will use **more energy**. There will be **more people**.	**More** means a larger number or amount. Use *more* before **noncount nouns** and **plural count nouns**.
(3) There will be **less pollution**. The lights use **less electricity**.	**Less** means a smaller amount. Use *less* before **noncount nouns**.
(4) There will be **fewer people**. That store will soon have **fewer workers**.	**Fewer** means a smaller number or amount. Use *fewer* before **plural count nouns**.
(5) It creates **a few jobs**. I have **a little coffee** in the morning.	We use **a few** (with **plural count nouns**) and **a little** (with **noncount nouns**) in **neutral** or **positive** statements. They mean "not a lot, but some."

Grammar Practice

MyEnglishLab
Grammar Plus 2
Activities 1 and 2

A   Notice the words in **bold**. Circle *C* for count nouns and *N* for noncount nouns. Then complete the sentences with *fewer* or *less*.

1. C / N   There will be ___fewer___ **people**.

2. C / N   Next year, I will take _____ **classes**.

3. C / N   In the future, we will have _____ **water**.

4. C / N   Solar energy creates _____ **pollution**.

5. C / N   We will have _____ bad **winters**.

6. C / N   A bicycle uses _____ **energy**.

B   Read the interview with a "futurist." Complete the sentences. Use *more, fewer,* or *less*.

A: Professor Cummings, do you think we will have **1.** _____ or

  2. _____ problems in the future?

B: I'm a positive person, so I say fewer. I think the world will have many good things in the future. But we need to make good decisions now.

A: What decisions will help us in the future?

B: We need to use technology to create **3.** _____ jobs. I hope we will use

  4. _____ machines to do hard work for us. This means there will be

  5. _____ dangerous jobs.

A: How will our health be different in the future?

B: I think we will be healthier. **6.** _____ people will need to see a doctor.
7. _____ children will die. We will have **8.** _____ trouble with diseases because science will find cures.

A: How will the environment be different in the future?

B: We will find new kinds of energy. We will get **9.** _____ energy from the sun. We will also get **10.** _____ power from the wind and from plants. This will mean **11.** _____ pollution. I don't pretend to know the future. But I know that good decisions now are important. Good decisions about work, energy, and health will create **12.** _____ challenges in the future.

C Circle the correct words to complete the questions. Then answer with your predictions, starting with *Yes, there . . .* or *No, there . . . .* Write complete sentences.

In 50 years, will there be . . .

1. Q: fewer / less people on Earth?

   A: _____

2. Q: more / less big cities?

   A: _____

3. Q: less / fewer problems with disease?

   A: _____

4. Q: fewer / less good jobs for people?

   A: _____

5. Q: less / fewer pollution?

   A: _____

6. Q: more / fewer energy?

   A: _____

Listening

A BEFORE LISTENING How will people fuel cars, heat homes, and power computers in the future? Discuss your ideas with a partner.

B 🎧 UNDERSTANDING MAIN IDEAS Listen to podcast. What does Todd predict? Check (✓) his predictions.

☐ **1.** Scientists will find new sources of energy.

☐ **2.** We will use more wind power.

☐ **3.** We will use less solar power.

☐ **4.** Solar energy will help us reduce pollution.

☐ **5.** We will get energy from plants.

C 🎧 UNDERSTANDING DETAILS Listen again. Circle the future energy sources that Todd predicts.

Speaking

A Work with a partner. What will life on Earth be like in 50 years? What questions do you want to ask a futurist? Write *yes / no* questions and *wh-* questions. Use the words.

1. Q: (Will) _____

2. Q: (What) _____

3. Q: (When) _____

4. Q: (How) _____

5. Q: (Will) _____

B Work with a partner. Ask and answer your questions from Part A. Take turns playing the role of a futurist. Make up answers. Look at the model.

> In the future will people live underwater, in the ocean?

> No, they won't. The oceans will be too warm for life.

Writing

MyEnglishLab

▶ Linking Grammar to Writing

A What will your life be like in five years? Take notes in the chart.

Five years from now	Your predictions
Your job	
Your family	
Your house	
Your city or town	
Your education	

B Write a paragraph about your future. Use your notes from Part A. Try to use the grammar from the chapter.

> Five years from now I will have a good job. I will work for a big company. I will make more money. I will work about 40 hours every week. I won't work on the weekends. I'll have a handsome husband and two beautiful children. We'll name them Talia and Dash. My parents will live with us. We will live in a modest house. It will use solar power, and we'll have a big garden. Our street will be very quiet . . .

C Read your paragraph to the class. Answer any questions.

MyEnglishLab

▶ Diagnostic Test

Grammar Summary

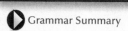

We use **be going to** to tell and ask about future plans and predictions. Use *be going to* + base verb. We often add **time signals**. Time signals usually come at the end of the sentence. In short answers to *yes / no* questions, use *be*.

Statements	Questions
He **is going to** buy a new car.	**Is** he **going to** go to bed?
They **are going to** open a bookstore.	**Are** they **going to** work?
She**'s going to** take a vacation.	Where **is** he **going to** live?
I**'m not going to** eat that.	When **are** you **going to** study French?
On Monday, we**'re going to** leave for Paris.	How many homes **are going to** have solar power **in 2050**?
It**'s going to** snow **tonight**.	Q: Are you **going to** be here **tomorrow**?
We **aren't going to** take lessons **this year**.	A: Yes, I **am**.

We use the **present progressive** to talk about future plans and schedules. With future plans, the present progressive is similar in meaning to *be going to*. We often add **time signals**. In short answers to *yes / no* questions, use *be*.

Statements	Questions
He**'s going** to Ohio for a visit. (*He's **going to go** to Ohio for a visit.*)	**Is** their flight **arriving** on time?
I**'m starting** piano lessons **next month**.	Who **is quitting**?
My friend **is leaving tomorrow**.	What **are** you **doing next weekend**?
The library **is closing at noon**.	Q: **Are** you **taking** classes **this fall**?
	A: No, we**'re not**.

Use **will** to make predictions and promises. Use *will* + base verb; *will* does not change form with the subject. The contracted form of *will* is *'ll* and *will not* is *won't*. We often add **time signals**. In questions, we use *will* to ask about predictions and to make requests. In short answers to *yes / no* questions, use *will* or *won't*.

Statements	Questions
The population **will** continue to grow.	**Will** you **turn on** the heater, please?
I **will** call you **tomorrow**.	**Who will discover** new kinds of energy?
I **won't** tell anyone.	Q: **Will** you **be** at Dave's party **tonight**?
She**'ll** have a good job.	A: Yes, we **will**. / No, we **won't**.

Use the quantifiers **more**, **less**, and **fewer** + nouns to make **comparisons** about amounts. *More* means a larger number or amount. *Less* means a smaller amount. *Fewer* means a smaller number or amount. We use *a few* and *a little* in neutral or positive statements to mean "not a lot, but some." Use *a few* with count nouns and *a little* with noncount nouns: *It creates a few jobs. I have a little coffee in the morning.*

More + plural count nouns and noncount nouns	*Less* + noncount nouns	*Fewer* + plural count nouns
There are **more people** here now.	This toilet uses **less water**.	We get **fewer breaks** at work.
We have **more homework** today.	This garden needs **less fertilizer**.	There are **fewer cars** here now.

Self-Assessment

A (5 points) Complete the sentences about the future. Use the words. More than one correct answer may be possible.

1. I plan to take the bus home tonight. I _____ (not / walk).

2. I dropped your favorite glass! I _____ (buy) you a new one! I promise.

3. It's cold this morning! Our classroom _____ (not / be) warm.

4. Wind power _____ (create) good jobs in the future.

5. We changed our plans. We _____ (not / buy) solar panels.

B (5 points) Circle the correct words.

1. Wind energy means **fewer / less** pollution.

2. This new system has **less / more** problems!

3. We need to use **less / fewer** electricity.

4. Our company has **more / less** workers.

5. The workers want **more / less** hours.

C (5 points) Complete the conversations. Write a *yes / no* question or a *wh-* question.

1. Q: _____

   A: Yes, I'm visiting my sister next weekend.

2. Q: _____

   A: Marina will become a famous scientist.

3. Q: _____

   A: We're going to live in Alaska.

4. Q: _____

   A: No, she's not going to finish on time.

5. Q: _____

   A: Yes, I'll go to the concert with you.

D (10 points) Read the story. There are 10 mistakes. Find and correct the mistakes.

My plans: I'm finishing my English courses next month. I'm no taking courses in the summer. I'm working. Next year, I'm take French. I'm going to getting my degree in environmental science in the spring.

My predictions: In five years, I'm going to being a math teacher. I think I wills be a very good teacher. No, I will get married. I going to live by myself. I will getting a teaching job. I not will work in the summer. I'll going to relax.

Unit Project: Planning a city of the future

A Work with a partner. Imagine and create a city that exists 50 years from now. Follow the steps.

1. Answer the questions. Take notes.

- **Name:** What is the name of your city?
- **Size:** How many people will live in the city?
- **Economy:** What kind of jobs will people have? Where will people work? How will the city get money to pay for things people need?
- **Energy:** What kind of energy will the city use for light, transportation, etc.?
- **Transportation:** How will people travel in the city?
- **Communication:** How will people communicate with each other? How will people find new information?
- **Education:** What kinds of schools will there be?

Other questions to consider:

- How will people have fun or relax?
- What kinds of foods will people eat?
- Will there be more or less crime, compared to cities today?

2. Use your notes to write a paragraph about your future city.
3. Draw a map of your future city. Create or find pictures that show special features of the city.

B Give a presentation about your city. Use visual aids to describe your city. Why is it a good place to live? Answer any questions. Look at the model.

The year is 2100. Our city is called Futureville. Here's a picture of Futureville. What will life in Futureville be like? Here are our ideas. First, cities in the future will be very large. Futureville will have 20 million citizens. Why? Because . . .

MyEnglishLab

▶ Unit Test

MyEnglishLab

▶ Search it!

Architecture

OUTCOMES

After completing this unit, I will be able to use these grammar points.

CHAPTER 15

Grammar Focus 1
Descriptive adjectives

Grammar Focus 2
Very, too, enough

CHAPTER 16

Grammar Focus 1
Comparative adjectives

Grammar Focus 2
As . . . as and other expressions

CHAPTER 15   House and Climate

 Getting Started

A Look at the pictures and read the statements. What are your preferences? Write *T* for the true statements and *F* for the false statements.

_____ **1.** I prefer to live in a very warm climate.

_____ **2.** Anything over 70 degrees Fahrenheit (21° C) is too hot.

_____ **3.** I want to live in a safe small town.

_____ **4.** I don't want to live in a concrete apartment building.

_____ **5.** I like interesting old houses.

_____ **6.** My house should be spacious enough for big parties.

_____ **7.** I want to have a beautiful, decorative backyard.

B Work with a partner. Compare your answers in Part A. Which picture best matches your preferences?

C Look back at the statements in Part A. Complete the tasks.

1. **Descriptive adjectives** modify—or give more information about—nouns. Circle the descriptive adjectives.
2. ***Very*** + adjective makes an adjective stronger. ***Too*** + adjective indicates a problem. ***Enough*** + adjective (or adjective + *enough*) means an acceptable amount. Complete the chart with examples from Part A.

Very + adjective	*Too* + adjective	Adjective + *enough*

Reading

A WARM-UP Work with a partner. What do you know about architecture and climate? Try to match the climates to the housing features.

Features	Climates
_____ 1. Steep, sloped roof	**a.** Rainy or snowy
_____ 2. Thin wooden walls	**b.** Strong sun
_____ 3. Strong wood	**c.** Mild climate
_____ 4. Light-colored buildings	**d.** Very cold

B PREDICTING What kind of houses do people in warm climates have? What about cold climates? Tell a partner your ideas. Then read the article. Were your ideas correct?

🏠 Housing Styles Around the World

Housing styles around the world vary. There are very beautiful small houses, large old concrete buildings, houses with flat roofs, and houses with sloped roofs. The greatest influence on style is climate. For example, in very cold areas, houses are made from strong wood. In places with floods and hurricanes, houses are on stilts to protect people from fast-moving water. In warm climates, people build their houses with green grass and mud.

Here are some examples of housing styles:
- Homes in Ireland have steep, sloped roofs. Why? Ireland gets enough rain every year to fill a large lake. When there's not enough slope, the roof will leak.
- In Spain, it is the opposite. This area receives little rainfall. It is dry enough to have a straight, flat roof.

- In Japan, there is a strong connection between the family home and the garden. Large green gardens often are as spacious as the living quarters. They are also comfortable enough to be part of the living space. Homes in Japan also have thin wooden walls because of the mild climate. The weather is dry and sunny.
- It is also very sunny in Santorini, Greece. Homeowners frequently paint their houses white to protect against the strong sun. Homes that are too dark absorb the heat.
- Lastly, in colder climates, such as Canada, Greenland, and parts of Russia, many houses are made from wood. The wood keeps very cold air outside.

While culture helps shape housing styles, climate is clearly the greatest influence.

C UNDERSTANDING DETAILS Complete the chart with information from the article.

Place	Housing features	Climate
Ireland	steep, sloped roofs	rainy
Spain		
Japan		
Santorini, Greece		
Canada, Greenland, Russia		

MyEnglishLab

▶ Reading Comprehension

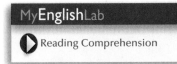

Grammar Focus 1 Descriptive adjectives

Examples	Language notes
(1) Japan has many **green** gardens. Houses keep **cold** air out.	**Descriptive adjectives** give us more information about nouns. The added information often appeals to the senses—sight, touch, taste, sound, smell.
(2) Who owns this **new house**? This house **is old**. *Incorrect:* Those houses are ~~olds~~.	As you learned in Unit 4, adjectives come **before** the **nouns** they modify or **after** the verb **be**. They do not change form to match the noun they modify.
(3) Many people live in **apartment** <u>buildings</u>. Our **family** <u>garden</u> is in the backyard.	**Nouns** can act like descriptive adjectives, modifying <u>other nouns</u>.
(4) Cities have **large apartment** buildings. Greenland has a **cold winter** climate.	We sometimes use **descriptive adjectives and nouns** together to describe a noun. Use: **adjective + noun** + noun

(5) They have a **beautiful small** house. [opinion, size]
 In Spain, there are **steep red** roofs. [shape, color]
 My aunt lives in a **cold old concrete** building.
     [weather-related, age, material]
 These **old Japanese** homes have beautiful
     gardens. [age, origin]
 This neighborhood has some **expensive large modern** homes. [opinion, size, age]
	We occasionally use two or three descriptive adjectives with nouns. With multiple adjectives, follow **adjective word order**, which is based on category:
	
	 1) opinion
	 2) size / shape / condition
	 3) weather-related
	 4) age
	 5) color
	 6) origin
	 7) material

Grammar Practice

MyEnglishLab

Grammar Plus 1
Activities 1 and 2

A   Complete the chart. Use the adjectives from the box.

~~big~~	hot	mud	thick
broken	huge	old-fashioned	unusual
circular	interesting	quiet	white
classic	Indian	Swiss	
cold	large	terrible	

Opinion	Size / Shape / Condition	Weather-related	Age	Color	Origin	Material
	big					

B Complete the sentences. Use the adjectives. Use correct adjective order and commas when necessary.

1. I prefer homes with _____ (sunny / large) kitchens.

2. She lives in a(n) _____ (concrete / tall / expensive) apartment building.

3. I would love to live in a _____ (light-colored / modern / clean) home near the ocean.

4. He prefers to live in a(n) _____ (English / old / charming) cottage.

5. How do you feel about _____ (dark / short / clay) houses?

C Work with a partner. Look at the pictures. Describe each home. Use two adjectives from the list, or your own ideas. Look at the model

1.

2.

3.

4.

American	dark	lovely	old-fashioned	traditional
beautiful	Japanese	modern	orange	typical
charming	light	old	square	wood

That's a charming wood cabin.

D Find and correct the mistake in each sentence.

1. Do you prefer small cute homes or beautiful large homes?

2. We are in an English old classroom.

3. How do you feel about houses American?

4. In cold climates, houses are made with wood thick strong.

5. Do you like modern busy cities or peaceful small towns?

6. Our neighbors are building an large attractive house.

Grammar Focus 2 *Very, too, enough*

Examples	Language notes
(1) Strong wood can keep **very** cold air outside. Our house is **very** big. *(It's great to have all that space.)*	**Very** is an adverb. It makes a description stronger. It often has a positive meaning.
(2) There are **very beautiful** small houses.	**Very** goes before the **adjective**.
(3) Our house is **too** big. That home is **too** expensive. *(We can't afford it.)*	**Too** is an adverb. It often means that something is not possible. It has an **unfavorable**—or negative—meaning.
(4) Homes that are **too dark** absorb a lot of heat.	**Too** goes before the **adjective**.
(5) There is **enough** space. [adjective] We have **enough**, thanks. [pronoun] The garden is large **enough** to play in. [adverb]	**Enough** can be an adjective, pronoun, or adverb. It means the right amount.
(6) Do we have **enough nails**? We get **enough rain** every year.	As an **adjective**, enough goes before **plural nouns** and **noncount nouns**.
(7) **A:** Is there **enough space** for a garden? **B:** Yes, there's **enough**.	After the **first reference**, we often drop the noun and enough becomes a **pronoun**.
(8) The wood is **strong enough**. Is the house **warm enough** for you?	As an **adverb**, enough goes after the **adjective**.
(9) There isn't **enough light**. There isn't **enough**. The kitchen isn't **big enough**.	**Not + enough** means less than the right amount. Use: **not enough** (+ noun) **not + adjective + enough**
(10) This condo is **too expensive to buy**. It is **dry enough to have** a flat roof.	**Too + adjective** and **adjective + enough** are often followed by **an infinitive**.

Grammar Practice

MyEnglishLab

Grammar Plus 2
Activities 1 and 2

A Match the explanations to the statements.

Statements	Explanations
_____ 1. The garden is big enough.	**a.** The children won't be able to play there.
_____ 2. It is very cold here in the winter.	**b.** I'll have enough space to plant vegetables.
_____ 3. That home is too expensive.	**c.** There's a problem with the heater.
_____ 4. The roofs are steep enough for the rain.	**d.** The daytime high is 22 degrees Fahrenheit (−5° Celsius).
_____ 5. That closet is very small.	**e.** It costs a lot of money.
_____ 6. That yard is too small.	**f.** All of our clothes won't fit.
_____ 7. This house is too cold.	**g.** The rain will run off. The slope is correct.
_____ 8. That home is very expensive.	**h.** We can't afford it.

B Complete the sentences. Use *too, very,* or *enough.*

1. The house is _____ run-down. We can't live in it.

2. That is a(n) _____ beautiful home. I want to live there!

3. This room is _____ hot. It's impossible to stay here.

4. The house is large _____ for the family. Everyone has a bedroom.

5. She is _____ comfortable. She is really enjoying the hotel.

6. The kids are _____ cold. They can't stay outside another minute.

7. The closet has enough space for clothes but not _____ for shoes.

C Work with a partner. Look at the world map. Choose a location and describe the conditions. Use *too, very,* or *enough.* Look at the model.

Death Valley, California, is very hot.

I agree. It's too hot for me.

Boulder, Colorado
76 in. (1.9 m) of snow in one day

Cherrapunji, India
366 in. (9.3 m) of rain in one month

Antarctica
−134˚ F (−92˚ C)

Death Valley, California
134˚ F (57˚ C)
record temperature

Arica, Chile
.03 in. (.07 cm)
of rain in one year

Belouve, LaReunion Island
53 in. (1.3 m)
of rain in one hour

Listening

A BEFORE LISTENING Look at the pictures. Where in the world do you think these houses are? Tell a partner your ideas.

B 🎧 UNDERSTANDING MAIN IDEAS Listen to the program. Check (✓) the descriptions you hear.

Huay Xai, Laos	West Mountains, Iran	Sana'a, Yemen
☐ wet	☐ cold	☐ rocky
☐ tall	☐ soggy	☐ underground
☐ sunny	☐ big	☐ dry desert
☐ unique	☐ dark-colored	☐ very large

C 🎧 UNDERSTANDING DETAILS Listen again. Circle the correct words.

Huay Xai, Laos

1. Here it is very **dry / wet**.

2. People live in **tree houses / caves**.

3. The homes are **above / below** the ground.

West Mountains, Iran

4. Here it is very **cold / moderate**.

5. Snow covers the mountains in **fall and winter / winter and spring**.

6. Homes have **big / small** windows.

Sana'a, Yemen

7. The area is **rocky / wet**.

8. People build their homes with **bricks / rocks**.

9. Homes are **very large / too small**.

Speaking

A Work with a partner. What do you want to know about the architectural style of houses in your partner's home country? Write your questions.

1. Q: _____

2. Q: _____

3. Q: _____

4. Q: _____

5. Q: _____

B Interview your partner. Look at the model.

> *Are houses in your country big or small?*

> *They're very big. Usually many family members live together.*

C Tell the class about the architectural style of houses in your partner's home country.

Writing

A Think about the climate and housing styles in your home country. Follow the steps.

1. Check (✓) the weather conditions that are typical:

   ☐ very cold   ☐ cold   ☐ hot   ☐ very hot   ☐ warm

   ☐ snowy   ☐ rainy   ☐ dry   ☐ very windy   ☐ sunny

2. Check (✓) the words that describe a typical home. Circle the words that describe your family's home or a home you know well:

   ☐ beautiful   ☐ peaceful   ☐ noisy   ☐ comfortable   ☐ new

   ☐ traditional   ☐ large   ☐ small   ☐ old   ☐ modern

B Write a paragraph about climate and housing styles in your home country. Try to use the grammar from the chapter.

> My hometown is Santo Domingo, Dominican Republic. The weather is very hot and dry in the summer. In the spring and fall, the weather is warm and rainy. Santo Domingo has many charming old homes. My house is old, too. It is very peaceful.

C Share your paragraph with a partner. Can you answer these questions about your partner's home and climate?

1. What is the climate like?
2. What are the architectural styles of homes?
3. What are some typical home features?

CHAPTER 16 International Designs

Getting Started

A Look at the pictures and answer the questions. Write *A* or *B*.

A

B

_____ **1.** Which Olympic Stadium looks larger?

_____ **2.** Which Olympic Stadium is more traditional?

_____ **3.** Which Olympic Stadium is more modern?

_____ **4.** Which Olympic Stadium is older?

B Look at the pictures in Part A again. Write *T* for the true statements and *F* for the false statements.

_____ **1.** Stadium A is as big as Stadium B.

_____ **2.** Stadium A is as new as Stadium B.

_____ **3.** Stadium A is as interesting as Stadium B.

_____ **4.** Stadium A is as colorful as Stadium B.

C Look back at Parts A and B. Complete the tasks.

1. To make comparisons, we use adjective + *-er* or *more* + adjective. Underline the **comparative adjectives** in Part A.

2. Complete the comparisons with the words you underlined. Then circle the word that follows each comparative adjective.

   • Stadium B is large. Stadium B is _____ than Stadium A.

   • Stadium A is traditional. Stadium A is _____ than Stadium B.

   • Stadium B is modern. Stadium B is _____ than Stadium A.

   • Stadium A is old. Stadium A is _____ than Stadium B.

3. When two things are the same in some way, we use *as* + **adjective** + *as* to compare them. Underline the words in Part B that show how the stadiums are the same.

Reading

A WARM-UP Look at the pictures. Try to match the countries in the box to the buildings.

_____ **Kremlin**   _____ **Jongno Tower**   _____ **Rose Tower**   _____ **Sears Tower**

| **a.** Dubai   **b.** Korea   **c.** Russia   **d.** the United States |

B SKIMMING Skim the conversation for mention of a building from Part A. Underline the sentence. Then go back and read the conversation again.

CHIN HO: I'm reading an article about architecture around the world. Is it true that everyone in Russia lives in an apartment?

ALINA: The cities in Russia are as crowded as the big cities in the United States. So, yes, people in cities often live in tall apartment buildings.

CHIN HO: Are they as modern as some U.S. apartment buildings?

ALINA: No, they're not as modern, generally. And they're larger and taller. Our apartments are more spacious and cheaper to rent. But some are as expensive as apartments in the United States. But the building materials are the same: both use concrete. What about Korean architecture? Is it true that there are a lot of tall skyscrapers?

CHIN HO: Yes, in the big cities. They have more modern buildings than the small towns and villages. Our modern buildings are taller and thinner than buildings in other countries—and prettier, in my opinion. They look like modern buildings in Dubai and Japan. For example, the Ryugyong Hotel is not very different from the Rose Tower.

ALINA: How interesting! What about the homes?

CHIN HO: In the villages, many people live in traditional homes. These are farther from the city than homes in the United States. And they're fancier, more decorative, and older than homes in the United States.

ALINA: They sound very unique. In my opinion, older architectural styles are less attractive than modern styles.

CHIN HO: I like variety. It's boring when everything is alike.

C UNDERSTANDING DETAILS Write *T* for the true statements and *F* for the false statements.

_____ **1.** Russian cities have large, tall apartment buildings.

_____ **2.** There are a lot of skyscrapers in the big Korean cities.

_____ **3.** Chin Ho doesn't like Korea's buildings.

_____ **4.** Buildings in Korea don't look like buildings in Dubai.

_____ **5.** Alina and Chin Ho agree that architecture is boring.

Grammar Focus 1 Comparative adjectives

Examples	Language notes
(1) Houses are **bigger** than apartments.	We use **comparative adjectives** to compare people, places, and things.
(2) tall → **taller** old → **older**	Comparative adjectives have special spelling rules. For **one-syllable adjectives**, add *-er*:
(3) big → **bigger** hot → **hotter**	For adjectives that **end in a vowel + consonant**, double the final consonant and add *-er*.
(4) safe → **safer** large → **larger**	For adjectives that **end in an -e**, add *-r*.
(5) easy → **easier** friendly → **friendlier**	For adjectives with **two syllables + y**, drop the *y* and add *-ier*.
(6) interesting → **more / less** interesting decorative → **more / less** decorative	For adjectives with **two or more syllables**, add *more* or *less*. **Note:** *Less* is the opposite of *more*.
(7) good → **better** bad → **worse** far → **farther / further**	Some adjectives are **irregular**. They do not follow a pattern.
(8) Our house **is older than** your house. Their house **is more decorative than** her house.	When comparing two things, use: **verb + comparative adjective + *than***
(9) That house is larger (**than this house**).	Often the ***than* phrase** is understood and dropped.
(10) **It's better to live** in the city. **It seems smarter to rent.**	***It* + verb + comparative adjective** is often followed by an **infinitive**.

See Appendix H on page A-4 for more examples and for spelling rules for comparative adjectives.

Grammar Practice

MyEnglishLab

Grammar Plus 1
Activities 1 and 2

 Complete the sentences. Use comparatives.

1. Penthouse apartments are _____ (private) than regular apartments.

2. Skyscrapers are _____ (tall) than houses.

3. Traditional houses are _____ (charming) than modern houses.

4. Buildings from the 21st century are _____ (modern) than buildings from the 20th century.

5. People in small towns are often _____ (friendly) than people in big cities.

6. Do you think it is _____ (good) to live in a big house or a small house?

7. Our cabin is _____ (far) from the beach than your beach house.

B Look at the two famous museums. Complete the sentences. Use the comparative form of adjectives in the list.

The British Museum

The Guggenheim Museum (in Spain)

beautiful	contemporary	luxurious
big	good	modern
colorful	interesting	unique

1. The British Museum _____ the Guggenheim Museum.

2. The British Museum _____ the Guggenheim Museum.

3. The Guggenheim Museum _____ the British Museum.

4. The Guggenheim Museum _____ the British Museum.

C Share your sentences from Part B with a partner. Which museum do you like better? Why? Look at the model.

> I like the Guggenheim better.

> Why?

> It's more unique, in my opinion.

D Choose one picture from Part B. Write sentences comparing a famous building in your home country with the picture.

Example: *The Guggenheim Museum is more modern than the Hermitage in Russia.*

1. _____

2. _____

3. _____

4. _____

5. _____

Grammar Focus 2 *As . . . as* and other expressions

Examples	Language notes
(1) The big cities in Russia are **as crowded as** the big cities in the United States.	To show how two things are **equal**, use: ***as* + adjective + *as***
(2) North American homes are **not as fancy as** Korean homes.	To show how two things are **not equal**, use: ***not* + *as* + adjective + *as***
(3) Our home is **just as decorative as** your home.	Add *just* to mean "equally": ***just* + *as* + adjective + *as***
(4) Korean homes are **almost as large as** U.S. homes.	Add *almost* to mean "not quite": ***almost* + *as* + adjective + *as***
(5) Our houses are **the same**. This Olympic Stadium is **the same as** that Olympic Stadium. Apartments in Russia are **the same** size **as** apartments in Europe. The building materials are **similar**. Our modern buildings are **similar to** buildings in Dubai. Our cultures are **different**. They are **different from** American buildings.	We can also make comparisons with these words: subject + verb + ***the same*** subject + verb + ***the same as*** + noun subject + verb + ***the same*** + noun + ***as*** + noun subject + verb + ***similar*** subject + verb + ***similar to*** + object subject + verb + ***different*** subject + verb + ***different from*** + object
(6) Our homes are **alike** in many ways.	Use *alike* as an adjective to say that two (or more) things are "similar." Use: subject + verb + ***alike***
(7) His room looks **like** her room. This seems **like** French architecture.	Use *like* as a preposition to say something is "similar to" something else: subject + verb + ***like*** + object

Grammar Practice

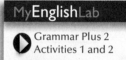

MyEnglishLab

Grammar Plus 2
Activities 1 and 2

 Look at the pictures and read the descriptions. Can you guess the names of the two famous buildings?

	Building A	Building B
Year built	1653	1377
Size	24,596 square feet (7,497 sq m)	8,000 square feet (2,438 sq m)
Climate	hot, dry	cold, snowy
Rating	★ ★ ★ ★ ★	★ ★ ★ ★ ★

B Use the information from the chart in Part A to complete the sentences. Use *(not) as . . . as, the same as,* or *different from*.

1. Building A is _not as old as_ (old) Building B.

2. Building B is _____ (big) Building A.

3. Building A is _____ (small) Building B.

4. Building A's climate is very _____ Building B's.

5. Building A's rating is _____ Building B's.

C What are characteristics of your "dream" home? Take notes in the chart. Then interview a partner and take notes. Look at the model.

What size is your dream home?

My dream home is small but with big rooms.

	Size	Style	Outdoor features	Distance to school	Noise
You					
Partner					

D Write sentences comparing your dream home to your partner's dream home. Use the words and the simple present.

Example: _My dream home is as big as Mila's._

1. (as . . . as) _____

2. (not as . . . as) _____

3. (almost as . . . as) _____

4. (the same . . . as) _____

5. (like) _____

E Find and correct the mistake in each sentence.

1. Houses in France are as older as houses in Spain.

2. Vera's neighborhood is as not nice as Tomas's neighborhood.

3. Do you like apartment buildings tall as this one?

4. Homes in the country are not as expensive homes in the city.

5. That castle is alike this castle.

Listening

A 🎧 UNDERSTANDING MAIN IDEAS Listen to the conversation between two neighbors. Are their homes the same or different? Circle your answers.

1. Size **Same** **Different**

2. Number of people **Same** **Different**

3. Age **Same** **Different**

4. Style **Same** **Different**

5. Convenience **Same** **Different**

B 🎧 UNDERSTANDING DETAILS Listen again. Circle the correct word. Then complete the sentence with the correct comparison.

1. **big / small**   Maggie's family is _____ Becca's family.

2. **quiet / noisy**   Maggie's home is _____ Becca's home.

3. **old / new**   Maggie's house is _____ Becca's house.

4. **traditional / modern**   Maggie's house is _____ Becca's house.

5. **far / close**   Maggie's workplace is _____ Becca's workplace.

C AFTER LISTENING Sketch a house with some of the features from Maggie's house or Becca's house. Talk about your sketch with a partner. What features are important to you?

Speaking

A Work with a partner. Look at the pictures of four famous leaders' homes. With your partner, circle the two you are most interested in.

Prince's Palace in Monaco

Vaduz Castle in Liechtenstein

Palacio da Alvorada in Brazil

The White House

B Take notes in the chart about one of the homes you circled in Part A. Your partner takes notes about the other.

Characteristics	Home #1	Home #2
Opinion		
Size / Shape		
Age		
Color		
Origin		
Material		

C With your partner, discuss the questions. Use your notes from Part B. Look at the model.

I think the Prince's Palace is more attractive.

Why?

- Which house is more attractive? Why?
- Which house is more unusual? Why?
- How are they different from one another?
- How are they similar to one another?
- Choose one to live in. Explain why.

Writing

MyEnglishLab

Linking Grammar to Writing

A Think about the city or town you live in now (Place 1). Make a list of the pros (positive features) and cons (negative features). Then think about another place you want to live in (Place 2). Add pros and cons to the chart.

	Pros	Cons
Place 1		
Place 2		

B Compare the two places. Write about the pros and cons. Try to use the grammar from the chapter.

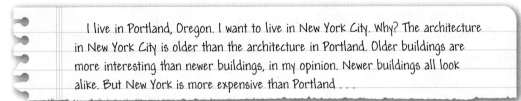

I live in Portland, Oregon. I want to live in New York City. Why? The architecture in New York City is older than the architecture in Portland. Older buildings are more interesting than newer buildings, in my opinion. Newer buildings all look alike. But New York is more expensive than Portland . . .

C Work in groups of three. Read and compare your paragraphs. What features do you agree on? What do you have different opinions about?

MyEnglishLab

Diagnostic Test

Grammar Summary

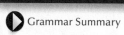

Descriptive adjectives give us more information about nouns. They come before the noun they modify or after the verb *be*. They do not change form to match the noun they modify. Nouns can also act like descriptive adjectives. For multiple adjectives, follow adjective word order.

Opinion	Size / Shape / Condition	Weather-related	Age	Color	Origin	Material
beautiful	big	hot	old	colorful	Mexican	glass
nice	tall	windy	brand-new	red	Chinese	clay
expensive	round	sunny	modern	dark	African	silver

Very makes a description stronger. It often has a positive meaning. *Too* means that something is not possible. It has an unfavorable—or negative—meaning. *Enough* means the right amount. After the first use of *enough* + noun, we often drop the noun. *Not* + *enough* means less than the right amount. *Too* + adjective and adjective + *enough* are often followed by an infinitive.

Very, too	*Enough*
Your garden is **very cute**.	We have **enough chairs**. / We have **enough**.
The rent is **too high**.	Are you **warm enough**?
It's **too cold** to open the windows.	There aren**'t enough closets**.

We use **comparative adjectives** to compare things. Comparative adjectives have special spelling rules. Some adjectives are irregular. When two things are being compared in a sentence, put the verb + comparative adjective + *than* in between. Often the second thing is not mentioned—it's understood. In those cases, we drop the *than* phrase. It's also common to use infinitives after comparative adjectives.

Comparisons		
short → **shorter**	friendly → **friendlier**	Renting is **cheaper than** buying.
hot → **hotter**	beautiful → **more / less** beautiful	Renting is **cheaper**.
large → **larger**	good → **better**	It's **cheaper** to rent.

We use *(not) as* + **adjective** + *as* to show how two things are equal (or not). Add *just* to mean "equally." Add *almost* to mean "not quite." We also use expressions with *the same, similar, different, alike,* and *like* to make comparisons.

Expressions with *as . . . as*	Other comparisons
Towns in France are **as cute as** towns in Italy.	Our bedrooms are **the same**.
Our home is **not as fancy as** their home.	My kitchen is **the same as** your kitchen.
Her garden is **just as large as** your garden.	Her car is **the same color as** his car.
Seattle rents are **almost as high as** New York rents.	The garages are **similar**.
	Moroccan homes are **similar to** Algerian homes.
	Our cultures are **different**.
	These are **different from** those.
	Our families are **alike** in many ways.
	This couch looks **like** Patty's couch.

Self-Assessment

A   (5 points) Complete the sentences. Put the adjectives in the correct order. Use commas.

1. In cold climates, homes have _____ (wood / thick) walls.

2. Do you prefer _____ (tiny / cute) apartments or
_____ (modern / large / family) homes?

3. _____ (contemporary / square / white) homes are
popular along beaches.

4. Those look like _____ (antique / charming) homes, but they are new.

B   (6 points) Complete the sentences. Use *too, very,* or *enough*.

1. Some deserts are _____ hot for humans. People can't live there.

2. It gets _____ cold in the mountains. But with a good coat, you're fine.

3. That sand is hot _____ to burn your feet! Put your shoes on!

4. This house doesn't have _____ windows. In fact, most houses don't have
_____, in my opinion.

5. I can't buy that house. It's _____ expensive.

C   (4 points) Look at the chart. Complete the comparisons.

	Houses near the ocean	Houses in the mountains
Color	light	dark
Size	large	tiny
Sound	noisy	peaceful
Cost	expensive	expensive

1. Houses near the ocean are _____ houses in the mountains.

                                          color

2. Houses near the ocean are _____ houses in the mountains.

                                          size

3. Houses in the mountains are _____ houses near the ocean.

                                          sound

4. Houses in the mountains are _____ houses near the ocean.

                                          cost

D   (10 points) Find and correct the mistake in each sentence.

1. Your house is as bigger as my house.

2. This neighborhood is just as safer as that one.

3. Do you like beach houses gooder?

4. My house is more far than your house.

5. Modern buildings are alike art, in my opinion.

6. Concrete is more strong than wood.

7. This school is similar my old school.

8. Do you think living in the country is different to living in the city?

9. The two castles are like in many ways.

10. Museums are just interesting as shopping malls.

Unit Project: Class map

A Work together as a class. Create a class map. Follow the steps.

1. With a partner, choose a country (not your own) to research. Make sure no one else in the class is researching the same country.
2. Decide with your partner who will research the country's climate and who will research its housing and other architectural styles.
3. As you do your research, think about these questions:

Climate
- What's the weather like in different parts of the country? How?
- What is interesting or unique about the climate in this country?

Architecture
- What's the architecture like in different parts of the country? Think about housing, office buildings, museums, sports complexes, and shopping areas, for example.
- What is interesting about the architecture here?
- How does the climate influence the architecture? Give examples.

4. Write a report about the country you researched. Describe its climate. Describe its architecture. Compare it to where you live now.

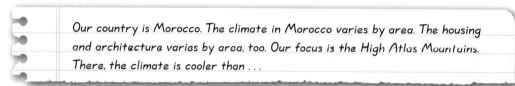

> Our country is Morocco. The climate in Morocco varies by area. The housing and architecture varies by area, too. Our focus is the High Atlas Mountains. There, the climate is cooler than . . .

5. Add visual aids to your report—for example, a weather forecast, pictures of geographic features, typical houses, famous buildings, etc.

B On a world map, place a pin on the country you researched. Then tape your report to the wall, connect a string from your pin to your report and invite your classmates to read.

MyEnglishLab
▶ Unit Test

MyEnglishLab
▶ Search it!

UNIT 9

Hidden History

OUTCOMES
After completing this unit, I will be able to use these grammar points.

CHAPTER 17

Grammar Focus 1
Simple past: Regular verbs

Grammar Focus 2
Simple past: Irregular verbs

CHAPTER 18

Grammar Focus 1
Simple past: Questions

Grammar Focus 2
Time signals

MyEnglishLab

 What do you know?

CHAPTER 17   Uncovering the Past

 Getting Started

A   Do you have a good memory? Test yourself. Follow the steps.

     1. Sit back-to-back with a partner.
     2. Describe what your partner is wearing.
     3. Turn around and check your answers.

B   Here's another test of your memory: What did you do yesterday? Check (✓) your answers.

☐ listened to music   ☐ wrote an email   ☐ went to class

☐ bought something in a store   ☐ exercised   ☐ worked at a job

☐ called a friend on the phone   ☐ studied for a test   ☐ drank coffee

C   Look back at the activities in Part B. Complete the tasks.

     1. In the simple past, "regular" verbs end in *-ed*. Circle the **simple past regular verbs**.
     2. In the simple past, "irregular" verbs have a variety of forms. Underline the **simple past irregular verbs**.
     3. Use the information in Part B to help you match the verb forms.

Base form	Irregular simple past form
_____ **1.** buy	**a.** wrote
_____ **2.** go	**b.** went
_____ **3.** drink	**c.** drank
_____ **4.** write	**d.** bought

Reading

A WARM-UP Look at the sketch of the bridge in Part B. It's from the 1600s. What tells you that this image is from the past?

B SCANNING What year did Dock Creek become Dock Street? Scan the article for the answer. Circle the year. Then go back and read the whole article.

From Dock Creek to Dock Street

Philadelphia is one of the oldest cities in the United States. In fact, the city is older than the country. A small group of people from Europe settled Philadelphia in 1682. The United States didn't become a country until 1776. Many people don't know about the interesting things in Philadelphia's past.

In the 1680s, a group of people from England came to live along the Delaware River in North America, near the Atlantic Ocean. Their leader was William Penn. Penn planned the new city and named it Philadelphia: the "City of Brotherly Love." Penn wanted the city to be modern and green. The city had public squares with grass and trees. Also, all of the streets were straight. They went from north to south or from east to west.

A creek flowed through the new town. The English settlers called it Dock Creek. They used it for their boats. They built their houses and businesses along the creek.

The city grew in the early 1700s. There were many houses and businesses along Dock Creek.

People used the creek as a sewer. They put their waste in it. It became dirty and smelled very bad. Sometimes it rained, and the streets flooded. People needed to get across the creek, but they did not want to get in the water. So they constructed bridges over the creek.

Then in 1820, in the middle of the Industrial Age, workers completely covered the creek. And people changed the name from Dock Creek to Dock Street. There was still a stream under the street, but many people forgot this. However, one thing made Dock Street different from all the other streets in the city: it didn't go in a straight line!

C UNDERSTANDING MAIN IDEAS Match the years to the events.

Events	Years
_____ 1. The creek became dirty.	a. 1682
_____ 2. People from Europe settled in Philadelphia.	b. early 1700s
_____ 3. Workers covered Dock Creek.	c. 1776
_____ 4. The United States became a country.	d. 1820

Grammar Focus 1 Simple past: Regular verbs

Examples	Language notes
(1) Present **Past** —— **X** —— **|** ————▶ Future Many interesting things **happened**.	We use the **simple past** to tell about actions that occurred before the present time.
(2) The stream **flowed** through the city.	Simple past verbs that end in -*ed* are called **regular verbs**. Most English verbs are regular. To form **statements** in the simple past, use: subject + **simple past verb**
(3) **want:** They **wanted** to cross the creek. **talk:** The man **talked** about the town's history.	Add -*ed* to verbs that end in: **consonant + consonant**
(4) **rain:** Sometimes it **rained**. **seem:** He **seemed** troubled.	Also add -*ed* to verbs that end in: **vowel + vowel + consonant**
(5) **plan:** Penn **planned** the city. **trim:** The man **trimmed** his beard.	Double the consonant and add -*ed* to short verbs that end in: **consonant + vowel + consonant** ***Note:*** If the stress is on the first syllable or if the word ends in -*w* or -*x*, do not double the consonant: *showed, visited.*
(6) **settle:** People from England **settled** there. **balance:** He **balanced** the box on his shoulder.	Add just -*d* to verbs that end in -*e*.
(7) **carry:** She **carried** her belongings in a bag. **study:** They **studied** the map of the city. *Incorrect:* They ~~studyed~~ the map of the city.	Change the *y* to *i* and add -*ed* to verbs that end in: **consonant + y**
(8) **I wanted** to cross the stream. **He wanted** to cross the stream. **They wanted** to cross the stream.	The form of regular simple past verbs is the **same for all subjects**.
(9) They **did not want** to use a boat. She **did not want** to use a boat. We **did not want** to use a boat.	To form **negative** statements, use: subject + ***did*** + ***not*** + **base verb** ***Note:*** *Did* is the simple past form of the helping verb *do*. (It is irregular.) It always has the same form in the simple past.
(10) The people **didn't swim** in the river.	In speech and informal writing, people commonly contract *did not* to **didn't**.

See Appendix I on page A-5 for more examples and for spelling rules for -ed endings.

Pronunciation of -*ed* endings
When the base verb ends in a /t/ or /d/ sound, the -*ed* ending is pronounced /ɪd/. This gives the word an extra syllable: *The city started in 1682.*

Grammar Practice

A Complete the sentences. Use the simple past form of the verbs.

1. They _lived_ (live) along the creek.

2. We _____ (change) the time of our meeting.

3. She _____ (wait) near the creek.

4. They _____ (call) it the "City of Brotherly Love."

5. I _____ (study) history in my old school.

6. My teacher _____ (plan) a field trip to a history museum.

B Complete the sentences. Use the simple past form of the verbs.

1. They _didn't want_ (not / want) to cross the creek.

2. We _____ (not / remember) its name.

3. The people _____ (not / need) help.

4. The owners _____ (not / fix) the buildings for many years.

5. Flooding _____ (not / happen) often.

6. The city _____ (not / change) quickly.

C Work with a partner. Take turns saying affirmative sentences in the simple past. Check (✓) the verbs that add a syllable. Look at the model.

> The streets flooded.

> Flooded. The -ed adds a syllable.

☑ 1. flood   ☐ 5. settle

☐ 2. work   ☐ 6. need

☐ 3. talk   ☐ 7. walk

☐ 4. want   ☐ 8. construct

The sign on the photo reads:

PHILADELPHIA
Founded by William Penn. Laid out in 1682. Chartered a city, 1701. Pennsylvania's capital until 1799: the nation's to 1800. County was one of Pennsylvania's original three, formed 1682 and consolidated with city in 1854. Name means "City of Brotherly Love."

Grammar Focus 2 Simple past: Irregular verbs

Examples	Language notes
(1) **have:** The city **had** squares. **be:** Their leader **was** William Penn.	**Irregular** verbs are verbs that do not follow a rule.
(2) **I was** tired. The **house was** dirty. **You were** late. The **travelers were** from England.	*Be* is a commonly used irregular verb. As you saw in Chapter 6 with *There was* and *There were*, *be* has two forms in the simple past: *I, he, she, it,* singular subjects + *was* *we, you, they,* plural subjects + *were*
(3) Dock Street **was not** straight. The stores **were not** busy.	To form **negative** statements, use *was not* or *were not*.
(4) Dock Street **wasn't** straight. We **weren't** ready.	The **contracted** forms **wasn't** and **weren't** are common in speech and informal writing.
(5) **put:** They **put** their waste in the creek. **cut:** I **cut** my hand yesterday.	Some irregular verbs do not change. They have **the same form as the base verb.**
(6) **become:** The United States **became** a country in 1776. **come:** The citizens **came** here in the 1700s. **forget:** Many people **forgot** about the creek. **grow:** The city **grew** in the 1700s.	In many irregular verbs, only **a vowel changes.**
(7) **build:** People **built** bridges over the creek.	In some irregular verbs, the *-d* ending changes to *-t*.
(8) **do:** We **did** our work in silence. **go:** They **went** from north to south. **have:** He **had** only two dollars. **make:** One thing **made** Dock Street different.	Some irregular past forms **do not follow a clear rule.**

See Appendix J on pages A-6–7 for more examples of irregular simple past verbs.

 ## Grammar Practice

My**English**Lab
▶ Grammar Plus 2
Activities 1 and 2

A Complete the chart with irregular simple past forms. (See Appendix J on pages A-6–7 for help.)

Base form	Simple past	Base form	Simple past	Base form	Simple past
be		give		say	
build		go		see	
buy		grow		send	
come		have		set	
drink		hurt		spend	
eat		know		take	
find		let		tell	
forget		make		think	
get		put		write	

B Complete the paragraph. Use the simple past form of the words.

Today, Dock Street in Philadelphia is a stone street. It goes through the old part of the city. Three hundred years ago, the street **1.** _____ (be) a small creek. People **2.** _____ (bring) their boats up the creek. They used it like a road.

People also **3.** _____ (have) businesses on the creek. Back then, people **4.** _____ (not / think) about protecting the water. People **5.** _____ (put) their waste in the creek. This **6.** _____ (make) the water very dirty.

Philadelphia Exchange, Omnibus Depot, and part of Dock Street

The city government **7.** _____ (build) bridges over the creek. Over time, the city **8.** _____ (grow), and people **9.** _____ (forget) about the creek. The creek **10.** _____ (become) a street.

C Work in small groups. Each person says one thing he or she did and did not do yesterday. The next person restates the information, then tells his or her own information. Use verbs from the chart in Part A. Look at the model.

> I got up early. I didn't spend money.

> Ana got up early. She didn't spend money. I went to English class. I wasn't late.

> Ana got up early. She didn't spend money. Bardhi went to English class. He wasn't late. I took a math test. I didn't eat lunch.

Listening

A BEFORE LISTENING Have you toured a museum? What did you see? What did you learn?

B 🎧 UNDERSTANDING MAIN IDEAS Listen to the radio feature. Circle the best title for the story.

　a. Remembering the Declaration of Independence

　b. Tourists rediscover Dock Creek

　c. Popular tourist sites in Philadelphia

C 🎧 UNDERSTANDING DETAILS Listen again. Complete the sentences.

　1. Philadelphia _____ the first capital of the United States.

　2. Leaders of the United States _____ the Declaration of Independence in Philadelphia.

　3. In the old city, most of the streets _____ straight.

　4. The streets _____ north and south and east and west.

　5. William Penn _____ the city in the 1600s.

　6. A museum _____ an exhibit about Dock Creek.

　7. The organizers _____ to have the exhibit indoors.

　8. They _____ a tour of the old city.

　9. The lines _____ the location of the old creek.

　10. Tourists _____ past colonial buildings beside the old creek.

　11. They _____ about the boats people used to travel through the city.

　12. They _____ past beautiful old homes.

　13. The visitor _____, "It was an interesting tour."

Speaking

A Read the list of events in William Penn's life. What do you think was Penn's biggest accomplishment?

Events in William Penn's life

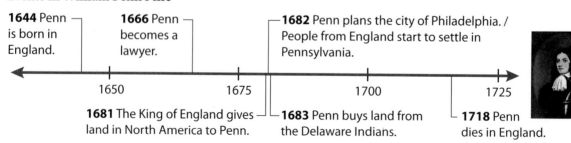

1644 Penn is born in England.

1666 Penn becomes a lawyer.

1682 Penn plans the city of Philadelphia. / People from England start to settle in Pennsylvania.

1650　1675　1700　1725

1681 The King of England gives land in North America to Penn.

1683 Penn buys land from the Delaware Indians.

1718 Penn dies in England.

B Work with a partner. Take turns telling about William Penn's life. Use the simple past. Make positive and negative statements. Look at the model.

> William Penn did not grow up in the United States. He grew up in England.

C With your partner, take the history quiz. Take turns asking and answering the items. Look at the model.

> William Penn was a doctor. True or false?

> False. He was a lawyer.

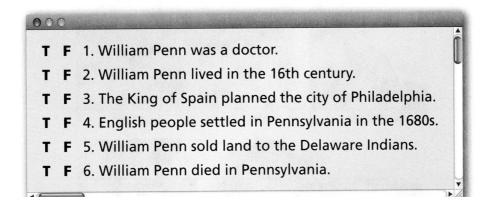

T F 1. William Penn was a doctor.
T F 2. William Penn lived in the 16th century.
T F 3. The King of Spain planned the city of Philadelphia.
T F 4. English people settled in Pennsylvania in the 1680s.
T F 5. William Penn sold land to the Delaware Indians.
T F 6. William Penn died in Pennsylvania.

Writing

MyEnglishLab
▶ Linking Grammar to Writing

A Imagine that you are writing an autobiography (a book about your life). Think about the topics in the list. Take notes.

• the place you grew up
• your family
• your life as a very small child
• your experiences in middle and high school as a child
• fun you had as a child
• places you lived as an adult
• work you did as an adult
• your studies as an adult

B Write a paragraph about your life. Use your notes from Part A. Try to use the grammar from the chapter.

> I grew up in Nanjing, a large city in China. I lived with my parents and my aunt. I do not remember very much about my life before school. . . .

C Share your writing with a partner. What is interesting about your partner's past?

MyEnglishLab
▶ Diagnostic Test

CHAPTER 18   City of Angels

Getting Started

A   Work with a partner. Guess the famous faces and places.

Answers (starting from upper left corner): Marilyn Monroe, actress (1926–1962); Venice Beach (1905–present); Felipe de Neve, governor (1728–1784); The Doors, band (1965–1973)

B   Match the answers to the questions.

Questions

_____ 1. When did Marilyn Monroe die?

_____ 2. Was Venice Beach always popular?

_____ 3. Did you see the Doors in concert?

_____ 4. Where was Felipe de Neve from?

Answers

a. Spain. But in the 1770s, he moved to Mexico.

b. Yes. On Dec. 12, 1970. It was their final show.

c. Yes. It was a resort town from the beginning. Workers built it a century ago.

d. At 12:30 A.M. on Aug. 5, 1962. There was a movie about her last year.

C   Look back at Part B. Complete the tasks.

1. Find the **_wh-_ questions in the simple past** and underline the verbs. What two verb patterns do you see?

   _Wh-_ word + _____ + subject + _____

   _Wh-_ word + _____ + subject

2. Find the **_yes / no_ questions in the simple past**. How are they different? _____

3. Look at the answers. What words introduce or tell information about time? Circle the **time signals**.

Reading

A WARM-UP Work with a partner. Draw a simple map of your city. What are the most important streets? What are the most important places (a river, a campus, etc.)?

B SKIMMING A group is touring an historic city, formerly a Spanish colony. Read the following questions. Skim the conversation for answers. Then go back and read the conversation again.

1. What did Felipe de Neve do? _____

2. Who was Vitruvius? _____

3. What laws did the King of Spain write? _____

A Tour of the City of Angels

GUIDE: On Friday we toured a modern art gallery. Yesterday we ate at a 1950s diner. And last night we enjoyed 1920s music. So today we continue our journey back in time. We are standing in a very old part of the city. Do you see the large square in the center? And the church on the square? This entire area is over 200 years old. Today, as in the past, streets lead away from the square into other parts of town.

TOURIST A: Did a lot of people live here in the 1700s?

GUIDE: No, there were only 48 people in the first settlement.

TOURIST B: Who built the town?

GUIDE: The local governor, Felipe de Neve, built this town in 1781. He represented the King of Spain.

TOURIST C: Why did he build it?

GUIDE: He developed this town and others to support nearby forts. The towns supplied things like food and tools to the forts.

TOURIST D: Did the governor do a good job? Was he popular?

GUIDE: Yes and yes, generally. He had help: he used a set of laws called the "Laws of the Indies."

TOURIST E: What were they about?

GUIDE: About 2,000 years ago, a Roman teacher named Vitruvius taught Roman leaders how to plan a good city. The King of Spain read about Vitruvius's ideas and liked them. So he used them to write the Laws of the Indies. According to the Laws, a town needed a square in the center, a church, and government buildings. Streets should go in straight lines from the square, they said. And farms and houses should be built along the streets. . . . At noon, we're heading over to the Felipe de Neve Branch Library, so we'll hear more about de Neve then. . . .

C UNDERSTANDING DETAILS Write *T* for the true statements and *F* for the false statements.

_____ **1.** Governor Felipe de Neve built the town in 1781.

_____ **2.** The town had a square in the center.

_____ **3.** The governor wanted the area to develop.

_____ **4.** The King of England wrote the "Laws of the Indies."

Grammar Focus 1 Simple past: Questions

Examples	Language notes
(1) **Was he** the governor? **Were they** from Mexico?	To form **yes / no questions** with **be** in the simple past, use: **Be** + **subject** + other information
(2) **Did** the governor **build** the town? **Did** they **write** the laws?	To form **yes / no questions** with **other verbs**, use: **Did** + subject + **base verb**
(3) **Q:** Was he a good governor? **A: Yes, he was. / No, he wasn't.** **Q:** Were they late? **A: Yes, they were. / No, they weren't.**	For **short answers** to *yes / no* questions with **be**, use: **Yes,** + subject + **was / were** **No,** + subject + **was not (wasn't) / were not (weren't)**
(4) **Q:** Did the people follow the laws? **A: Yes, they did. / No, they didn't.**	For **short answers** to *yes / no* questions with **other verbs**, use: **Yes,** + subject + **did** **No,** + subject + **did not (didn't)**
(5) **Who was** the governor? **What were** their names?	To form **wh- questions** with **be**, use: **Wh- word** + **was / were** + subject
(6) **When did** he **become** the governor? **Why did** the king **use** his ideas? **How did** they **design** the streets?	To form **wh- questions** with **other verbs**, use: **Wh- word** + **did** + subject + **base verb**
(7) **Who chose** the governor? **What caused** the problem?	When the *wh-* word is the **subject**, use: **Wh- word** + **simple past verb**

Grammar Practice

 A Read each answer. Then write a *yes / no* question or a *wh-* question.
Use the *wh-* words.

MyEnglishLab
> Grammar Plus 1
> Activities 1 and 2

1. Q: *Did the history class begin on Monday?* _____

   A: Yes, the history class began on Monday.

2. Q: _____

   A: Yes, new settlers went to the colony.

3. Q: (Who) _____

   A: The governor made a plan for the city.

4. Q: _____

   A: No, the governor wasn't from Italy.

5. Q: (Where) _____

   A: The old town square was next to the church.

6. Q: (Why) _____

   A: They settled here because it's beautiful.

B Read the conversation. There are six mistakes. Find and correct the mistakes.

STUDENT: Why did they chose this place for the town? Did it has gold?

GUIDE: No, it don't. It was near a fort. The governor wanted to grow food for the fort.

STUDENT: Were the people speak Spanish?

GUIDE: Yes, the first settlers do. They came from Mexico.

STUDENT: How you did learn about the history of this town?

GUIDE: I studied history at the university.

C Work with a partner. Learn about your partner's past. Ask about your partner's childhood. Use the ideas from the list. Use the simple past. Look at the model.

Where were you born?

I was born in Bhutan.

Topic ideas

Where: born?
go on vacation?

Did you: study English in school?
like school?

Who: best friend?

What: foods eat?
sports play?
kinds of music like?

Were you: a good student?
an only child?

Grammar Focus 2 Time signals

Examples	Language notes
(1) It was here **yesterday**. I arrived **last night**. The party began **an hour ago**. The tour was **on Friday**.	We use **time signals** to explain when a past event occurred.
(2) Today is Sunday. We took a tour **yesterday**. *(yesterday = Saturday)* Today is Sunday. We went to a museum **the day before yesterday**. *(the day before yesterday = Friday)*	Use *yesterday* to mean one day ago and *the day before yesterday* to mean two days ago.
(3) I started my class **last month**. We heard the news **last Friday**. She worked **the night before last**.	Use *last* to indicate "the previous": *last* ___ *(night, week, weekend, month, year, Friday, summer)* *the* ___ *before last (night, week, year)*
(4) They built the city **200 years ago**. I finished my paper **three days ago**. He left **a week ago**.	Use *ago* to express an amount of time: number + ___ *ago (hours, days, months, years)*
(5) I started this class **in January**. It became part of the United States **in 1848**.	Use *in* with **months** and **years**.
(6) Our last test was **on Tuesday**. Final exams were **on the 12th**.	Use *on* with **days** and **dates**.
(7) The meeting began **at 6:30 P.M.** The train arrived **at midnight**.	Use *at* with **time**.

Grammar Practice

MyEnglishLab

Grammar Plus 2
Activities 1 and 2

A Complete the sentences about you. Use time words and expressions.

1. I got up _____ _____ o'clock today.
   time

2. I began to study English _____ years _____.
   number

3. I was born _____ _____. It's a beautiful month.
   month

4. I was born _____ the _____. It's a very lucky date.
   date

5. I went to _____ yesterday. In other words, I went there _____
   place

   _____.
   day of the week

B Work with a partner. Take turns asking and answering the questions. Write your partner's answers in complete sentences.

1. **Q:** What did you eat for lunch yesterday?

   A: _____

2. **Q:** When did you start this class?

   A: _____

3. **Q:** When did you buy that pen?

   A: _____

4. **Q:** What time did you come to class today?

   A: _____

5. **Q:** What year did you start high school?

   A: _____

C Read the paragraph. There are five mistakes. Find and correct the mistakes.

When is the real birthday of the United States? Some people say the country began at July 4, 1776. Some people disagree. Here is why: Congress voted for independence from Great Britain in July 2, 1776. On July 4, Congress adopted the Declaration of Independence. Leaders signed it on August. But Great Britain did not accept U.S. independence at 1776. They accepted it on 1783.

Listening

A BEFORE LISTENING Look at the picture. What city do you think it is? What are the clues?

B 🎧 UNDERSTANDING MAIN IDEAS Listen to the Q&A session with a group of tourists. Answer the questions.

1. Where were many of the first settlers from? _____

2. Was the town always part of the United States? _____

3. How many people live there now? _____

4. What is it called now? _____

C 🎧 UNDERSTANDING DETAILS Listen again. Complete the sentences with time signals.

1. The town started _____.

2. Mexico became independent _____.

3. The town became part of the United States _____.

Speaking

A What can you learn from your classmates? Complete the questions with information you want to know.

1. When do *people in the United States celebrate Independence Day* _____?

2. When _____?

3. What time _____?

4. What year _____?

5. What month _____?

6. How many years ago _____?

B Now walk around the classroom and talk to your classmates. Ask each person only one question. Look at the model.

> When do people in the United States celebrate Independence Day?

> On the fourth of July.

Writing

A You are going to write a conversation based on an interview with a classmate. Choose Topic A or Topic B.

Topic A: Moving to a new place
When / move to a new place?
Where?
How feel / first day of new job or school?
Make new friends?

Topic B: Studying English
When / begin to study English?
Where?
Difficulties learning English at first? Examples?
Recent successes learning English? Examples?

B Use the questions from Part A to interview a classmate. Take careful notes or use a recording device.

C Write an introduction explaining the interview. Use your notes or recording to recreate the interview. Write out both the questions and the answers. Try to use the grammar from the chapter.

> On Tuesday, I interviewed my classmate Samir about his life. This is our conversation.
>
> **Sandra:** Samir, when did you come to this country?
> **Samir:** I came here three years ago. I came with my parents and my sister.
> **Sandra:** How did you feel in the beginning?
> **Samir:** In the beginning I was surprised. I was shocked. I studied English in my country. When I came here, I didn't understand anyone! I stayed in my house. I didn't want to go out.
> **Sandra:** Did your feelings change?
> **Samir:** Oh, yes! Last summer I got a job at a restaurant and made some friends there. They helped me . . .

Grammar Summary

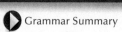

We use the **simple past** to tell about actions that occurred before the present time. Simple past verbs that end in *-ed* are called **regular verbs**. Use *did + not +* base verbs to make statements negative. In speech and informal writing, we commonly contract *did not* to *didn't*.

Regular verbs	
start: The city **started** in 1781. **happen:** Nothing **happened**. **plan:** He **planned** the city.	**bake:** She **baked** all morning **cry:** They **cried** when they heard the news. **live:** She **didn't live** in Los Angeles.

Verbs in the simple past that do not follow the *-ed* rule are called **irregular verbs**. Some have patterns: (A) Some irregular verbs do not change from their simple present form. (B) Some change their vowel. (C) Some change the *-d* ending to *-t*. Others, such as *be, make,* and *go*, do not follow a clear rule. Only *be* has different forms with singular *(was)* and plural *(were)* subjects.

Irregular verbs	
patterns	**other forms**

(A) **shut:** She **shut** the door quietly.
(B) **come:** They **came** to Philadelphia from England.
    give: My parents **gave** me some help.
    know: They **knew** the answer.
    get: They **got** a room in a hotel.
(C) **send:** He **sent** the letter yesterday.
	be: The horses **were** in the field.
	make: The artist **made** the lines.
	go: They **went** out for the evening.
	take: We **took** the train to Los Angeles.
	see: They **saw** the old square in the city.
	find: She **found** the map of the city.
	think: We **thought** about the question.

To form **yes / no questions** with *be* in the simple past, begin the sentence with *Was* or *Were*. With other verbs, use *Did +* subject + base verb. For short answers, use the past form of *be* (with *be*) or *do* (with other verbs). To form **wh- questions** with *be* in the simple past, use a *wh-* word + *was / were*. With other verbs, use a *wh-* word + *did +* subject + base verb. When the *wh-* word is the subject, use the simple past form of the verb.

Yes / No questions	Wh- questions
Q: **Were** you in Los Angeles? **A:** Yes, I **was**. / Yes, we **were**. / No, I **wasn't**. / No, we **weren't**. **Q:** **Did** she **take** the train from Los Angeles? **A:** Yes, she **did**. / No, she **didn't**.	**When were** you there? **How did** they **get** enough food? **Who made** the decision? (Who = *subject*)

We add **time signals** to sentences in the simple past to help explain when a past event occurred.

Time signals	
She stopped by **the day before yesterday**. He died **the night before last**. We had a party **last week**. The city started **200 years ago**.	The family left town **in 1785**. Our paper was due **on Tuesday**. The train came **at 3:05**.

Self-Assessment

A (5 points) Complete the sentences. Use the simple past form of the words.

1. William Penn _____ (make) a plan for the city.

2. I _____ (not / go) home this week.

3. My friend _____ (take) math last semester.

4. Many people _____ (come) to this city in the 1800s.

5. Paul _____ (not / study) for the test.

B (6 points) Complete the sentences with time expressions.

1. He went back to England _____ 1693.

2. I went to work _____ 4:30.

3. Sarah stayed up late _____ night.

4. The weather was very nice _____ November.

5. They went to Pacific City _____ Saturday.

6. Today is Sunday. _____ was Saturday.

C (5 points) Read each answer. Then write a *yes / no* question or a *wh-* question.

1. Q: _____

   A: The first governor was William Penn.

2. Q: _____

   A: Los Angeles became a city in 1781.

3. Q: _____

   A: Yes, she came to school today.

4. Q: _____

   A: They named the town New Amsterdam.

5. Q: _____

   A: No, he wasn't angry. He was just tired.

D (9 points) Read the paragraph. There are nine mistakes. Find and correct the mistakes.

New York City begin almost 400 years ago, at 1625. Or maybe the city started in 1623, or in 1653. People disagree about the year. The first settlers from Europe were came to the area on May 1623. They was from Holland, and they named the colony New Amsterdam. The Dutch settlers purchase the area from the local Indians on 1626. The colony becomes a Dutch city in 1653. In 1664, the Dutch settlers give up the area, and it become a colony of Great Britain. Later it was the first capital of the United States and the place of President George Washington's inauguration.

Unit Project: Guided tour

A Work with a partner. Give your classmates a "guided tour" of a city you know well. Follow the steps.

1. Collect information for your project. Use the list of questions to help you.

   • Where is the city?
   • When did the city begin?
   • Who built the city? Who first lived there?
   • What important things happened in the city's history?
   • How do you know about the city? Did you live there or visit there? When?

2. Organize your information in an outline.

I. Introduction: Name of city and why we chose it
II. Location of the city: Interesting geographic features
III. The past: The history of the city
A. Who: The first people in the city
B. What and when: Important events in the city's history
IV. Now: The city today
A. Our experiences with the city
B. Our suggestions to a visitor
V. Summary

3. Create visual aids—for example: photos, graphs, drawings.

B With your partner, give the class "a tour" of your city. Look at the model.

We're going to tell you about the history of the city of Buenos Aires. Buenos Aires is a big city in South America. It's the capital of Argentina. The city began in 1536—almost 500 years ago. The first people were from Spain. The city was a very important port city. It was the place of a lot of trading between Europe and America. . . .

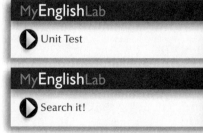

MyEnglishLab
▶ Unit Test

MyEnglishLab
▶ Search it!

UNIT 10

Pathways

OUTCOMES

After completing this unit, I will be able to use these grammar points.

CHAPTER 19

Grammar Focus 1
Past progressive: Statements

Grammar Focus 2
Past progressive: Questions

CHAPTER 20

Grammar Focus 1
Time clauses: *While* and *when*

Grammar Focus 2
Simple past vs. past progressive

CHAPTER 19 Their Stories

Getting Started

A What were you doing one year ago? Five years ago? Write the letter(s) in the chart.

a. I was living with my family.
b. I was learning a new culture.
c. I was making new friends.
d. I was renting an apartment.
e. I was studying English.
f. I was working.
g. I was raising my children.
h. I was planning my wedding.

1 year ago	
5 years ago	

B Interview a classmate. What was happening 10 years ago? Circle the answers.

1. Where were you living? _____		
2. Were you living alone?	**Yes**	**No**
3. Were you living with friends or family?	**Yes**	**No**
4. Were you happy?	**Yes**	**No**

C Look back at Parts A and B. Complete the tasks.

1. We use the **past progressive** (*was / were* + base verb + *-ing*) to talk about ongoing events in the past. Look at Part A. Underline the past progressive forms.
2. Look at Part B. Which question isn't in the past progressive? What form is it in? Why?

_____

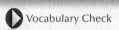
Reading

A WARM-UP Look at the map of the United States in 1860 on page 192. During this time, the country was divided in two: the North and the South. Why was the country was divided? Discuss ideas with a partner.

B SCANNING Scan the book excerpt to complete the statement below. Then go back and read the whole excerpt.

The author was living in the _____ at the beginning of the story.
a. the North   **b.** the South

The Journey Begins
by Susan Tallmon

The Slaveholders' Rebellion, as we called the Civil War, began in 1861. My husband George and I were living in Iowa. That is where I grew up. George was teaching in a small school. He left his job and joined the Army. He wanted to fight the slaveholders. The Army sent his group down the Mississippi River to Louisiana.

I stayed home in Iowa while George was fighting in the war. Soon after George left, I had our baby. In 1864, George wrote to me about his new assignment. He was leading a special Army unit of former slaves. He asked me to come to stay with him. In February, I took our baby, Grace, and traveled by boat down the Mississippi River, to Baton Rouge, the capital of Louisiana. I planned to teach in a school for former slaves. On the boat, Grace became very sick. She had a fever, and she was coughing all the time. Was I making a terrible mistake? What was I thinking? I was taking my new baby on a dangerous journey.

I arrived in Baton Rouge on February 25. Grace was very sick with a fever, and I was sick, too. George wasn't at the boat landing. Why wasn't he waiting for me? I asked for information about George. He was working in a camp miles away, people told me. I walked a long way to his camp. Finally, I found him.

In March we moved from the camp in Baton Rouge to a place called Arlington Plantation. The slaveholders weren't living at the plantation anymore. We used their big beautiful plantation house as a school for former slaves. I was recovering from my illness, but our baby daughter was not getting better. When she died, George and I were heartbroken, but we had to continue our work.

While I was at Arlington Plantation, I spoke to many people who lived there. Their stories seemed so interesting. One of the women was Martha Miller, a former slave . . .

C UNDERSTANDING DETAILS **Answer the questions.**

1. Where was the author living and when? Complete the information with dates and places.

   a. _____: Iowa

   b. February, 1864: _____

   c. _____: Arlington Plantation

2. Did the author recover from her illness? _____

3. Did her daughter get better? _____

4. What was the author doing at Arlington Plantation?

   _____

Grammar Focus 1 Past progressive: Statements

Examples	Language notes
(1) Present **Past** —— XXX —— | ————→ Future He **was reading** in the kitchen. I **was trying** to write a letter. We **were living** in Iowa. You **were trying** to be a better neighbor.	We use the **past progressive** to describe **actions** in progress in the past.
(2) **He was** leading former slaves. **They were** returning to the war.	As in the simple past, **be** has two forms in the past progressive. Use: *I, he, she, it,* singular subjects + **was** *we, you, they,* plural subjects + **were**
(3) I **was traveling**. She **was coughing** all the time.	To form **statements** in the past progressive, use: subject + **was / were** + **base verb** + **-ing**
(4) Our daughter **was not getting** better. George **wasn't waiting** for me.	To form **negative** statements, use: subject + **was / were** + **not** + **base verb** + **-ing**

See Appendix E on page A-3 for more examples and for spelling rules for -ing *endings..*

Grammar Practice

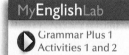

MyEnglishLab
Grammar Plus 1
Activities 1 and 2

A Complete the sentences. Use the past progressive form of the verbs.

1. We _____ (live) in Iowa in 1862.

2. The men _____ (return) to the war.

3. George _____ (not / teach) in the school.

4. He _____ (lead) former slaves.

5. He _____ (not / wait) for me when I arrived.

6. I _____ (recover).

7. Our baby _____ (cough) all the time.

8. She _____ (not / get) better.

B Circle the verb in each sentence. Then rewrite the sentence. Use the past progressive.

1. We reached Baton Rouge.

We were reaching Baton Rouge.

2. I cleaned my room.

_____

3. George cried bitterly.

_____

4. I talked to the women.

_____

5. She asked about my life.

_____

6. We used the house for classrooms.

_____

7. They moved fast.

_____

8. We held school in the countryside.

_____

C Complete the sentences. Use past progressive and the information in the timeline.

	1842	1853 1854 1856		1863 1864	1865
Martha	lives in South Carolina	lives and works in Louisiana			
Susan	grows up in New York	lives in Iowa		teaches in Louisiana	lives in Iowa
Eliza	lives in Kentucky	lives in Louisiana		stays in Texas	

1. In 1842, Martha *was living* _____ in South Carolina.

2. In 1843, Eliza _____.

3. In 1854, Martha and Eliza _____.

4. In 1856, Susan _____.

5. In 1863, Eliza _____.

6. In 1864, Susan _____.

7. In 1865, Susan _____ not _____ in Louisiana anymore.

She _____ again.

Grammar Focus 2 Past progressive: Questions

Examples	Language notes
(1) **Were** you **preparing** a grocery list? **Why was** she **cleaning** the house? **Was** he **fighting** in the war? **How were** people **changing**?	Use the **past progressive** to ask questions about **actions in progress** in the past.
(2) **Was** George **teaching** in a small school? **Were** you **living** in Iowa?	To form **yes / no questions**, use: **Was / Were** + subject + **base verb** + **-ing**
(3) **How was** she **doing**? **Where were** you **living**?	To form **wh- questions**, use: **Wh- word** + **was / were** + subject + **base verb** + **-ing**
(4) **Who was living** on the plantation? **What was happening** in the South in the 1880s?	When the **wh-** word is the **subject**, use: **Wh- word** + **was** + **base verb** + **-ing**
(5) **Q:** Was she living in Iowa? **A: Yes, she was. / No, she wasn't.** **Q:** Were they teaching in Louisiana? **A: Yes, they were. / No, they weren't.** **Q:** What was she doing? **A: Teaching former slaves.**	For **short answers** to **yes / no questions**, use: **Yes,** + subject + **was / were** **No,** + subject + **wasn't / weren't** For **wh- questions**, give information.

Grammar Practice

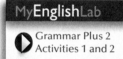

MyEnglishLab

Grammar Plus 2
Activities 1 and 2

A Write a *yes / no* question or a *wh-* question. Use the information. Use the past progressive.

1. Q: (you / sleep / on the boat)   *Were you sleeping on the boat?*

2. Q: (he / work in the army / in 1861) _____

3. Q: (What / you / think / about that day) _____

4. Q: (they / fight / in Louisiana) _____

5. Q: (Where / the children / go to school) _____

6. Q: (Why / Susan / take a boat) _____

B Read each answer. Then write a *yes / no* question or a *wh-* question. Use the past progressive.

1. Q: *Were they living in Iowa?*

   A: Yes, they were living in Iowa.

2. Q: _____

   A: No, they weren't teaching in a schoolhouse.

3. Q: _____

   A: They were living on the plantation.

4. Q: _____

   A: No one. She was traveling alone.

C Write a *yes / no* question and two *wh-* questions about each person. Use the past progressive. Use information from the list.

People	Actions	Places	Years
Eliza	live	Iowa	1844
George	stay	Louisiana	1861
Martha	teach	South Carolina	1864
Susan	work	Texas	1865

1. _____

   _____

   _____

2. _____

   _____

   _____

3. _____

   _____

   _____

4. _____

   _____

   _____

D Work with a partner. Use the timeline to ask and answer questions. Take turns. Look at the model.

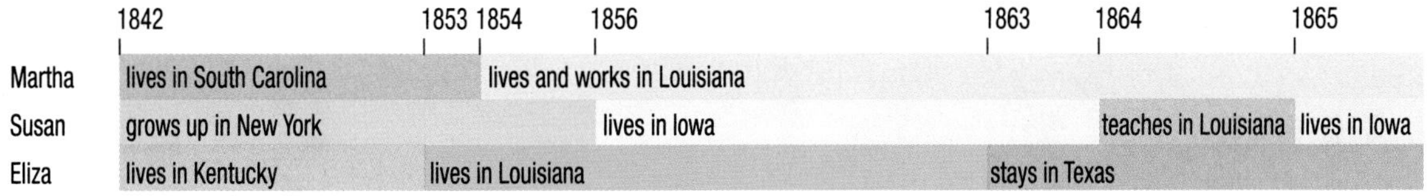

	1842	1853 1854	1856		1863	1864	1865
Martha	lives in South Carolina		lives and works in Louisiana				
Susan	grows up in New York		lives in Iowa			teaches in Louisiana	lives in Iowa
Eliza	lives in Kentucky	lives in Louisiana			stays in Texas		

Was Martha living in South Carolina in 1844?

Yes, she was. Was Susan living in South Carolina in 1844?

No, she wasn't. She was living in New York. . . .

Listening

A BEFORE LISTENING Work with a partner. Discuss the questions.

• What do you think slaves' children's lives were like?
• Do you think they learned to read?
• Did they have time to play?

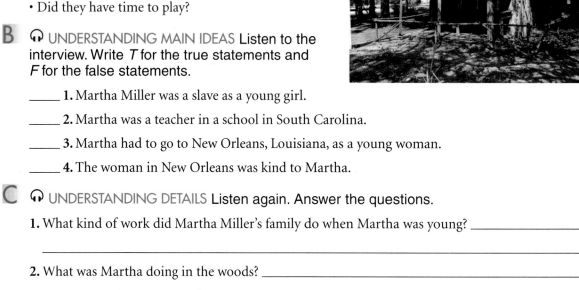

B 🎧 UNDERSTANDING MAIN IDEAS Listen to the interview. Write *T* for the true statements and *F* for the false statements.

_____ **1.** Martha Miller was a slave as a young girl.

_____ **2.** Martha was a teacher in a school in South Carolina.

_____ **3.** Martha had to go to New Orleans, Louisiana, as a young woman.

_____ **4.** The woman in New Orleans was kind to Martha.

C 🎧 UNDERSTANDING DETAILS Listen again. Answer the questions.

1. What kind of work did Martha Miller's family do when Martha was young? _____

_____

2. What was Martha doing in the woods? _____

_____

3. Why did Martha go to New Orleans? _____

_____

4. What did the woman do with Martha when the woman went shopping? _____

_____

Speaking

A Work with a partner. Tell your partner about someone interesting you know. Explain what is interesting about the person. Then listen as your partner tells about his or her interesting person. Ask questions about the person, using the ideas in the list. Take notes.

• What was the person doing one year ago? five years ago? ten years ago?
• Where: going to school? working? living?
• Friends? Interests?

B On the board, draw a timeline based on your classmate's answers. Use it to tell the class what you learned. Look at the model.

> *Ali's girlfriend Yesenia is a professional dancer. Ten years ago, she was living with her parents in Chia, Colombia, and attending high school. Five years ago, she moved to New York. She was taking business classes and studying ballet. Last year she was performing every night in . . .*

10 years ago	5 years ago	1 year ago
Living in Chia, Colombia, at home, attending high school	Living in New York, going to school and studying ballet	Performing . . .

Writing

A Imagine your grandparents when they were your age. What was happening in the world?

B Write a paragraph about when your grandparents were your age. What was happening in their lives? What was happening around them? Use the questions in the list to help you. Try to use the grammar from the chapter.

Questions

• Where were they living?
• What big events were happening in the country? In the world?
• What were they doing? Were they working? Were they starting a family?
• What challenges were they facing?

> *My grandparents were my age, 20, in 1960. They were living in southern Thailand. . . .*

C Share your paragraph with a partner. Are your stories similar? How?

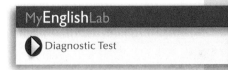

CHAPTER 20   Intersecting Lives

Getting Started

A Look at the pictures. Match the pictures to the statements.

a.

b.

c.

d.

Statements

_____ **1.** When she arrived, the kids gathered around her.

_____ **2.** This wealthy family was living here when the war started.

_____ **3.** While they were fighting in the war, they were fighting for their freedom.

_____ **4.** People watched while the protestors were marching.

B What stories do the pictures tell? Discuss with a partner.

C Look back at the statements in Part A. Complete the tasks.

1. We often use **when** time clauses (*when* + noun + verb) in sentences about the past. Circle the verb forms you see after *when*.
2. We also use **while** time clauses (*while* + noun + verb) in sentences about the past. Underline the verb forms you see after *while*.

Reading

A WARM-UP Have you heard the term "Yankee"? What does it mean to you? Discuss with a partner.

B SKIMMING Skim the interview between Susan Tallmon and Martha Miller. Answer the questions. Then go back and read the article again.

1. Was Martha Miller living in New Orleans when the war started? _____

2. Did she leave New Orleans during the war? _____

3. Was she hoping to start a new life? _____

An interview with former slave Martha Miller
by Susan Tallmon

ST: Were you living in New Orleans when the war started?

MM: Oh, yes. In 1862, the Yankees came to New Orleans. Everyone was very excited. The white people in New Orleans were becoming very nervous.

ST: Did you leave New Orleans during the war?

MM: Yes. When the Yankees came, everything changed in New Orleans. I was working as a slave in the home of a woman while all of this was happening. She was very upset. She wasn't giving me much food. One morning, the mistress threw some old bread at me. When I refused to eat it, she went crazy! She tried to hit me in the face with a whip. I picked up everything in the room, and I threw it all at her. I ran into the street. When I found some Yankee soldiers, I asked them to help me. They came with me to the house. The soldiers told the mistress I was leaving. She screamed at them while I was collecting my things. I only got a few of my clothes. Then I left the house—and New Orleans. That was my last day as a slave!

ST: Were you hoping to start a new life?

MM: Yes, I was. And I did start a new life. The Yankee soldiers took me to a plantation near Baton Rouge. The owner wasn't living there anymore, and a lot of former slaves were working there. While I was living there, I met a white man, Mr. Miller. He was running the plantation. We fell in love. I became the head of my own household. I had time to read and to sew. I was able to buy nice clothes.

ST: When did you come here to Arlington?

MM: After some time, Mr. Miller and I moved here to Arlington Plantation to live. And then I met you.

C UNDERSTANDING DETAILS Circle the correct answers.

1. ___ were happy when the Yankees came to New Orleans.
   a. Southern whites
   b. Slaves

2. ___ helped Martha escape from New Orleans.
   a. Martha's owner
   b. Yankee soldiers

3. When Martha was living in Baton Rouge, she ___.
   a. became a seamstress
   b. fell in love

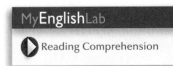

Grammar Focus 1 Time clauses: *While* and *when*

Examples	Language notes
(1) **While he was fighting in the war**, she was caring for the children.	To tell about related events, use: *while* clause + main clause
When the baby died, she was heartbroken.	*when* clause + main clause
(2) **While I was traveling**, I met many soldiers.	**While** clauses are often in the **past progressive**.
(3) **When I got off the boat**, he wasn't waiting.	**When** clauses are often in the **simple past**.
(4) **While I was living in the house, I worked** as a slave. I **worked** as a slave **while I was living in the house.**	We often use these forms with *while* clauses: *while* clause + main clause in **simple past**
While I was sleeping, my husband **was reading.** My husband **was reading while I was sleeping.**	*while* clause + main clause in **past progressive** **Note:** A sentence may begin with the *while* clause or the main clause. Use a **comma** when the *while* clause begins the sentence.
(5) **When I heard the noise, I got up.** I **got up when I heard the noise.**	We often use these forms with *when* clauses: **when** clause + main clause in **simple past**
When the war started, I was living in New Orleans. I **was living** in New Orleans **when the war started.**	**when** clause + main clause in **past progressive** **Note:** A sentence may begin with the *when* clause or the main clause. Use a **comma** when the *when* clause begins the sentence.

When clauses with simple past in main clause	
When the president arrived, [1st action]	the crowd cheered. [2nd action]
The receptionist answered [2nd action]	when I called. [1st action]
When clauses with past progressive in main clause	
When the president arrived, [2nd action]	the crowd was gathering. [1st action (ongoing)]
The receptionist was eating lunch [1st action (ongoing)]	when I called. [2nd action]
While clauses with simple past in main clause	
While we were hiking, [1st action (ongoing)]	we saw a bear. [2nd action]
It began to rain [2nd action]	while they were sleeping. [1st action (ongoing)]
While clauses with past progressive in main clause	
Actions occurring at same time	
While we were hiking,	we were looking out for bears.
It was raining	while they were sleeping.

Grammar Practice

A Complete the sentences. Circle the correct words.

1. **When / While** he was living in Springfield, he went to school.

2. The soldiers heard a strange sound **when / while** they were sleeping.

3. **When / While** the army arrived, the slaveholders left.

4. **When / While** I saw my husband, I cried.

5. He was teaching **when / while** she was taking care of the children.

6. The slaves celebrated **when / while** the soldiers arrived.

B Complete the sentences. Use the simple past or past progressive form of the verbs.

1. When you called, I _____ (sleep).

2. When my roommate _____ (fall) asleep, I turned off the TV.

3. We came inside when it _____ (get) dark.

4. His family was surprised when he _____ (not / come) home.

5. When his mother died, he _____ (fly) home for her funeral.

C Complete the sentences. Use your own ideas.

1. When I saw my friend, _____.
   simple past

2. When the package arrived, _____.
   past progressive

3. While I was eating breakfast, _____.
   simple past

4. While I was sitting in class, _____.
   past progressive

5. _____ when I met him.
   simple past

6. _____ when the phone rang.
   past progressive

7. _____ while we were walking to class.
   simple past

8. _____ while I was standing in line at the post office.
   past progressive

9. My friend and I were talking when _____.
   simple past

10. I went shopping while _____.
    past progressive

Grammar Focus 2 Simple past vs. past progressive

Examples	Language notes
(1) Present **Past** ——— **X** ——— | ———→ Future He **left** the plantation in 1889.	Use the **simple past** to talk about an action that began and ended in the past.
(2) Present **Past** ——— **XXX** ——— | ———→ Future She **was living** at Arlington at that time.	Use the **past progressive** to talk about actions in progress in the past.
(3) There **was** enough food to eat. *Incorrect:* There ~~was being~~ enough food to eat. We **liked** the Natural History Museum. *Incorrect:* We ~~were liking~~ the Natural History Museum.	We use the simple past—not the past progressive—with most **non-action verbs**. As you learned in Chapter 11, non-action verbs describe states of being, possession, senses, emotions, and mental activities. Examples include *be, hate, like, love, prefer, want, believe, know, have,* and *understand.*
(4) We **never left** the South. The store **closed two months ago**.	We commonly use **adverbs of frequency** and **time signals** with the **simple past**. They include: every day the day before yesterday often last _____ (night, week) sometimes _____ (an hour, two months) ago rarely in _____ (a month, two years) never on _____ (Tuesday, the 21st) generally at _____ (2:00, noon) normally from _____ to _____ (10:00 / 11:00, April / May) yesterday when _____ (you called, I left)
(5) They **were living** in Ohio **then**. **A year ago** the business **wasn't doing** well.	We also use **time signals** with the **past progressive**. They include: then one _____ (hour, day) ago at / during that time while _____ (you were sleeping, he was eating) in _____ (2003, June)

See Appendix F on page A-4 for more non-action verbs.

Grammar Practice

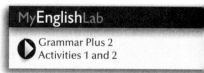

MyEnglishLab

▶ Grammar Plus 2
Activities 1 and 2

A Complete the paragraph. Use the verbs from the box. There is one extra verb.

called	decided	deciding	was calling	was studying

My best friend **1.** _____ me last week from Australia. We talked for two hours! She **2.** _____ English at a university there last semester. Now she's living there while she's **3.** _____ what to do next. She didn't ask my opinion. But I **4.** _____ to tell her anyway. I said, "Come home! I miss you."

B Complete the sentences. Use the simple past or past progressive form.

1. I _____ (watch) TV 10 hours a day while I

   was living in Texas. It was too hot to go outside.

2. She _____ (fall) asleep while she

   _____ (babysit).

3. When they _____ (get) married, George

   _____ (have) a job as a teacher.

4. My roommate and I _____ (be) unhappy

   when we _____ (see) the electric bill.

   During that time, we _____ (not / earn)

   much money.

5. I _____ (not / like) New Orleans when we _____

   (go on vacation) there.

C Write true statements about you. Use the correct form of the verbs from the list. Use time signals and time clauses with *while* and *when*.

Past progressive	Simple past
come	feel (happy, nervous, etc.)
go	hear
live in	learn
study	meet
work	see

Examples: 1. *I met my wife in 2003.*
          2. *While I was living in Spain, I learned Spanish.*

1. _____

2. _____

3. _____

4. _____

5. _____

6. _____

Listening

MyEnglishLab
▶ Listen for it.

A BEFORE LISTENING Discuss the questions with a partner.

Have you ever had to move to a new place?

How did you feel about leaving the old place?

B 🎧 UNDERSTANDING MAIN IDEAS Listen to the radio program. Write *T* for the true statements and *F* for the false statements.

_____ **1.** Eliza and her husband were plantation owners.

_____ **2.** Eliza raised money for the Yankees during the war.

_____ **3.** The Yankees brought food to the people.

_____ **4.** Eliza stayed at Arlington Plantation after the war.

C 🎧 UNDERSTANDING DETAILS Listen again. Complete the transcript. Use the words from the box.

20	6,000	pack	sugar
1832	army	refused	uniforms
1862	food	slave	

I was born in Kentucky in **1.** _____. I married James McHatton when I was
2. _____. I was a young wife when we moved to Arlington. We owned a big,
beautiful **3.** _____ plantation. I loved life at Arlington.

When the Civil War came, we women worked together to support our **4.** _____.
We made **5.** _____. We raised **6.** $_____. But the Yankees captured New
Orleans before we could send the money.

In the spring of **7.** _____, the Yankees came nearer. They took Baton Rouge.
The Yankees were taking all the **8.** _____. Hundreds of hungry people came to
Arlington. They were looking for food, and I tried to help them.

One day we got a report. The Yankees were coming to Arlington. I was alone. I asked
some of our slaves to help me **9.** _____. Some helped, some **10.** _____.
While I was riding away, Hannah, the old **11.** _____, stood in the doorway of
her cabin. She was standing up very straight. She said, "Good-bye, madam. I wish
you no harm."

Speaking

A Complete the timeline with important events in your life. Add more years if necessary. Then interview a classmate and add his or her information.

My Life		My Partner's Life
_____	1990	_____
_____	1995	_____
_____	2000	_____
_____	2005	_____
_____	2010	_____
_____	Today	_____

B Join another pair and share your timelines. Use *when* and *while* to describe events happening around the same time. Look at the model.

> My partner Nihija was five years old when I was born.
> While I was learning to walk, she was learning to read!

Writing

A By 1866, slavery was illegal throughout the United States. All slaves were free. Look at the picture. Imagine you are one of the people in the picture. Imagine the person's activities and feelings. Take notes.

B Use your notes from Part A to write a caption (a description of a picture). Try to use the grammar from the chapter.

> That's me in the dress on the left. I was five years old. At that
> time, I was living with my aunt and uncle and cousins. My parents
> were working in the city.

C Work in small groups. Share your captions. Whose point of view are the captions written from?

Grammar Summary

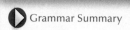

Use the **past progressive** to describe actions in progress in the past. The past progressive follows the same *-ing* spelling rules as the present progressive. Add *not* after *be* to form negative statements. For *yes / no* questions, use *Was / Were* + subject + base verb + *-ing*.

Statements	
She **was talking** to a neighbor. We **were drinking** coffee. They **weren't listening** to me.	I **wasn't feeling** well. The war **was ending**. They **weren't getting** better.
Yes / No questions	**Wh- questions**
Q: Was he **leading** former slaves? **A:** Yes, he **was**.	**Q: What were** they doing? **A:** Sleeping.
Q: Were you **working** at that time? **A:** No, we **weren't**.	**Q: Where was** he **living**? **A:** In Louisiana.

Use *while* and *when* **clauses** along with a main clause to talk about related events. *While* clauses are often in the past progressive, and *when* clauses are often in the simple past. Use a comma when the *while* or *when* clause begins the sentence.

Time clauses with *while*	Time clauses with *when*
While I was living there, I studied English. He was eating breakfast **while he was finishing his homework**.	**When we heard the noise,** we ran. I was sleeping **when he called**.

Use the **simple past** to talk about an action that began and ended in the past. Use the **past progressive**, on the other hand, to describe ongoing action in the past. Use the simple past—not the past progressive—with most non-action verbs. We use time signals with both forms.

Simple past	Past progressive
They **knew** her family. She **worked** there from 1850 to 1855.	They **were getting to know** her family. He **was studying** at NYU in 1975.

Self-Assessment

A (5 points) Complete the sentences. Use the past progressive form of the verbs.

1. She _____ (live) in a big city.

2. Her brothers _____ (not / fight) in the war.

3. I _____ (take) a nap with my baby.

4. My friends _____ (visit) for the weekend.

5. We _____ (not / expect) many people.

B (5 points) Write a *yes / no* question or a *wh-* question. Use the information and the past progressive.

1. **Q:** (she / write / an email)

   _____

2. **Q:** (the students / plan / their project / in the library)

   _____

3. **Q:** (Why / your teacher / laugh)

   _____

4. **Q:** (What / her boss / say / to her)

   _____

5. **Q:** (When / the dog / bark)

   _____

C (8 points) Use the information to complete the sentences. Use the simple past and the past progressive.

1. _____ (we hear the news) while

   _____ (we watch TV).

2. _____ (I learn a lot) when

   _____ (I take that class).

3. While _____ (we visit our cousins last summer),

   _____ (we see that movie).

4. When _____ (she graduate from college),

   _____ (her parents buy her a car).

D (7 points) Read the story. There are seven mistakes. Find and correct the mistakes.

When I was a child, we lives in a house in the countryside. While I was go to school, my parents are working. When my mother and father finish work, they were came to get me at school. I was always happy to come home. While I doing my homework, my father fixed dinner and my mother teached piano lessons.

Unit Project: Letter to your grandchildren

 A Write a personal history. Imagine that you are writing it for your grandchildren who will read it in 50 years. Follow the steps.

1. Collect the information that you need to tell your personal history. For example, interview family and friends. Do library and Internet research. Use your own memories as well. Consider the following questions as you do your research:

   - **Your family:** When did your parents start your family? What important events were happening when your parents were young?

   - **Growing up:** What were your experiences with your family and friends? What important events were happening in your country or the world when you were growing up? How did these events affect you and your family?

   - **Your adult life:** What important things happened in your life as an adult? Did you move to a new country? If so, what was that like? What important events were happening in the world when you became an adult?

2. Write your personal history. Write at least one paragraph about one of these topics: your family, growing up, your adult life.

3. Use visual aids to help tell your story. For example, include photos of your family or important events.

B Give a class presentation about your personal history. Use your visual aids. Answer any questions.

My parents got married in the 1970s. They were working on a farm in Brazil when they met. While they were living there, Pelé retired from Brazilian soccer. They had four children. My brother was born in 1985, and my sister was born in 1988. My parents were driving to a Madonna concert when my sister announced her arrival. (They arrived at the hospital just in time!) I was born in 1990. That's the year Nelson Mandela was released from prison. . . .

MyEnglishLab

Unit Test

MyEnglishLab

Search it!

Appendices

A Spelling rules for -s endings on regular plural nouns

Rules	Examples
For nouns that end in a **vowel + y**, add -s.	boy → boys day → days toy → toys way → ways
For nouns that end in a **vowel + o**, add -s.	radio → radios zoo → zoos
For nouns that end in **-s, -ss, -sh, -ch**, or **-x**, add **-es**.	bus → buses business → businesses, class → classes brush → brushes match → matches box → boxes
For nouns that end in a **consonant + o**, add -es.	potato → potatoes tomato → tomatoes
For nouns that end in a **consonant + y**, change the y to i and add -es.	activity → activities body → bodies city → cities company → companies country → countries dictionary → dictionaries party → parties
For nouns that end in **-f** or **-fe**, change the -f to v and add -(e)s.	leaf → leaves life → lives wife → wives
For **most other nouns**, add -s.	book → books car → cars computer lab → computer labs pencil → pencils student → students

B Spelling of irregular plural nouns

	Examples
child → **children**	She has five **children**.
man → **men**	Eduardo and Bob are **men**.
woman → **women**	Emma and Madison are **women**.
foot → **feet**	We have two **feet**.
tooth → **teeth**	We have 32 **teeth** in our mouths.
deer → **deer**	A **deer** is an animal. Many **deer** are walking in the meadow.
fish → **fish**	There is one **fish** in the pond. There are hundreds of **fish** in the lake.

C Pronunciation and spelling rules for final -s on verbs with *he, she, it* subjects

Pronunciation rules	Examples
For base verbs that end in the *voiceless* sound /f/, /p/, /t/, or /k/, the pronunciation of the final -s is /s/. **Note:** /θ/ is also a voiceless sound but is rarely the last sound in verbs in English.	stuffs sleeps, helps writes, fits likes, walks
For base verbs that end in the **voiced** sound /b/, /d/, /g/, /l/, /m/, /n/, /ŋ/, /r/, /v/, or /ð/ or in a vowel sound, the pronunciation of the final -s is /z/.	rubs reads sags falls comes runs sings cares lives breathes goes, tries
For base verbs that end in the sound /s/, /z/, /ʃ/, /ʒ/, /tʃ/, or /dʒ/, the pronunciation of the final -s is /ɪz/.	misses, mixes closes, excuses brushes measures watches judges

Spelling rules	Examples
For verbs that end in a **vowel + y**, add -s.	buy → buys pay → pays
For verbs that end in a **consonant + y**, change the y to i and add -es.	cry → cries dry → dries
For verbs that end in -*ch*, -*s*, -*sh*, -*x*, or -*z*, add -es.	catch → catches discuss → discusses brush → brushes mix → mixes buzz → buzzes
For **most other verbs**, add -s.	call → calls like → likes put → puts talk → talks

D Subject pronouns, object pronouns, and possessive adjectives

Subject pronouns	Object pronouns	Possessive adjectives
I	me	my
you	you	your
he	him	his
she	her	her
it	it	its
we	us	our
they	them	their

E Spelling rules for *-ing* endings

Rules	Examples of common verbs	
For verbs that end in a **consonant + -e**, drop the final -e and add *-ing*.	arrive → arriving become → becoming believe → believing care → caring change → changing close → closing come → coming describe → describing drive → driving	give → giving have → having hope → hoping lose → losing make → making promise → promising take → taking use → using write → writing
For many verbs that end in a **consonant + vowel + consonant**, double the final consonant. (For two-syllable verbs, this rule applies only if the stress is on the second syllable.) *Exceptions:* w, x, and y endings	begin → beginning control → controlling cut → cutting forget → forgetting get → getting buy → buying enjoy → enjoying fix → fixing grow → growing	plan → planning put → putting run → running sit → sitting stop → stopping know → knowing play → playing show → showing
For **most other verbs**, add *-ing* with no change to the verb.	agree → agreeing answer → answering ask → asking do → doing go → going happen → happening	help → helping keep → keeping learn → learning open → opening see → seeing try → trying

F Non-action verbs: Verbs not commonly used in progressive tenses

Categories	Examples
Verbs that describe possession	belong, have, own, possess
Verbs that describe senses	feel, hear, see, smell, taste, touch
Verbs that describe emotions	desire, dislike, hate, like, love, need, please, surprise
Verbs that describe mental activities	believe, realize, remember, understand
Verbs that describe states of being	appear, be, consist, seem, sound

G Noncount nouns

Examples		
advice	ice	tea
bread	information	traffic
cheese	mail	vocabulary
coffee	meat	water
food	milk	weather
furniture	money	work
help	salt	
homework	sugar	

Note: Some noncount nouns can be made plural in special cases: For the party we want to serve a variety of **foods** including different **meats** and **cheeses**.

H Spelling rules for comparative adjectives

Rules	Examples
For **most one-syllable** adjectives, add -er.	soft → soft**er** strong → strong**er** tall → tall**er**
For one-syllable adjectives that end in **-e**, only add -r.	safe → safe**r** nice → nice**r**
For adjectives that end in a **consonant + vowel + consonant**, double the final consonant and add -er.	red → red**der** sad → sad**der** wet → wet**ter**
For two-syllable adjectives that end in a **consonant + -y**, delete the y and add -ier.	easy → eas**ier** busy → bus**ier**
For adjectives with **three or more syllables**, add the word *more* (or *less*) before the adjective. **Note:** Sometimes -ier, not more or less, is added—often to adjectives with the prefix un-.	interesting → **more** interesting beautiful → **more** beautiful common → **more** common unhappy → unhapp**ier**
Some adjectives have **irregular** forms.	bad → **worse** good → **better** far → **farther** or **further**

Spelling rules for *-ed* endings

Rules	Examples	
For verbs that end in **-e**, add **-d**.	agree → agreed arrive → arrived believe → believed care → cared change → changed close → closed complete → completed	decide → decided describe → described die → died hope → hoped promise → promised use → used
For verbs that end in a **consonant + -y**, change *-y* to *-i* and add *-ed*.	apply → applied carry → carried cry → cried	dry → dried study → studied try → tried
For verbs that end in **consonant + vowel + consonant**, double the last consonant and add *-ed*. (For two-syllable verbs, this rule applies only if the stress is on the second syllable.) ***Exceptions:*** *w, x,* and *y* endings	drop → dropped occur → occurred permit → permitted plan → planned allow → allowed enjoy → enjoyed fix → fixed	ship → shipped step → stepped stop → stopped flow → flowed show → showed
For **most other verbs**, add *-ed*, with no change to the verb.	add → added answer → answered end → ended explain → explained	happen → happened help → helped learn → learned open → opened

J Verbs with irregular simple past forms

Group A: Verbs with vowel sound changes in the simple past	
base form	simple past form
become	became
begin	began
break	broke
come	came
draw	drew
drink	drank
drive	drove
eat	ate
fall	fell
find	found
forget	forgot
get	got
give	gave
grow	grew
hold	held
know	knew
lead	led
lie	lay
meet	met
read	read
rise	rose
run	ran
see	saw
sit	sat
speak	spoke
take	took
understand	understood
write	wrote

J (continued) Verbs with irregular simple past forms

Group B: Verbs with *d* or *t* ending (sound) in the simple past	
base form	simple past form
bring	brought
build	built
buy	bought
do	did
feel	felt
have	had
hear	heard
keep	kept
leave	left
lose	lost
make	made
mean	meant
pay	paid
say	said
send	sent
spend	spent
stand	stood
tell	told
think	thought

Group C: Verbs with simple past forms that do not change	
base form	simple past form
cut	cut
hurt	hurt
let	let
put	put
set	set

Group D: Verbs with simple past forms that are unrelated to their base forms	
base form	simple past form
be	was, were
go	went

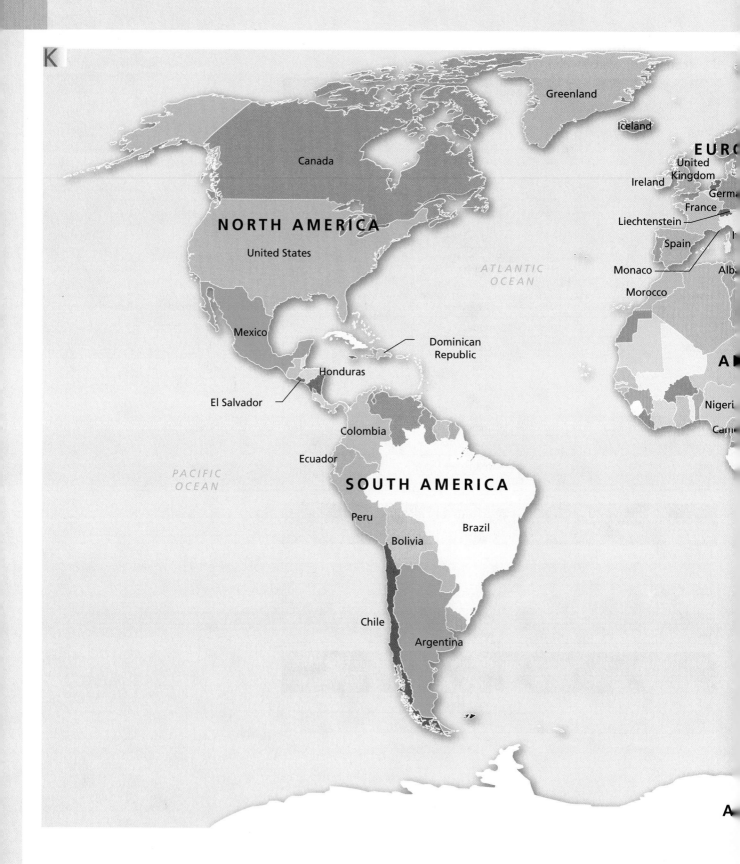

K

Greenland

Iceland

EUR○

Canada

United Kingdom

Ireland

Germa

France

NORTH AMERICA

Liechtenstein

Spain

United States

ATLANTIC OCEAN

Monaco

Alb.

Morocco

Mexico

Dominican Republic

A

Honduras

Nigeri

El Salvador

Cam

Colombia

Ecuador

PACIFIC OCEAN

SOUTH AMERICA

Peru

Brazil

Bolivia

Chile

Argentina

A

Russia

ASIA

Mongolia

elarus
Czech Republic
Ukraine
Hungary
Romania
Bulgaria
Kosovo
ce   Turkey

Iran   Afghanistan

Egypt

Dubai

Pakistan

India

China

South
Korea

Japan

Taiwan

PACIFIC
OCEAN

Yemen

Laos

Thailand

Bangladesh

Vietnam

Philippines

Ethiopia

Malaysia

cratic
blic
Congo

Kenya

Indonesia

Fiji

Zimbabwe

INDIAN
OCEAN

AUSTRALIA

uth
rica

TICA

Index

A few, 142
A little, 142
Adjectives
    comparative, 158, 160, 166
    demonstrative, 14, 20
    descriptive, 150, 152, 166
    explanation of, 66, 68, 84
    irregular, 160
    placement of, 152, 166
    possessive, 98, 104
    use of, 68, 84
Adverbs of frequency, 24, 30, 38, 42
Advice, 88, 90, 104
Affirmative statements
    in future, 132, 140
    in past progressive, 192, 206
    in present progressive, 110
    in simple past, 56, 58, 172
    in simple present, 6, 12, 20, 26, 42
Ago, 182
Alike, 162
Almost, 162
Always, 30, 42
Amounts, 48, 56, 58
Apostrophe, 98
As . . . as, 158, 162, 166
At, 50, 52, 62

Be
    descriptive adjectives with, 166
    in past progressive, 192
    sentence patterns with, 78, 84
    short answers with, 12
    in simple past, 56, 58, 174
    in simple present, 6, 12, 16, 20
    wh- questions with, 16, 20, 72
    yes / no questions with, 12, 20, 72
Be going to, 130, 132, 146
Be + there questions, 58, 62
Between, 50, 62

Commas, 152
Comparative adjectives, 158, 160, 166

Comparisons, 142, 146, 158, 162
Contractions
    with *be*, 6, 12
    with *do + not*, 26, 42
    explanation of, 2, 6
    in future, 132, 140
    with *should*, 90
    in simple past, 56
    in simple present, 6, 12, 16, 26, 42, 48
    with *there is / there are*, 48
    with *wh-* words *+ is*, 16
    with *will*, 140
Count nouns
    explanation of, 120, 126
    plural, 120, 122
    quantifiers with, 122, 142, 146
    singular, 120
    with units of measure, 120

-d, 172, 174
Demonstrative adjectives, 14, 20
Demonstrative pronouns, 14, 20
Descriptive adjectives, 150, 152, 166
Did not / Didn't, 172
Different (from), 162
Do / Does, 28, 36, 38, 72
Do not / Does not, 26, 42

-ed, 170, 172, 186
Enough, 150, 154, 166
-er, 158, 160

Fewer, 142, 146
Frequency, adverbs of, 24, 30, 38, 42
Future
    with *be going to*, 130, 132
    time signals for, 132, 146
    wh- questions in, 132
    will in, 138, 140, 146
    yes / no questions in, 132, 140, 146

Gerunds
    explanation of, 96, 100, 104
Go + gerund, 100, 104
Go / Goes, 28

Have / Has, 28
Helping verbs, 68, 104
How, 16
How many, 122, 126
How much, 122, 126

In, 50, 62, 182
Infinitives, 88, 92, 104
-ing, 100, 104, 108, 110, 192
Irregular adjectives, 160
Irregular plural nouns, 4
Irregular verbs, 28, 42, 174, 186
Is / Are, 72

Just, 162

Less, 142, 146
Like, 162

Many, 48
Modals, 90, 104
More, 142, 146

Near, 50, 62
Negative statements
    in future, 132, 140
    infinitives in, 92
    no in, 48
    in past progressive, 192
    in present progressive, 110
    should in, 90
    in simple past, 56, 58, 172
    in simple present, 6, 12, 20, 26, 42, 48
Never, 30, 42
No, 48, 56
Non-action verbs, 114, 126, 202
Noncount nouns
    explanation of, 120, 126
    quantifiers with, 122, 142, 146
    with units of measure, 120, 126
None, 122

Not enough, 154, 166
Noun phrases
  explanation of, 78
  gerund in, 100
  with preposition, 80
Nouns
  count, 120, 122, 126
  explanation of, 2, 4, 20, 68, 84
  modifying other nouns, 152
  noncount, 120, 122, 126
  plural, 4, 68, 84, 98
  possessive, 98, 104
  proper, 4
  singular, 4, 68, 84, 98

Object of preposition, 80, 84
Object pronouns
  explanation of, 80, 84
  with infinitive, 104
Objects
  explanation of, 66, 70, 72, 84
  gerund as, 100
  infinitives with, 92, 104
Occasionally, 30, 42
Often, 30, 42
On, 50, 62, 182

Partitives, 120
Past. *See* Simple past
Past progressive
  affirmative statements in, 192, 206
  explanation of, 190, 202
  negative statements in, 192, 206
  simple present vs., 202, 206
  time signals in, 202
  use of, 202, 206
  wh- questions in, 194, 206
  when clauses in, 200
  while clauses in, 200
  yes / no questions in, 194, 206
Place, prepositions of, 50, 62
Plural nouns
  count and noncount, 120, 122
  explanation of, 68
  possessive of, 98

Plural pronouns, 4
Plural subject, 70
Possessive adjectives, 96, 98, 104
Possessive nouns, 98, 104
Predictions, 132, 140
Prepositional phrases, 50, 68, 78, 80, 84
Prepositions
  with gerunds, 96
  object of, 80, 84
  of place, 46, 50, 62
  use of, 46, 50, 62, 68, 84
Present. *See* Simple present
Present progressive
  affirmative statements in, 110
  explanation of, 108, 110, 126
  negative statements in, 110
  questions in, 112
  simple present vs., 114
  to talk about future, 130, 134, 146
  time signals in, 110, 126, 146
  use of, 110, 114, 126, 132
  wh- questions in, 112, 134
  yes / no questions in, 112, 134
Progressive. *See* Past progressive; Present progressive
Pronouns
  demonstrative, 14, 20
  explanation of, 2, 4, 20, 68
  object, 80, 84, 104
  plural, 2, 4, 20
  singular, 2, 4, 20
  subject, 4, 20, 68, 84, 98
  use of, 4, 20, 68
Pronunciation
  of final -*s*, 28
Proper nouns, 4

Quantifiers
  with count and noncount nouns, 122, 126, 142, 146
  use of, 122, 138, 142, 146

Questions. *See also Wh-* questions; *Yes / No* questions
  be + there, 58, 62
  about count and noncount nouns, 122, 126
  explanation of, 10, 20, 72, 84
  forms of, 72, 84
  in future, 132, 140, 142, 146
  in past progressive, 194, 206
  in present progressive, 112, 134
  in simple past, 178, 180, 186
  in simple present, 12, 16, 36, 38, 72, 84

Rarely, 30, 42
Regular verbs, 172, 186. *See also* Verbs

-*s* / -*es*, 98
Sentences
  explanation of, 70, 84
  parts of, 70, 84
Short answers
  to *wh-* questions, 38, 72
  to *yes / no* questions, 12, 20, 36, 72, 90, 92, 112, 140, 146
Should / Shouldn't, 88, 90, 104
Similar (to), 162
Simple past
  affirmative statements in, 56, 58, 172
  be in, 56, 58
  be + there questions in, 58, 62
  contractions in, 56
  irregular verbs in, 170, 174, 186
  negative statements in, 56, 58, 172, 174
  past progressive vs., 202, 206
  questions in, 180
  regular verbs in, 170, 172, 186
  there + be statements in, 56, 58
  time signals in, 30, 114, 182, 186

use of, 172, 186, 202, 206
wh- questions in, 178, 180, 186
when clauses in, 200
while clauses in, 200
yes / no questions in, 178, 180, 186
Simple present
  affirmative statements in, 6, 12, 20, 26, 42
  be in, 6, 12, 16, 20
  be + there questions in, 58, 62
  contractions in, 6, 12, 16, 26, 42
  explanation of, 6, 26, 42, 108
  negative statements in, 6, 12, 20, 26, 42
  present progressive vs., 108, 114, 126
  there + be in, 48, 58, 62
  time signals in, 30, 114
  use of, 26, 42, 114, 126
  wh- questions in, 16, 20, 38, 42
  yes / no questions in, 12, 20, 36, 42, 72
Singular nouns
  count and noncount, 120, 122
  explanation of, 68
  possessive of, 68
Singular pronouns, 4
Singular subject, 70
Sometimes, 30, 42
Statements. *See* Affirmative statements; Negative statements
Subject
  explanation of, 66, 70, 84
  gerund as, 100
Subject pronouns
  explanation of, 4, 20, 84
  list of, 68, 96, 98

Than, 160, 166
That, 14, 20
The same (as), 162
There + be
  in simple past, 58
  in simple present, 56, 58, 78
There is / There are, 46, 48, 62, 84
These, 14,20
This, 14, 20
Those, 14, 20
Time signals
  with future, 132, 146
  with past progressive, 202
  placement of, 30
  with present progressive, 110, 126, 134, 146
  with simple past, 114, 182, 186, 202
  with simple present, 30, 42, 114
  with *while* and *when*, 198, 200, 206
Too, 150, 154, 166

Units of measure, 120
Usually, 30, 42

Verbs
  explanation of, 24, 66, 68, 70, 84
  helping, 68, 104
  irregular / other forms, 28, 42, 174, 186
  modal, 90, 104
  non-action, 114, 126, 202
  regular, 26, 42, 172, 186
  use of, 70
Very, 150, 154, 166
Volume, 120

Was / Wasn't, 174
Weight, 120

Were / Weren't, 174
Wh- questions. *See also* Questions
  with *be*, 16, 20, 72
  with *be going to*, 132, 146
  contractions in, 16
  explanation of, 10, 20, 84
  in future, 132, 140
  gerunds in, 100
  infinitives with, 92
  in past progressive, 194, 206
  in present progressive, 112, 134
  should in, 90. 104
  in simple past, 178, 180, 186
  in simple present, 16, 20, 38, 42, 72
  with *will*, 140, 146
When clauses, 198, 200, 206
While clauses, 198, 200, 206
Will, 138, 140, 146

Yes / No questions
  with *be*, 12, 72
  with *be going to*, 132, 146
  about count and noncount nouns, 122, 126
  explanation of, 10, 20, 84
  in future, 132, 140
  gerunds in, 78
  infinitives with, 92
  in past progressive, 194, 206
  in present progressive, 112, 134
  short answers to, 36, 42, 72, 90, 92, 112, 140, 146
  should in, 90, 104
  in simple past, 178, 180, 186
  in simple present, 12, 20, 36, 42, 72
  with *will*, 140, 146
Yesterday, 182

Credits